Dr. Martin Luther King Jr.

ON LOVE

Dr. Martin Luther King Jr.

ON LOVE

DR. MARTIN LUTHER KING JR.

MartinLuther King Jr. *Library*

CV 08.13.2024 1117

Contents

CONTENTS

Dr. Martin Luther King Jr.

ON LOVE

Foreword

In Martin Luther King Jr.'s last sermon at Ebenezer Baptist Church in Atlanta, Georgia, where his father had been pastor since the time King Jr. was a child, and he himself was then co-pastor, he essentially delivered his own eulogy. He did not trumpet his achievements: his Nobel Prize for Peace, his victories in winning landmark legislation in the battle for civil rights, or his stature as one of the greatest intellects and spiritual leaders in modern history. Instead, he said that he hoped he would be remembered after death as "someone who tried to love somebody."

To understand another human being thoroughly is always a challenge, and King spelled out that difficulty in his 1960 sermon "The Three Dimensions of a Complete Life": "You look here this morning, and I know you're saying, 'We see Martin Luther King.' I hate to disappoint you. You merely see my body. You can never see my mind; you can never see my personality; you can never see the me that makes me me. So in a real sense everything that we see in life is something of a shadow cast by that which we do not see. Plato was right: 'The visible is a shadow cast by the invisible.'"

In King's writings, the question of what animated him, the beam that silhouetted his essence, seems to be made visible in the subject he highlighted and turned to repeatedly: love. Over the course of his life as a preacher and in his unwavering endurance pressing for civil rights, love stands out as the value that propelled his actions, bolstered his commitment, and ignited his courage. Love's beam shone through his whole public life, from his earliest sense of love as the law of the universe to that plea late in his life to be known for his commitment to love.

For King, love was clearly inseparable from God, a love that encompassed everyone and created all. He repeatedly leaned on the call to love our fellow men "because God loves them."

In the pages that follow, we see King examining love through myriad prisms: as a creative force, a political principle, a means of psychological stability.

He elucidates its varied forms—filial, parental, romantic, platonic, humanitarian, and holy love—considering their respective powers, limitations, and misinterpretations. He explores the need for each of us to love ourselves as a first step toward greater love of others. Only through love can one follow activist and spiritual leader Mohandas K. Gandhi's strategy of nonviolent resistance.

We even sense that King's belief in God's love for each of us was the only value that could sustain him as he endured severe duress over the years of his life, including some twenty-nine arrests, solitary confinement, two firebombings of his home, constant death threats against himself and his family, manufactured tax fraud charges that were ultimately dismissed, snarling dogs, fire hoses, a stabbing, beatings . . . All this he experienced in only thirty-nine years of life.

Some of the sermons and speeches included in these pages have been excerpted to highlight the material where King specifically addressed the topic of love. Whether the speech or sermon is excerpted is indicated in the introduction to each chapter and ellipses are included in the text where material was omitted.

As a preacher traveling the country and the world, King would at times give the same sermons in different locations, but with variations.

We have generally included a significant version of a sermon and then added any relevant variations chronologically.

All King's writings in their complete form are of course deeply valuable for study and should be read in full. But we believe that this presentation of King's evolving philosophy will help readers better trace his views on love, his most sustaining value.

It is helpful to remember King's basic biography before reading this collection. Martin Luther King Jr. was born in 1929 to a family firmly tied to the Baptist church. When young Martin was only two, his father became senior pastor at the Ebenezer Baptist Church in Atlanta; his maternal grandfather was a preacher there as well, and his great-grandfather had also been a preacher elsewhere. The impulse toward civil action ran deep: King's father had decided to become a minister out of admiration for other preachers who stood up for racial justice, and he had become head of Atlanta's NAACP.

King Jr. entered Morehouse College in Atlanta at the age of fifteen and graduated in 1948. His father then named him an associate pastor at his church. That same year, King began his studies at Crozer Theological Seminary near Chester, Pennsylvania, one of eleven Black pupils among a student body of about one hundred. In his junior year, he was elected president of his class.

He began his doctoral studies at Boston University in 1951. Three years later, he became the pastor of Dexter Avenue Baptist Church in Montgomery, Alabama, and he received his PhD the following year.

King's commitment to nonviolent protest was tested early. He was first arrested on January 26, 1956, for his participation in the Montgomery Bus Boycott. The circumstances were indicative of the harassment he would regularly receive over the course of his life: As he was driving through Montgomery, he picked up some of the bus boycotters waiting on a street corner and was immediately tailed by police officers on motorcycles. At his next stop, they charged him with driving 30 miles per hour in a 25-miles-per-hour zone.

King's activism brought about many changes, including legislative ones. In 1957 and 1960, while King was a vocal, active leader insisting on equal treatment for Black Americans, President Dwight D. Eisenhower signed two pieces of civil rights legislation. King's continued activism helped bring about the passage of the Civil Rights Act of 1964, outlawing segregation and employment discrimination based on race, color, sex, religion, or country of origin.

While King increasingly addressed specific failings of US policies both at home (particularly poverty and unequal opportunity) and abroad (particularly the war in Vietnam and the threat of nuclear war), he held on to his belief in the transformative power of love if only we would all strive to remember we possessed it.

King was assassinated on April 4, 1968, at the Lorraine Motel in Memphis, Tennessee. He was in that city to participate in a march to support striking sanitation workers. He was thirty-nine years old.

Elizabeth Mitchell, Executive Editor
Ghjulia Romiti, Assistant Editor

Rediscovering Lost Values

EXCERPT FROM SERMON AT THE SECOND BAPTIST CHURCH

Detroit, Michigan

"There is a law of love in this universe."

At age twenty-five, Dr. Martin Luther King Jr. traveled to Detroit to address the Lansing NAACP and visit the historic Second Baptist Church, where his uncle was a pastor. A few weeks earlier, he had preached his first "audition" sermon at Dexter Avenue Baptist Church in Montgomery, Alabama: "Three Dimensions of Life." Over the years, he developed that sermon, and a version of it appears later in this book (page 160).

In the sermon at the Second Baptist Church excerpted here, King focused on society's lost foundational values. He observed that occasionally one must return to the past so as to move ahead. God, he asserted, is the only timeless entity, the only essence that resists passing fads, desires, and needs. Therefore, King said, he will focus on God, on what lasts.

He went on to describe love as the immutable law of life. After this passage, he criticized moral relativism—that something is good because everyone is doing it—and reminded his listeners that God is in control.

The responses of the congregation are indicated in parentheses.

• • •

[Excerpt]

. . . The first principle of value that we need to rediscover is this—that *all* reality hinges on moral foundations. In other words, that this is a moral universe, and that there are moral laws of the universe, just as abiding as the physical laws. [*Congregation: Lord help us*] I'm not so sure we all believe that. We, we never doubt that there are physical laws of the universe that we must obey. We never doubt that. And so we just don't jump out of airplanes or jump off of high buildings for the fun of it—we don't do that. Because we, we unconsciously know that there is a final law of gravitation, and if you disobey it, you'll suffer the consequences—we know that. Even if we don't know it in its Newtonian formulation, we, we know it intuitively, and so we just don't jump off the highest building in Detroit for the fun of it—we, we, we don't do that. Because we *know* that there is a law of gravitation which is final in the universe. (*Lord*) If we disobey it, we'll suffer the consequences.

But I'm not so sure if we know that there are, are moral laws, just as abiding as the physical law. I'm not so sure about that. I'm not so sure we really believe that there is a law of love in this universe, and that if you disobey it you'll suffer the consequences. (*Yes*) I'm not so sure if we really believe that. . . .

The Impassable Gulf
(The Parable of Dives and Lazarus)

SERMON AT DEXTER AVENUE BAPTIST CHURCH
Montgomery, Alabama

**"There is a gulf. But the gulf can be bridged by a little love
and compassion. Bridge the gulf before it becomes too late.
It is now passable. But it can become impassable."**

King accepted the role of a pastor of Dexter Avenue Baptist Church
in February 1954, at age twenty-five but postponed his start date until
the fall. In May, the Supreme Court decided that school segregation
was unconstitutional in *Brown v. Board of Education.*

As King would later say, when he took on the pastorship he "had not
the slightest idea that I would later become involved in a crisis in which
nonviolent resistance would be applicable." But the Supreme Court
decision had established the essential lawlessness of segregation.

The Montgomery Bus Boycott was two months in the offing when
King delivered this sermon, reproduced here in full. It reinforces the
need for the transformative power of love to make white citizens com-
passionate toward their fellow Black citizens and the role of God's love
to bridge the gulf between.

The full parable from Luke, on which the sermon is based, is also
included here for reference.

· · ·

LUKE 16:19–31, NIV

The Rich Man and Lazarus

There was a rich man who was dressed in purple and fine linen and lived in luxury every day. At his gate was laid a beggar named Lazarus, covered with sores and longing to eat what fell from the rich man's table. Even the dogs came and licked his sores.

The time came when the beggar died and the angels carried him to Abraham's side. The rich man also died and was buried. In Hades, where he was in torment, he looked up and saw Abraham far away, with Lazarus by his side. So he called to him, "Father Abraham, have pity on me and send Lazarus to dip the tip of his finger in water and cool my tongue, because I am in agony in this fire."

But Abraham replied, "Son, remember that in your lifetime you received your good things, while Lazarus received bad things, but now he is comforted here and you are in agony. And besides all this, between us and you a great chasm has been set in place, so that those who want to go from here to you cannot, nor can anyone cross over from there to us."

He answered, "Then I beg you, father, send Lazarus to my family, for I have five brothers. Let him warn them, so that they will not also come to this place of torment."

Abraham replied, "They have Moses and the Prophets; let them listen to them."

"No, Father Abraham," he said, "but if someone from the dead goes to them, they will repent."

He said to him, "If they do not listen to Moses and the Prophets, they will not be convinced even if someone rises from the dead."

• • •

This dramatic parable, told in first-century Palestine, has long been stenciled on the mental sheets of succeeding generations. It was this parable which served as the spark setting off the humanitarian flame in the life of Albert Schweitzer. He concluded that Africa, so long exploited and crushed by Western civilization, was a beggar lying at Europe's doorstep, so he willingly relinquished the charming melodies of Bach on the organ and the prestige that comes from an attractive professorship in one of Europe's greatest universities to establish a hospital in Africa. This parable has that kind of power.

We must not take this story as a theology of the afterlife. It is not a Baedeker's guide to the next world.* Its symbols are symbols and not literal fact. Jesus accepted the Hereafter as a reality but never sought to describe it.† There is always the danger that we will transform mythology into theology. We must remember that there is always a penumbra of mystery which hovers around every meaningful assertion about God and the afterlife. He who seeks to describe the furniture of heaven and the temperature of hell is taking the mystery out of religion and incarcerating it in the walls of an illogical logic.‡ Jesus had no such intentions. He was merely telling a parable to get over a basic truth about this life. He who takes this parable as a description of

---

* German publisher Karl Baedeker began producing a series of travel handbooks in the mid-nineteenth century.

† George Arthur Buttrick, *The Parables of Jesus* (Garden City, NY: Doubleday, Doran & Company, Inc., 1928), p. 139: "Let it be remembered that the story is a parable. Its symbols are symbols, not literal facts. Jesus took for granted a Hereafter, but did not describe it."

‡ Reinhold Niebuhr, *The Nature and Destiny of Man: A Christian Interpretation, Vol. 2* (New York: Charles Scribner's Sons, 1943), p. 294: "It is unwise for Christians to claim any knowledge of either the furniture of heaven or the temperature of hell; or to be too certain about any details of the Kingdom of God in which history is consummated."

the history and geography of the afterlife is transplanting it violently from its native soil to a barren literalism where it cannot live.

First of all, let us get the picture vividly in our minds. There are two main characters in this drama: Dives, the rich man, and Lazarus, the beggar at his gates. Dives dresses in the finest clothes. He is richly housed in a palatial home and richly fed with the best of foods. Then Lazarus enters in ghastly contrast. He lies outside the rich man's gate and is not only very poor but is very ill, covered with sores, and is so weak that he cannot even push the unclean dogs away when they come and lick his sores. His circumstances are so tragic that he counts it good fortune to be fed with crumbs from the rich man's table.*

The second scene of the drama is cast in the next world. Lazarus is now in Abraham's bosom, and Dives is in torment. Dives requests that Lazarus may come and ease his torment, by bringing one drop of water. But Father Abraham answers, "No, you had your good things in the earth life while Lazarus had only evil things, and now the situation is reversed. Besides all this," says Abraham, "there is now a gulf between us and you which is fixed."[†]

So we can see that it is Dives who ends up being condemned in this parable. We are naturally forced to raise the question, Why?

There is no hint that Dives was condemned because he gained

---

* Buttrick, *The Parables of Jesus*, pp. 137–38: "There are two main characters: the unnamed Rich Man and Lazarus, the beggar at his gates. We see the Rich Man richly clothed—his outer garment was dyed in the costly purple of the murex; his inner garment was woven from Egyptian flax. We see him richly housed—'gates' betokens the portico of a palatial home. We see him richly fed and living merrily. Then Lazarus enters in ghastly contrast. He is daily carried to the Rich Man's porch. His rags do not cover his ulcerated body. Unclean dogs which infest the street come to lick his sores, and he has no strength to drive them off. He counts it good fortune to be fed with scraps from the Rich Man's table."

† Cf. Luke 16:25–26.

his wealth by dishonest means.* From all indications he gained his wealth from the discipline of an industrious life. He probably had the genius for wise investment. His wealth did not come through some corrupt racket or vicious exploitation.

Moreover, Dives was not a bad man by the world's accepted standards.† He was probably well respected in his community. He possessed at least a modicum of humanness. He probably dispensed the customary charities. The fact that the beggar was brought to his gate daily implies that he had been fed.‡

There is no implication in that parable that being rich was Dives's crime. We must remember that Dives in hell was talking to Abraham in heaven, and Abraham was considered the richest man of his day. Dives's riches would have hardly been more than the interest which Abraham received from his boundless extension of his wealth. So this is not a parable condemning wealth. Jesus never condemns wealth per se. It is the inordinate worship of wealth that he condemns. Jesus always warned men that wealth is highly dangerous. But if the possessor of wealth does not allow it to suggest a false security and regards himself as a steward, then wealth can be a rich opportunity.§ There is nothing inherently vicious about

---

* Buttrick, *The Parables of Jesus*, p. 138: "Dives was not unscrupulous; the story gives no hint that he came by his wealth dishonestly."

† Buttrick, *The Parables of Jesus*, p. 138: "He was not cruel in the word's accepted meaning."

‡ Buttrick, *The Parables of Jesus*, p. 138: "The fact that a beggar was brought there daily implies that he had been fed. . . . Dives dispensed the customary charities."

§ In a handwritten version of this sermon that King filed in the same folder, he crossed out the following words in this sentence: "But if the possessor of wealth does not allow it ~~to bind him to himself~~ suggest a false security . . ." (King, "The Impassable Gulf [The Parable of Dives and Lazarus]," October 2, 1955).

wealth, and there is nothing inherently virtuous about poverty. If there is a hell, there will be plenty of poor folks in it.

What, then, were the sins that led to Dives's damnation?

First, Dives's overabsorption in self prevented him from seeing others. He was victimized with the tragic disease of egocentrism. He passed Lazarus every day, but he never really saw him.* He was too much absorbed in himself to be able to see. He was a man of large affairs, and he had to think of his stacks and banks, his house and estate. Soon Dives was so close to himself that he couldn't see Lazarus, although the beggar was as near him as the doorstep. Dives became locked up in Dives. He became so involved in his possessions that he became overabsorbed in the possessor. Dives's crime was not his wealth but inordinate self-love.†

Secondly, Dives was condemned because his selfishness caused him to lose the capacity to sympathize. There is nothing more tragic than to find a person who can look at the anguishing and deplorable circumstances of fellow human beings and not be moved. Dives's wealth had made him cold and calculating; it had blotted out the warmth of compassion. Dives could look at men crushed by the battering rams of circumstance and not be moved. Dives could watch hungry fellow men smothering in the airtight cage of poverty and not be moved. Dives could watch his brothers being blown asunder by the chilly winds of adversity and not be moved. He saw men hungry and fed them not; he saw men sick and visited them not; he saw men naked and clothed them not.

---

* Buttrick, *The Parables of Jesus*, p. 138: "He passed Lazarus several times a day, but he never really *saw* him."

† Buttrick, *The Parables of Jesus*, p. 138: "Being rich was not his crime; being rich, the story hints, was his opportunity. His crime was worldly self-love."

And so he was not fit for the Kingdom of God. He was only fit for a place of torment.[*]

Finally, Dives's greatest sin was that he accepted the inequalities of circumstance as being the proper conditions of life. There is a gulf that originates in the accident of circumstance. Circumstances make it possible for some people to get an education, while other people are denied the opportunity. Circumstances make some people rich, social prestige, while others are left gnawing on the crumbs of obscurity. There are certain gulfs in life which originate in the accident of circumstance. So in the parable Lazarus was poor, not because he wanted to be, but because tragic circumstances had made him so. On the other hand, Dives was rich because fortunate circumstances had made him so. There is a circumstantial gulf between Lazarus and Dives. Now Dives's sin was not that he made this gulf between him and Lazarus; this gulf had come into being through the accidents of circumstance. The sin of Dives was that he felt that the gulf which existed between him and Lazarus was a proper condition of life. Dives felt that this was the way things were to be. He took the "isness" of circumstantial accidents and transformed them into the "oughtness" of a universal structure.[†] He adjusted himself to the patent inequalities of circumstance.

Dives is the white man who refuses to cross the gulf of segregation and lift his Negro brother to the position of first-class citizenship because he thinks segregation is a part of the fixed structure of the universe. Dives is the India Brahman who refuses to bridge the gulf between himself and his brother because he feels that the gulf

---

[*] Cf. Matthew 25:41–46.

[†] Cf. Reinhold Niebuhr, *Beyond Tragedy: Essays on the Christian Interpretation of Tragedy* (New York: Charles Scribner's Sons, 1938), pp. 137–38.

which is set forth by the caste system is a final principle of the universe. Dives is the American capitalist who never seeks to bridge the economic gulf between himself and the laborer because he feels that it is natural for some to live in inordinate luxury while others live in abject poverty.

Dives's sin was not that he was cruel to Lazarus, but that he refused to bridge the gap of misfortune that existed between them. Dives's sin was not his wealth; his wealth was his opportunity. His sin was his refusal to use his wealth to bridge the gulf between the extremes of superfluous, inordinate wealth and abject, deadening poverty.

So when Dives cries to Abraham to send him one drop of water at Lazarus's hands, Abraham replies: "There is a fixed gulf between you now." There was a time that Dives could have bridged the gulf. He could have used the engineering power of love to build a bridge of compassion between him and Lazarus. But he refused. Now the gulf is fixed. The gulf is now an impassable gulf. Time has run out. The tragic words "too late" must now be marked across the history of Dives's life.

The Bible talks about another gulf. This time it is a gulf between God and man. This gulf originated in the circumstance of sin. In this situation God is the Dives; He is the rich man, rich in grace, rich in love, rich in power. Man is the Lazarus, poor in power, covered with the sores of sin, lying at the gates of God's throne, begging for the crumbs of God's grace. Man, like Lazarus, was too weak to bridge the gap. He was not totally helpless. He had enough power left to at least struggle up to the gate and desire the bread of grace. But he could not bridge the gulf; only God could do this. The beauty of the Christian gospel is that God, the divine omnipotent Dives, is not like the Dives of the parable. He is always seeking to bridge the gulf. He is not so concerned with Himself that He overlooks others. The

Christian God is not the God of Aristotle that merely contemplates upon himself; He is not only a self-knowing God but He is an ever-loving God. He does not think that the gulf that exists between Him and man is a proper condition of life. He knows that the gulf should not exist. So at the climax of the Christian gospel, we find God in Christ seeking to bridge the gulf. This is the meaning of that dramatic scene that took place on Calvary. The cross is the boundless bridge of God's love connecting time and eternity, man and God.

Whenever we find God, He is seeking to bridge the gulf. Said Paul, "God was in Christ reconciling the world unto himself."* Said the writer of the fourth Gospel, "For God so loved the world, that He gave His only begotten Son."† Said John the Revelator, "Behold, I stand at the door, and knock."‡ God is life's supreme Dives that seeks to bridge that gap between Himself and every Lazarus.

The story doesn't end here. It ends only as it is reproduced in the life of man. "As I loved you, so love the brethren."§ In other words, God is saying, "As I have bridged the gulf between man and God, so bridge you the gulf between man and man." Each of us is a potential Dives, maybe not rich in material goods, but rich in education, rich in social prestige, rich in influence, rich in charm. At our gate stands some poor Lazarus who has been deprived of all of these. There is a gulf. But the gulf can be bridged by a little love and compassion. Bridge the gulf before it becomes too late. It is now passable. But it can become impassable.

---

* 2 Cor. 5:19, KJV.

† John 3:16, KJV.

‡ Rev. 3:20, KJV.

§ Cf. John 13:34.

As Described in *The Autobiography of Martin Luther King, Jr.*

Montgomery, Alabama

"I . . . [would] attempt to combine two apparent irreconcilables. I would seek to arouse the group to action by insisting that their self-respect was at stake and that if they accepted such injustices without protesting, they would betray their own sense of dignity and the eternal edicts of God Himself. But I would balance this with a strong affirmation of the Christian doctrine of love."

On December 1, 1955, Rosa Parks, a Black woman, was riding at the front of the Black section of a city bus when the arrival of a white passenger meant she was supposed to give up her seat. Jim Crow laws in the South mandated the racial segregation of public facilities. Montgomery, Alabama, had a policy ordering Black passengers to seat themselves in the back of public buses, while white passengers would fill the front. If a white passenger needed a seat, a Black passenger had to stand. She refused, and was arrested and fined. In response, Black residents of Montgomery announced a boycott of city buses until they were integrated. Four days later, Martin Luther King Jr. was elected president of the Montgomery Improvement Association, the organizing body of the boycott, and thus became the spokesperson for the protests.

In this excerpt from *The Autobiography of Martin Luther King, Jr.*, King recounted his experience from that time, as he considered how to give the community direction in pursuing their civil rights.

[Excerpt]

... I went home for the first time since seven that morning, and found Coretta relaxing from a long day of telephone calls and general excitement. After we had brought each other up to date on the day's developments, I told her, somewhat hesitantly—not knowing what her reaction would be—that I had been elected president of the new association. I need not have worried. Naturally surprised, she still saw that since the responsibility had fallen on me, I had no alternative but to accept it. She did not need to be told that we would now have even less time together, and she seemed undisturbed at the possible danger to all of us in my new position. "You know," she said quietly, "that whatever you do, you have my backing."

Reassured, I went to my study and closed the door. The minutes were passing fast. I had only twenty minutes to prepare the most decisive speech of my life. I became possessed by fear. Now I was faced with the inescapable task of preparing, in almost no time at all, a speech that was expected to give a sense of direction to a people imbued with a new and still unplumbed passion for justice. I was also conscious that reporters and television men would be there with their pencils and sound cameras poised to record my words and send them across the nation.

I was now almost overcome, obsessed by a feeling of inadequacy. In this state of anxiety, I wasted five minutes of the original twenty. With nothing left but faith in a power whose matchless strength stands over against the frailties and inadequacies of human nature,

I turned to God in prayer. My words were brief and simple, asking God to restore my balance and to be with me in a time when I needed His guidance more than ever.

With less than fifteen minutes left, I began preparing an outline. In the midst of this, however, I faced a new and sobering dilemma: how could I make a speech that would be militant enough to keep my people aroused to positive action and yet moderate enough to keep this fervor within controllable and Christian bounds? I knew that many of the Negro people were victims of bitterness that could easily rise to flood proportions. What could I say to keep them courageous and prepared for positive action and yet devoid of hate and resentment? Could the militant and the moderate be combined in a single speech?

I decided that I had to face the challenge head-on, and attempt to combine two apparent irreconcilables. I would seek to arouse the group to action by insisting that their self-respect was at stake and that if they accepted such injustices without protesting, they would betray their own sense of dignity and the eternal edicts of God Himself. But I would balance this with a strong affirmation of the Christian doctrine of love. By the time I had sketched an outline of the speech in my mind, my time was up. Without stopping to eat supper (I had not eaten since morning) I said good-bye to Coretta and drove to the Holt Street Church. Within five blocks of the church I noticed a traffic jam. Cars were lined up as far as I could see on both sides of the street.

It took fully fifteen minutes to push my way through to the pastor's study. By now my doubts concerning the continued success of our venture were dispelled. The question of calling off the protest was now academic. The enthusiasm of these thousands of people swept everything along like an onrushing tidal wave.

It was some time before the remaining speakers could push their way to the rostrum through the tightly packed church. When the meeting began it was almost half an hour late. The opening hymn was the old familiar "Onward Christian Soldiers," and when that mammoth audience stood to sing, the voices outside swelling the chorus in the church, there was a mighty ring like the glad echo of heaven itself.

The chairman introduced me. I rose and stood before the pulpit. Television cameras began to shoot from all sides. The crowd grew quiet.

Without manuscript or notes, I told the story of what had happened to Mrs. Parks. Then I reviewed the long history of abuses and insults that Negro citizens had experienced on the city buses:

We are here this evening for serious business. We are here in a general sense because first and foremost we are American citizens and we are determined to apply our citizenship to the fullness of its meaning. We are here also because of our love for democracy, because of our deep-seated belief that democracy transformed from thin paper to thick action is the greatest form of government on earth. . . .

You know, my friends, there comes a time when people get tired of being trampled over by the iron feet of oppression. There comes a time, my friends, when people get tired of being plunged across the abyss of humiliation, where they experience the bleakness of nagging despair. There comes a time when people get tired of being pushed out of the glittering sunlight of life's July, and left standing amid the piercing chill of an alpine November.

And we are not wrong. We are not wrong in what we are doing. If we are wrong, the Supreme Court of this nation is wrong. If we are wrong, the Constitution of the United States is wrong. If we are wrong, God Almighty is wrong. If we are wrong, Jesus of Nazareth was merely a utopian dreamer that never came down to earth. And we are determined here in Montgomery to work and fight until justice runs down like water and righteousness like a mighty stream.

I want to say that in all of our actions we must stick together. Unity is the great need of the hour, and if we are united we can get many of the things that we not only desire but which we justly deserve. And don't let anybody frighten you. We are not afraid of what we are doing, because we are doing it within the law. There is never a time in our American democracy that we must ever think we're wrong when we protest. We reserve that right.

We, the disinherited of this land, we who have been oppressed so long, are tired of going through the long night of captivity. And now we are reaching out for the daybreak of freedom and justice and equality. May I say to you, my friends, as I come to a close . . . that we must keep . . . God in the forefront. Let us be Christian in all of our actions. But I want to tell you this evening that it is not enough for us to talk about love. Love is one of the pivotal points of the Christian faith. There is another side called justice.

Standing beside love is always justice and we are only using the tools of justice. Not only are we using the tools of persuasion but we've come to see that we've got to use the tools of coercion. Not only is this thing a process of education but it is also a process of legislation.

As we stand and sit here this evening and as we prepare ourselves for what lies ahead, let us go out with a grim and bold determination that we are going to stick together. We are going to work together. Right here in Montgomery, when the history books are written in the future, somebody will have to say, "There lived a race of people, a black people, 'fleecy locks and black complexion,' a people who had the moral courage to stand up for their rights. And thereby they injected a new meaning into the veins of history and of civilization."

As I took my seat the people rose to their feet and applauded. I was thankful to God that the message had gotten over and that the task of combining the militant and the moderate had been at least partially accomplished. The people had been as enthusiastic when I urged them to love as they were when I urged them to protest.

As I sat listening to the continued applause I realized that this speech had evoked more response than any speech or sermon I had ever delivered, and yet it was virtually unprepared. I came to see for the first time what the older preachers meant when they said, "Open your mouth and God will speak for you." While I would not let this experience tempt me to overlook the need for continued preparation, it would always remind me that God can transform man's weakness into his glorious opportunity.

Now the time had come for the all-important resolution. Ralph Abernathy read the words slowly and forcefully. The resolution called upon the Negroes not to resume riding the buses until (1) courteous treatment by the bus operators was guaranteed; (2) passengers were seated on a first-come, first-served basis—Negroes seating from the back of the bus toward the front, whites from the front toward the back; (3) Negro bus operators were employed on predominantly Negro routes. At the words, "All in favor of the motion stand," every person to a man stood up, and those who were already standing raised their hands. Cheers began to ring out from both inside and outside.

As I drove away my heart was full. I had never seen such enthusiasm for freedom. And yet this enthusiasm was tempered by amazing self-discipline. The unity of purpose and esprit de corps of these people had been indescribably moving. No historian would ever be able fully to describe this meeting and no sociologist would ever be able to interpret it adequately. One had to be a part of the experience really to understand it. . . .

Love vs. Bombs

EXCERPT FROM THE ARTICLE "WALK FOR FREEDOM"

"I urged the people to continue to manifest love, and to continue to carry on the struggle with the same dignity and with the same discipline that we had started out with."

As spokesperson for the Montgomery Bus Boycott, King received many written, shouted, and telephoned threats. Toward the end of January, he received a late-night call as he tried to fall asleep next to his wife, Coretta. The caller used a racial epithet and warned him of violence coming by the end of the week. King's baby daughter was asleep in another room.

King, in despair, went to his kitchen, heated up coffee, and, with his head in his hands, considered how he could "move out of the picture without appearing a coward." In *The Autobiography of Martin Luther King, Jr.*, King recalled his prayer: "Lord, I'm down here trying to do what's right. I think I'm right. I am here taking a stand for what I believe is right. But Lord, I confess that I'm weak now, I'm faltering. I'm losing my courage. Now I am afraid. . . . I am at the end of my powers. I have nothing left."

King remembered hearing Jesus's voice: "Martin Luther, stand up for righteousness. Stand up for justice. Stand up for truth. And lo, I will be with you. Even until the end of the world."

King later wrote, "Almost at once my fears began to go. My uncertainty disappeared. I was ready to face anything."

In an article published in *Fellowship Magazine*, King reflected on the strategy employed during the boycott and what happened after that phone call. He took the following text, which directly links love and the struggle for justice, from an interview conducted by Rev. Glenn E. Smiley for a film called *Walk for Freedom*.

[Excerpt]

. . . Love is our great instrument and our great weapon, and that alone. On January 30 my home was bombed. My wife and baby were there; I was attending a meeting. I first heard of the bombing at the meeting, when someone came to me and mentioned it, and I tried to accept it in a very calm manner. I first inquired about my wife and daughter; then after I found out that they were all right, I stopped in the midst of the meeting and spoke to the group, and urged them not to be panicky and not to do anything about it because that was not the way.

I immediately came home and, on entering the front of the house, I noticed there were some 500–1000 persons. I came in the house and looked it over and went back to see my wife and to see if the baby was all right, but as I stood in the back of the house, hundreds and hundreds of people were still gathering, and I saw there that violence was a possibility.

It was at that time that I went to the porch and tried to say to the people that we could not allow ourselves to be panicky. We could not allow ourselves to retaliate with any type of violence, but that we were still to confront the problem with *love*.

One statement that I made—and I believe it very firmly—was: "He who lives by the sword will perish by the sword."* I urged the people to continue to manifest love, and to continue to carry on the struggle with the same dignity and with the same discipline that we had started out with. I think at that time the people did decide to go home, things did get quiet, and it ended up with a great deal of calmness and a great deal of discipline, which I think our community should be proud of and which I was very proud to see because our people were determined not to retaliate with violence. . . .

* Matthew 26:52

Sermon on the Porch

King's Parsonage, Montgomery, Alabama

"We want to love our enemies. I want you to love our enemies. Be good to them. Love them and let them know you love them."

This text below presents the full sermon that King delivered from his porch in the immediate aftermath of the bombing of his home.

We believe in law and order. Don't get panicky. Don't do anything panicky at all. Don't get your weapons. He who lives by the sword will perish by the sword. Remember that is what God said. We are not advocating violence. We want to love our enemies. I want you to love our enemies. Be good to them. Love them and let them know you love them. I did not start this boycott. I was asked by you to serve as your spokesman. I want it known the length and breadth of this land that if I am stopped, this movement will not stop. If I am stopped, our work will not stop. For what we are doing is right. What we are doing is just. And God is with us.

The "New Negro" of the South: Behind the Montgomery Story

EXCERPT FROM ARTICLE APPEARING IN *SOCIALIST CALL* BASED ON SPEECH AT NAACP LEGAL DEFENSE AND EDUCATION FUND ANNUAL DINNER

New York City

"The law cannot make a man love me—religion and education must do that . . . but it can keep him from lynching me."

King delivered this speech at a dinner commemorating the second anniversary of the *Brown v. Board of Education* Supreme Court decision desegregating schools. The speech began with a discussion of whether race relations in the United States should be viewed with optimism or pessimism. King contended they should be viewed with realism. Much had been accomplished, he noted, but far more work was needed to reach the promised land.

Then King went on to talk about the bus boycott victory in Montgomery in increasing Black people's self-respect, something that could never be reversed. Finally, King reflected on what creates love and whether a hated man must wait for love's protection or if the law can intervene first.

Earlier that year, eighty-nine leaders of the boycott, including King, had been indicted for violating a 1921 state law against boycotts. The state narrowed its prosecution to King, and he was convicted just two months before this speech. The following excerpt is from the article based on this speech published in the *Socialist Call* in June 1965.

[Excerpt]

. . . There are those who contend that integration can come only through education, if for no other reason than that morals cannot be legislated. I choose, however, to be dialectical at this point. It isn't either legislation or education; it's both legislation and education. I quite agree that it is impossible to change a man's internal feeling merely through law. This was never the intention of the law.

The law does not seek to change one's internal feelings; it seeks to control the external effects of those internal feelings. For instance, the law cannot make a man love me—religion and education must do that . . . but it can keep him from lynching me. The law cannot make an employer have compassion for me, but it can keep him from refusing to hire me because of the color of my skin. Religion and education must change one's internal feelings, but it is scarcely a moral act to encourage others to patiently accept injustice until a man's heart gets right. All that we seek through legislation is to control the external effects of one's internal feelings.

Along with this emphasis on legislation, we must have the moral courage to stand up and protest against injustice wherever we find it. Wherever we find segregation we must have the fortitude to passively resist it.

We must not think in terms of retaliatory violence. To attempt to use the method of violence in our struggle would be both impractical and immoral. Violence creates many more problems than it solves. There is a voice crying through the vista of time saying: "He who lives by the sword shall perish by the sword." History is replete with the bleached bones of nations who failed to follow this truth. So we must not seek to fight our battles for freedom with weapons or arms. The method must be that of nonviolent resistance, using love as the regulating ideal. The Negro in his struggle for justice must never succumb to the temptation of becoming bitter. . . .

Living Under the Tensions of Modern Life

SERMON DELIVERED AT DEXTER AVENUE BAPTIST CHURCH

Montgomery, Alabama

"The Christian God is an other-loving God. He reaches out with His long arm of compassion and love and embraces all of His children. It gives life a meaning and a purpose that it could never have without Him. I say that if there is not a God, there ought to be one; and since there ought to be a God, there is a God; and if man doesn't find the God of the universe, he'll make him a God."

By September 1956, King had been leading a weary people through nine months of the Montgomery boycott. The sermon is included in full because it represents one of King's fuller expressions of love as a psychologically healing force. The exact date of this sermon is unknown.

King's interest in Sigmund Freud and Carl Jung represented relatively modern thinking. Although Freud and Jung had visited the United States to lecture as early as 1909, psychoanalysis and psychotherapy had not gained widespread attention until World War II, when soldiers were evaluated for their mental fitness and the strains of war caused a greater need for care.

· · ·

[*Gap in recording*] . . . use as the subject this morning, "Living Under the Tensions of Modern Life."* We use as a basis for our discussion together the twenty-eighth verse of the eleventh chapter of the Gospel as recorded by Saint Matthew: "Come unto me, all ye that labor and are heavy laden, and I will give you rest."

There can be no gainsaying of the fact that modern life is characterized by endless tensions. On all levels of life, men are experiencing disruption and conflict, self-destruction and meaninglessness. And if we turn our eyes around our nation, we discover that the psychopathic wards of our hospitals are filled today. Fear and anxiety have risen to the throne of modern life, and very few persons escape the influence of their powerful domination. It is probably true to say that we live today in one of the most, if not the most, frustrated generations of all human history. Now, what accounts for this tension, this anxiety, this confusion so characteristic of modern life? What is the causal basis for all of the tensions of our modern world? I will say that if we are to find the cause, we must look for more than one cause, and it's a plurality of causes that have all conjoined to make for the tensions of our generation.

First, there is a tension that comes as a result of the competitive struggle to make a living. It is true to say that our whole capitalistic economy is based on the profit motive under more or less competitive conditions. And whether we want to or not, we all find

---

* Harry Emerson Fosdick's sermon "Living Under Tension" may have inspired the title of King's sermon (Fosdick, *Living Under Tension* [New York: Harper & Brothers, 1941], pp. 1–10). King's secretary, Maude Ballou, made a September 1956 entry in her diary, referring to a sermon with this title: "Went to hear Martin preach yesterday. Inspiring, meaningful and timely" (Ballou, Diary. 7/1956–11/26/1956 [AD], 48 pp. LDRP-NN-Sc: Box 11. 561126-017).

ourselves engaged in the competitive struggle to make a living. Sometimes we come to the point of feeling that life is a sort of endless struggle to pay bills and to pay taxes and to buy food to eat. We go to work to make the money to buy the food to gain the strength to go back to work, and life sometimes seems to be an endless chain of monotony, an endless round of sameness. The competitive struggle to make a living makes for tensions throughout modern life, and that is why Karen Horney, the great psychologist, contends that it is this struggle to make a living in the competitive structure of our economic system that makes for the neurotic personality of our times.* There is some truth there, that tension grows out of the competitive struggle to make a living in this modern world.

Then again, we find that that tension grows out of the whole of modern urbanization and the industrial structure of our modern life. We live in an age in which men live in big cities and mass populations. It is a machine age in which we have vast industrial [orders?]. And there is a danger that men will feel in such a system that they are lost in the crowd. So men get in the big cities and feel a sense of lostness, feel that they are lost amid all of the vast numbers that they encounter every day. And then, there is a danger that men will feel that they are mere cogs in a vast industrial machine because it is an industrial world, and man so often becomes depersonalized; the machine becomes the end. This sense of not belonging, this sense of loneliness, characterizes modern life. And so many of us are lonely in a crowd because there is that basic drive that characterizes the whole of human nature: to want to belong, to have a sense of status. And there is so much in our modern world that makes us feel that we don't belong, that we are merely cogs in a vast industrial wheel that moves on.

---

* Karen Horney, *The Neurotic Personality of Our Time* (New York: W. W. Norton, 1937).

And then, there is a tension that results from the fears accompanying a war-torn world. We find ourselves today standing amid the threat of war at every hand, and we often wonder what will happen. We feel at times that the future is uncertain, and we look out and feel that the future is shrouded with impenetrable obscurities, that we don't know how things will turn out. Every young man that grows up in this world has to face the fact that he just doesn't know how the future will turn out because there is the endless round of preparing for war. And we know today that, through atomic development, we have now come to the point that we tread a narrow [*word inaudible*] that skirts a blazing inferno that Dante could never dictate.* We know that we stand today at any moment to be plunged across the abyss of atomic destruction. And all of that causes us to fear and live in tension and agony, wondering how things will turn out. This is a part of the general fear and tension and anxiety of modern life.

Then, there is the tension that comes as a result of man's general finite situation. Man has to face the fact that he's finite, that he is inevitably limited, that he's caught up within the categories of time and space. And he faces this thing that he may not be. That's why one great school of modern philosophy, known as existentialism, cries out that the great threat of modern life is the threat of nonbeing and every man has to live under the threat of nonbeing, that he must face this fact sooner or later in his life, that hovering over him is the threat of nonbeing.† He finds his self asking with Shakespeare, "To be or not to be, that's the question," but he faces the fact

---

* King is referring to Dante Alighieri's *Inferno* (c. 1314), the first volume of his epic poem *The Divine Comedy*.

† King may be referring to Jean-Paul Sartre's *Being and Nothingness* (New York: Philosophical Library, 1956).

that he may not be.* And he knows that there will come a moment that he will have to go into his room and pull down the shades and turn out the lights and take off his shoes and walk down to the chilly waters of death. And he confronts this *threat* of nonbeing that drives through the whole structure of modern life. And because of that he lives in tension and dismay and despair because he knows that hanging over him is the cloud of nonbeing, the threat of nothingness. He wonders, "Where does it go from here?" This is the tension of modern life, and these things account for the tension. These things all come together and leave all of us standing amid the tension of modern life.

But then in the midst of all of that, a voice rings out through all of the generations saying, "Come unto me, all ye that labor and are heavy-laden, and I'll give you rest." That voice cries out to us, saying, "Come unto me, all ye that are laboring everyday trying to make a living. You're caught in this round of life, in this chain of life. All of those who are laboring trying to explain life, all of those who are laboring under all of the problems of life, those who are heavy-laden with burdens of despair, those who are laden with fear, those who are laden with anxieties and disappointment, *come* unto me and I will give you rest." That's the voice that comes crying out to modern life, which gives us a little solace to carry us on. And if we didn't hear that voice, we couldn't make it. That voice simply says to us that the answer to the tension of modern life is to sufficiently commit ourselves to Christ and to be sure that we have a truly religious bit of life. For until a man discovers a religious attitude of life, he lives life in eternal frustration, and he finds himself

---

* Shakespeare, *Hamlet*, act 3, scene 1.

crying out unconsciously with Shakespeare's Macbeth that life "is a tale told by an idiot, full of sound and fury, signifying nothing."* Until he gets some *religion*, he cannot stand up amid the tensions of modern life. That is why H. G. Wells can cry out and say that a man who is not religious begins at nowhere and ends at nothing.† For religion is like a mighty wind that knocks down doors and breaks down walls and makes that possible, and even easy, which seems difficult and impossible. It is religion, it is a proper religious faith, that is the answer to the tensions of life.

I have a statement here from a man you should know, the great psychiatrist Jung, who was greatly influenced by Sigmund Freud but who went a little beyond Freud. But most of his life spent, had been spent counseling people who have confronted the problems of life, the agony of modern life. And this is what Jung says. He says:

> During the past thirty years, people from all the civilized countries of the earth have consulted me. I have treated many hundreds of patients, the larger number being Protestants, the smaller number Jews, and not more than five or six believing Catholics. Among all my patients, in the second half of life— that is to say over thirty-five—there has not been one whose problem in the last resort was not that of finding a religious outlook on life.‡

---

* Shakespeare, *Macbeth*, act 5, scene 5.

† Cf. H. G. Wells, *Mr. Britling Sees It Through* (New York: The Macmillan Company, 1916), p. 442.

‡ C. G. Jung, *Modern Man in Search of a Soul* (London: Routledge and Kegan Paul, 1981), p. 264. Harry Emerson Fosdick also quoted Jung in his essay "The Principle of Self-Acceptance," (Fosdick, in *On Being a Real Person* [New York: Harper & Brothers, 1943], p. 74).

That's not a preacher talking; that's a psychiatrist talking. That's a psychoanalyst talking. He's saying, in substance, that people face the frustrations and bewildering experiences in life so often because they do not have the proper religious bent on life. So the experiences of life come before them as mighty winds and knock them down because they have nothing within to face them. Facing the tensions of modern life through the proper religious faith. That's what Jesus is saying, "Come unto me. Sufficiently commit yourself to religion, and you will make it."

Now what does religion give us? What does genuine religion give us? What is it that Christ gives us to help us face the tensions of life and to stand up amid the tensions of life? What is it that he gives us to keep us going? What is it that genuine religion has to offer for us to live the difficult [*reign?*] of life? I think the first thing is that religion gives us a capacity to accept ourselves. And I think that is one of the first lessons that all of us should learn, the principle of self-acceptance.* This accounts for one of the big problems in modern life. So many people have been plunged across the abyss of emotional fatalism because they did not learn this simple lesson, the lesson of self-acceptance. So many of us hide this tragic gap between our desired self and our actual self. We find ourselves living life trying to be what we are not and what we can't be. So genuine religion says to us in no uncertain terms, "Accept yourself." You cannot be anybody else. You can't be me and I can't be you. And your great prayer in life should be, "Lord help me to accept my tools. However dull they are, help me to accept them. And then Lord, after I have accepted my tools, then help me to set out and do what

---

* Fosdick discussed religion's role in promoting self-respect in "The Principle of Self-Acceptance," pp. 73–78.

I can do with my tools." For there is a bit of latent creativity within all of us, seeking to break forth, and that creativity is often blocked because we are trying to be somebody else, trying to be what we aren't. There is nothing more tragic than to see an individual whose ambitions outdistance his capacity. That's a tragic sight.

So that we have in life this responsibility to be sure that we are willing to face our capacities as they are and do the best we can with them, and that's all God requires. That's all that stands before you is to do it well. And when you stand before the judgment of all eternity, there is a great reward: "Well done, thy good and faithful servant. You have been good, faithful over a few things. Come up high, and I'll make you rule over many.'" That is true for the two-talent man as well as the five-talent man, and it would have been true of the one-talent man if he had used it.†

We must live by this principle of self-acceptance. Oh, I know a lot of things in life that I would like to have, and I just have to face the fact that I don't have them and live by it. That means accepting everything, even your looks. I wish the Lord had made me tall, tan, and handsome, and it would have been much better for my sake. I would have enjoyed that the mirror would have been much more meaningful to me. But I can't spend all of my life worrying because the Lord didn't make me that way. We must come with that bit of humor to see that *we* must accept *ourselves* as we are. That becomes the first lesson of life, and genuine religion gives us that so that we

---

* Cf. Matt. 25:21, 23.

† King is referring to Jesus's Parable of the Talents, in which he praises those with five and two talents for using them constructively but condemns the person with one talent for burying it in the ground (Matt. 25:14–30). In this context, "talent" refers to a monetary unit or weight measurement and not an aptitude.

rise above the *competitive* tension of life because we accept ourselves as we are, and we begin to say, like Moses said in *Green Pastures*, "Lord, I ain't much but I's all I got."* And we live by that principle, and you live through life with a harmony that men all around you can never understand because you learned a great secret, the secret and the principle of self-acceptance.

But not only that, high religion, genuine religion, gives you the capacity to accept the realities of life, not only yourself but the external circumstances that beat up against you in life. That is one of the things that makes, also, for a lot of the problems of modern life: that so many people have not mastered this art of accepting life in a balanced perspective. We must come to see that life is a pendulum swinging between two opposites—a pendulum swinging between disappointment and fulfillment, between success and failure, between joy and sorrow. And that's life. And we never mask the life, and we think that life must be only joyous and happy and that we must live in terms of fulfillment. Disappointment is just as much a part of life as fulfillment. Failure is just as much a part of life as success, sorrow as much a part of life as joy. That is the thing that religion helps us to see. That is the greatness of Jesus. And He goes one day out, standing amid the Good Friday's light. He knows that Good Friday much as a part, is as much a part of life as Easter, and life somehow is a pendulum swinging between Good Friday and Easter, swinging between agony and triumph, swinging between darkness and light. And he who learns that has learned the lesson of life; so that he doesn't break down when he faces the other side

---

* Cf. Marc Connelly, *The Green Pastures: A Fable* (New York: Farrar & Rinehart, 1929), p. 68. See also Fosdick, *On Being a Real Person*, p. 78: "Says Noah in the play *Green Pastures*, 'I ain' very much but I'se all I got.'"

of the pendulum. When the bitter moment of life come, he doesn't break down, nor does he get overjoyous when the sweet moment of life come because he knows that this is the endless trend of life. This is the way it moves. This is what carries life on. Why it is that way maybe we do not fully understand, but it is. Religion says, "Yes, there is a crown you wear, but before the crown you wear there is a cross you must bear." We learned that when we learned to live close to Jesus, and we go unto Christ. He gives us the rest that comes for learning, from learning this lesson, that life is a pendulum, and it can throw us around and throw us [*wild when we let it?*]. But one day we might be rich, and that doesn't bother us. One day we might be poor, and that doesn't bother us. One day we might be happy, and that doesn't particularly bother us; and one day we might be unhappy, and that doesn't particularly bother us because we know that life is going to swing right back to the other opposite.

We learned that and we learned then to live with a harmony, with an inner peace, that the world can't understand. That is why Jesus says, "My peace I leave with you, not as the world giveth."* The world can't understand this peace for it is an inner peace; it is a tranquil soul amid the external accidents of circumstance. Christ gives us that. If we will only come unto Him, He gives us the capacity to accept the opposites of life. Not only that. Religion at its best, and when we go unto Christ we discover this, that there is something called forgiveness for the sins we commit. That too is a great release, isn't it? That is another lesson that we must all learn if we are to live amid the tensions of modern life.

The psychologists tell us on every hand that a lot of people are frustrated and disillusioned today because they have inner guilt

---

* Cf. John 14:27.

feelings, and these inner feelings of guilt begin to accumulate. You know enough about psychoanalysis, I'm sure, to understand what they're talking about, for when they talk about this thing they're talking about something realistic. Freud used to talk about this thing in his psychological system about [words inaudible] man here having an impression, and if it doesn't become an expression it becomes a repression. But all of the psychologists tell us that it's dangerous to repress our emotions, that we must always keep them on the forefront of consciousness. And we must do something else—not repress but sublimate. That's another big psychological word that we use in the modern world: "sublimation." But religion gives you the art of sublimation, and so you don't repress your emotions, you substitute the positive for the negative of repression. You sublimate instead of repressing, and that is what religion gives us when we go unto Christ. There is something saying to us at all times that you can be forgiven. If you commit a sin, you don't have to give your life in a long state of worrying about it because you're going to make mistakes. That's normal. It's altogether human to sin and to make mistakes and to fall short of the mark. But what religion says [is] that when you fall short of the mark, if you will humble yourself and bow before the feet of Jesus and confess your sins, then he gives you a sense of forgiveness, and you can stand up with it and keep going. And you no longer get bogged down in the past, but you move on in the future. That's the way to live life.

I was talking with a young lady some few weeks ago who had made a grave mistake, she felt, in life, and she hated to face [the public?]. She hated to face anybody, and she hated to face herself. And here she was with this guilt feeling deep down within her, afraid to face herself and afraid to face life. And I said to her, "You must see something else. You made a mistake, yes, but all of us make them. Maybe ours are not seen as much as yours. Maybe yours is glaring, and it's a mistake that everybody could see, but in our private lives all of us make them just as bad." And if I say to you this morning, "Bow down before the feet of Jesus, and there is your God, of Jesus, with the grace of God expressed in His being that will forgive us and say to us, 'Rise up and go on.'" That's what Jesus said to that woman when those men stood around her to cast their stones and they wanted to [*words inaudible*]. Jesus looked at them and said, "He who is without sin cast the first stone." They began to drop their stones and run from that situation because they knew deep down within that they too were involved in the guilt of life. But then Jesus looked at that lady and said, "Go and sin no more," as if to say, "Don't get bogged down in the path and worry because you've committed adultery. Everybody has committed it, but turn around into the future and move on out, and you will become somebody because you have accepted my grace and my forgiving power."*

There is a man lost in the foreign country of life, but then something comes to him and it says he came to himself. But he didn't stop there; that passage says that he got up and decided to walk up the dusty road that he had once come down. And as he started up that road, there was at the end of that road a father with an outstretched arm saying, "Come home, and I will accept you." And he reaches back and gets the fatted calf and said, "Come on into the fold, and you can be made all over again."† And that is the meaning of repentance. It means a right about-face, not only feeling sorry for your sins but turning around and deciding to move on and not do it anymore. And if you make the same mistake again, you try to

---

* Cf. John 8:3–11.

† King is referring to the Parable of the Prodigal Son in Luke 15:11–32.

turn around again and go on. And that is the joy, and that is the great example that the Christian religion gives to us. Christ says, "I will forgive you seventy times seven. I'll keep on forgiving you if you will keep on repenting."* This saying gives you a balanced life. That's just good psychology that Jesus discovered years ago. He is saying simply what psychiatrists are saying today: keep your emotions on the forefront of conscious, and don't repress them because if you keep on doing that you will have a deep sense of guilt that will make a morbid personality and you will become a civil war fighting against yourself. "Come unto me, all ye that labor and are heavy laden with sin, and I will give you the rest of forgiveness."

And then, finally, I must conclude now. There is something else that religion does. There is something else that Jesus does. It reminds us that at the center of the universe is a God who is concerned about the welfare of His children. Religion gives us that. High religion gives it in terms of a great personality. Religion at its best does not look upon God as a process, not as some impersonal force that is a mere moral order that guides the destiny of the universe. High religion looks upon God as a personality. Oh, it's not limited like our personalities. God is much higher than we are. But there is something in God that makes it so that we are made in His image. God can think; God is a self-determined being. God has a purpose. God can reason. God can love.

Aristotle used to talk about God as "Unmoved Mover," but that's not the Christian God. Aristotle's God is merely a self-knowing God, but the Christian God is an other-loving God. He reaches out with His long arm of compassion and love and embraces all of His children. It gives life a meaning and a purpose that it could never

---

* Cf. Matt. 18:21–22.

have without Him. I say that if there is not a God, there ought to be one; and since there ought to be a God, there is a God; and if man doesn't find the God of the universe, he'll make him a God. He's got to find something that he would worship and give his ultimate allegiance to. And I say this morning that the Christian religion talks about a God, a personal God, who's concerned about us, who is our Father, who is our Redeemer. And this sense of religion and of this divine companionship says to us, on the one hand, that we are not lost in a universe fighting for goodness and for justice and love all by ourselves. It says somehow that although we live amid the tensions of life, although we live amid injustice, no matter what we live amid, it's not going to be like that always.

There's a good dose of psychology there. And I'm glad the slaves were the greatest psychologists that America'd ever known, for they learned something that we must always learn. And they said it in their broken language, "I'm so glad that trouble don't last always."* They had learned something in their lives. And that's what real, determined faith in God gives you. Gives you the conviction that although trouble is rampant, that although you stand amid the forces of injustice, it will not last always because God controls the universe. And you can live without tension then. You can live under it.

Oh, I know all of us sometimes worry about our particular situation. We worry about the fact that we live now amid the tension of the Southland. We worry about what will happen, what's going

---

* In the published version of King's sermon "Knock at Midnight," King attributed this quote to Howard Thurman (Martin Luther King Jr., *Strength to Love* [Boston: Beacon Press, 1963], pp. 49, 144; Howard Thurman, *Deep River: Reflections on the Religious Insight of Certain of the Negro Spirituals* [New York: Harper & Brothers, 1955], pp. 28–29).

to happen in this whole struggle toward integration. We hear those who will come on the television and say that the brain of the Negro is less than that of white, that it is inferior. We hear those who say that they will use any means to block the Negro from his advance. They attempt to keep the Negro segregated and exploited and keep him down under the iron yoke of oppression. And we begin to wonder, and sometimes I know we ask the question: "Why is it? Why does God leave us like this? Seventeen million of his children here in America, leaving us under these conditions. Why is it?" But then there is something that comes out on the other side and says to us that it ain't gonna last always. There is that conviction that grows, "I'm so glad that segregation don't last always." And there is something that cries out to us and says that Kasper and Engelhardt and all of the other men that we hear talking—grim men that represent the death groans of a dying system—and all that they are saying are merely the last-minute breathing spots of a system that will inevitably die.* For justice rules this world, love and goodwill, and it will triumph. They begin to wonder over the nation, how is it that we can keep walking in Montgomery? How is it that we can keep burning out our rubber? How is it that we can keep living under tension? And we can cry out to the nation, "We can do it because we know that as we walk God walks with us." [*Congregation: Yes*]

---

* King is referring to vocal segregationist John Kasper, who aggressively opposed integration in Clinton, Tennessee, in the fall of 1956, and Alabama state senator Sam Engelhardt Jr., who was chair of the Central Alabama Citizens' Council and supported the 1956 Alabama Pupil Placement Act, which was designed to circumvent the implementation of *Brown v. Board of Education*. See Martin Luther King Jr., Robert E. DuBose, H. J. Palmer, H. H. Hubbard, S. S. Seay, and Ralph Abernathy to the Montgomery County Board of Education, August 28, 1959, in *The Papers of Martin Luther King, Jr. Volume V: Threshold of A New Decade. January 1959-December 1960* (Berkeley: University of California Press, 2005.)

We know that God is with us in all of the experiences of life. And we can walk and never get weary because we know that there is a great camp meeting in the promised land of freedom and justice.* Then it gives us this faith in God, gives us the assurance that in nothing we confront in life do we stand alone, for there is cosmic companionship. As we face our individual troubles, as we face our individual problems, there is a God that stands with us. And isn't that consoling that at long last we can find something permanent, for we live in life and life is so elusive. As I've said it is this pendulum swinging between joy and sorrow, between disappointment and fulfillment, but there is something beyond all of that which is permanent. If we put our ultimate faith in that, we don't worry about anything. Oh, when we get our ultimate faith in God, everything in life can come to us, and yet we don't despair because we know that there is something permanent.

And I say to you this morning, I'm not going to put my ultimate faith in these little gods that are here today and gone tomorrow. I'm not going to put my ultimate faith in a few dollars and cents and a few Cadillac cars and Buick convertibles. I'm going to put my ultimate faith in the God of the universe who is the same yesterday, today, and forever.† When all of these gods have passed away, He's still standing. And He is the eternal companion.

And now I can understand what the old people meant. They cried out in their poetic manner, not being able to talk about God in philosophical and theological categories. They could only talk about him in terms of their particular poetic imaginations expressed in the scripture. They could cry out throughout all the ages, "He's a

---

* King is paraphrasing the spiritual "There's a Great Camp Meeting."
† Cf. Heb. 13:8.

rock in a weary land and a shelter in the time of storm. He is a lily of the valley and a bright and morning star." And then when they gave out they wouldn't stop there because they gave out a language and they just started crying out, "He's my everything. He's my sister and my brother; He's my mother and my father. He's all together lovely; He's fairest among ten thousand. And I'm going to worship Him forever because I believe that He can guide us throughout life.'" Come unto me, all ye that are laborers, beat down and burdened down because of the problems of modern life. Come unto me and I will give you the rest that will carry you through the generations. I will give you a peace that the world can never understand. My peace I leave with you, not as the world giveth, but a peace that passeth all understanding.† God grant, if we will discover this, we will be able to live amid the tensions of modern life.

Oh God, our gracious heavenly [*recording interrupted*] Grant, oh God, that we will accept ourselves and accept the realities of life. And learn to come to Thee for forgiveness so that we can wash our guilt away, then devote our whole lives to Thee. Grant, oh God, that as we do this, we will rise out of the tensions of modern life. We can live in the world, and yet above it. We can live in the tension, and yet beyond it. In the name and spirit of Jesus, we pray. Amen.

---

* King is citing Charles W. Fry's hymn "The Lily of the Valley" (1881).

† Cf. Phil. 4:7 and John 14:27.

Paul's Letter to American Christians

SERMON AT DEXTER AVENUE BAPTIST CHURCH

Montgomery, Alabama

"I still believe that love is the most durable power in the world. Over the centuries men have sought to discover the highest good. . . . What is the summum bonum of life? I think I have an answer, America. I think I have discovered the highest good. It is love."

In this sermon, delivered at Dexter Avenue Baptist Church, King used the rhetorical device of an imaginary letter from the apostle Paul. At the time, King was twenty-seven years old and had been leading the bus boycott for almost a year.

He refers in the sermon to the Supreme Court decision in *Brown v. Board of Education* declaring school segregation to be unconstitutional. In the decision's wake, elected officials in the South vowed to fight integration and attempted to nullify the decision.

A week after King delivered this sermon, the Supreme Court ruled that Alabama's bus segregation laws were unconstitutional and the buses could now be integrated.

We use the full version of this address because it's important to see how King builds his case for love as the only way.

• • •

I would like to share with you an imaginary letter from the pen of the apostle Paul. The postmark reveals that it comes from the city of Ephesus. After opening the letter I discovered that it was written in Greek rather than English. At the top of the first page was this request: "Please read to your congregation as soon as possible, and then pass on to the other churches."

For several weeks I have worked assiduously with the translation. At times it has been difficult, but now I think I have deciphered its true meaning. May I hasten to say that if in presenting this letter the contents sound strangely Kingian instead of Paulinian, attribute it to my lack of complete objectivity rather than Paul's lack of clarity.

It is miraculous, indeed, that the apostle Paul should be writing a letter to you and to me nearly nineteen hundred years after his last letter appeared in the New Testament. How this is possible is something of an enigma wrapped in mystery. The important thing, however, is that I can imagine the apostle Paul writing a letter to American Christians in 1956 AD. And here is the letter as it stands before me.

I, an apostle of Jesus Christ by the will of God, to you who are in America, Grace be unto you, and peace from God our Father, through our Lord and Savior, Jesus Christ.

For many years I have longed to be able to come to see you. I have heard so much of you and of what you are doing. I have heard of the fascinating and astounding advances that you have made in the scientific realm. I have heard of your dashing subways and flashing airplanes. Through your scientific genius you have been able to dwarf distance and place time in chains. You have been able to carve highways through the stratosphere. So in your world you have made it possible to eat breakfast in New York City and dinner in Paris,

France. I have also heard of your skyscraping buildings with their prodigious towers steeping heavenward. I have heard of your great medical advances, which have resulted in the curing of many dread plagues and diseases and thereby prolonged your lives and made for greater security and physical well-being. All of that is marvelous. You can do so many things in your day that I could not do in the Greco-Roman world of my day. In your age you can travel distances in one day that took me three months to travel. That is wonderful. You have made tremendous strides in the area of scientific and technological development.

But America, as I look at you from afar, I wonder whether your moral and spiritual progress has been commensurate with your scientific progress. It seems to me that your moral progress lags behind your scientific progress. Your poet Thoreau used to talk about "improved means to an unimproved end." How often this is true. You have allowed the material means by which you live to outdistance the spiritual ends for which you live. You have allowed your mentality to outrun your morality. You have allowed your civilization to outdistance your culture. Through your scientific genius you have made of the world a neighborhood, but through your moral and spiritual genius you have failed to make of it a brotherhood. So, America, I would urge you to keep your moral advances abreast with your scientific advances.

I am impelled to write you concerning the responsibilities laid upon you to live as Christians in the midst of an un-Christian world. That is what I had to do. That is what every Christian has to do. But I understand that there are many Christians in America who give their ultimate allegiance to man-made systems and customs. They are afraid to be different. Their great concern is to be accepted socially. They live by some such principle as this:

"everybody is doing it, so it must be all right." For so many of you, Morality is merely group consensus. In your modern sociological lingo, the mores are accepted as the right ways. You have unconsciously come to believe that right is discovered by taking a sort of Gallup poll of the majority opinion. How many are giving their ultimate allegiance to this way?

But American Christians, I must say to you as I said to the Roman Christians years ago, "Be not conformed to this world, but be ye transformed by the renewing of your mind."* Or, as I said to the Philippian Christians, "Ye are a colony of heaven."† This means that although you live in the colony of time, your ultimate allegiance is to the empire of eternity. You have a dual citizenry. You live both in time and eternity; both in heaven and earth. Therefore, your ultimate allegiance is not to the government, not to the state, not to nation, not to any man-made institution. The Christian owes his ultimate allegiance to God, and if any earthly institution conflicts with God's will, it is your Christian duty to take a stand against it. You must never allow the transitory evanescent demands of man-made institutions to take precedence over the eternal demands of the Almighty God.

I understand that you have an economic system in America known as Capitalism. Through this economic system you have been able to do wonders. You have become the richest nation in the world, and you have built up the greatest system of production that history has ever known. All of this is marvelous. But, Americans, there is the danger that you will misuse your Capitalism. I still con-

---

* Rom. 12:2, KJV

† Phil. 3:20, NKJV: "For our citizenship is in heaven, from which we also eagerly wait for the Savior, the Lord Jess Christ."

tend that money can be the root of all evil.* It can cause one to live a life of gross materialism. I am afraid that many among you are more concerned about making a living than making a life. You are prone to judge the success of your profession by the index of your salary and the size of the wheel base on your automobile, rather than the quality of your service to humanity.

The misuse of Capitalism can also lead to tragic exploitation. This has so often happened in your nation. They tell me that one-tenth of 1 percent of the population controls more than 40 percent of the wealth. Oh, America, how often have you taken necessities from the masses to give luxuries to the classes. If you are to be a truly Christian nation, you must solve this problem. You cannot solve the problem by turning to communism, for communism is based on an ethical relativism and a metaphysical materialism that no Christian can accept. You can work within the framework of democracy to bring about a better distribution of wealth. You can use your powerful economic resources to wipe poverty from the face of the earth. God never intended for one group of people to live in superfluous inordinate wealth, while others live in abject deadening poverty. God intends for all of His children to have the basic necessities of life, and He has left in this universe "enough and to spare" for that purpose. So I call upon you to bridge the gulf between abject poverty and superfluous wealth.

I would that I could be with you in person, so that I could say to you face-to-face what I am forced to say to you in writing. Oh, how I long to share your fellowship.

Let me rush on to say something about the church. Americans, I must remind you, as I have said to so many others, that the church

---

* 1 Tim. 6:10.

is the Body of Christ. So when the church is true to its nature, it knows neither division nor disunity. But I am disturbed about what you are doing to the Body of Christ. They tell me that in America you have within Protestantism more than 256 denominations. The tragedy is not so much that you have such a multiplicity of denominations, but that most of them are warring against each other with a claim to absolute truth. This narrow sectarianism is destroying the unity of the Body of Christ. You must come to see that God is neither a Baptist nor a Methodist; He is neither a Presbyterian nor an Episcopalian. God is bigger than all of our denominations. If you are to be true witnesses for Christ, you must come to see that, America.

But I must not stop with a criticism of Protestantism. I am disturbed about Roman Catholicism. This church stands before the world with its pomp and power, insisting that it possesses the only truth. It incorporates an arrogance that becomes a dangerous spiritual arrogance. It stands with its noble Pope, who somehow rises to the miraculous heights of infallibility when he speaks ex cathedra. But I am disturbed about a person or an institution that claims infallibility in this world. I am disturbed about any church that refuses to cooperate with other churches under the pretense that it is the only true church. I must emphasize the fact that God is not a Roman Catholic and that the boundless sweep of His revelation cannot be limited to the Vatican. Roman Catholicism must do a great deal to mend its ways.

There is another thing that disturbs me to no end about the American church. You have a white church, and you have a Negro church. You have allowed segregation to creep into the doors of the church. How can such a division exist in the true Body of Christ? You must face the tragic fact that when you stand at 11:00 on

Sunday morning to sing "All Hail the Power of Jesus' Name" and "Dear Lord and Father of All Mankind," you stand in the most segregated hour of Christian America. They tell me that there is more integration in the entertaining world and other secular agencies than there is in the Christian church. How appalling that is.

I understand that there are Christians among you who try to justify segregation on the basis of the Bible. They argue that the Negro is inferior by nature because of Noah's curse upon the children of Ham. Oh, my friends, this is blasphemy. This is against everything that the Christian religion stands for. I must say to you, as I have said to so many Christians before, that in Christ "there is neither Jew nor Gentile, there is neither bond nor free, there is neither male nor female, for we are all one in Christ Jesus."* Moreover, I must reiterate the words that I uttered on Mars Hill: "God that made the world and all things therein . . . hath made of one blood all nations of men for to dwell on all the face of the earth."†

So, Americans, I must urge you to get rid of every aspect of segregation. The broad universalism standing at the center of the gospel makes both the theory and practice of segregation morally unjustifiable. Segregation is a blatant denial of the unity which we all have in Christ. It substitutes an "I-it" relationship for the "I-thou" relationship.‡ The segregator relegates the segregated to the status of a thing rather than elevate him to the status of a person. The underlying philosophy of Christianity is diametrically opposed to

---

* Gal. 3:28, KJV: "There is neither Jew nor Greek, there is neither bond nor free, there is neither male nor female: for ye are all one in Christ Jesus."

† Acts 17:24, 26, KJV.

‡ See Martin Buber, *I and Thou* (Edinburgh: T. & T. Clark, 1937).

the underlying philosophy of segregation, and all the dialectics of the logicians cannot make them lie down together.

I praise your Supreme Court for rendering a great decision just two or three years ago. I am happy to know that so many persons of goodwill have accepted the decision as a great moral victory. But I understand that there are some brothers among you who have risen up in open defiance. I hear that their legislative halls ring loud with such words as "nullification" and "interposition." They have lost the true meaning of democracy and Christianity. So I would urge each of you to plead patiently with your brothers and tell them that this isn't the way. With understanding goodwill, you are obligated to seek to change their attitudes. Let them know that in standing against integration, they are not only standing against the noble precepts of your democracy but also against the eternal edicts of God Himself. Yes, America, there is still the need for an Amos to cry out to the nation: "Let judgment roll down as waters, and righteousness as a mighty stream."*

May I say just a word to those of you who are struggling against this evil. Always be sure that you struggle with Christian methods and Christian weapons. Never succumb to the temptation of becoming bitter. As you press on for justice, be sure to move with dignity and discipline, using only the weapon of love. Let no man pull you so low as to hate him. Always avoid violence. If you succumb to the temptation of using violence in your struggle, unborn generations will be the recipients of a long and desolate night of bitterness, and your chief legacy to the future will be an endless reign of meaningless chaos.

In your struggle for justice, let your oppressor know that you are

---

* Amos 5:24, KJV.

not attempting to defeat or humiliate him or even to pay him back for injustices that he has heaped upon you. Let him know that you are merely seeking justice for him as well as yourself. Let him know that the festering sore of segregation debilitates the white man as well as the Negro. With this attitude you will be able to keep your struggle on high Christian standards.

Many persons will realize the urgency of seeking to eradicate the evil of segregation. There will be many Negroes who will devote their lives to the cause of freedom. There will be many white persons of goodwill and strong moral sensitivity who will dare to take a stand for justice. Honesty impels me to admit that such a stand will require willingness to suffer and sacrifice. So don't despair if you are condemned and persecuted for righteousness' sake. Whenever you take a stand for truth and justice, you are liable to scorn. Often you will be called an impractical idealist or a dangerous radical. Sometimes it might mean going to jail. If such is the case, you must honorably grace the jail with your presence. It might even mean physical death. But if physical death is the price that some must pay to free their children from a permanent life of psychological death, then nothing could be more Christian.* Don't worry about persecution, America; you are going to have that if you stand up for a great principle. I can say this with some authority, because my life was a continual round of persecutions. After my conversion, I was rejected by the disciples at Jerusalem. Later I was tried for heresy at Jerusalem. I was

---

* In a speech to the National Committee for Rural Schools, King attributed this statement to Kenneth Clark, replacing "Christian" with "honorable." See King, "Desegregation and the Future," December 15, 1956, p. 478. *The Papers of Martin Luther King, Jr. Volume III: Birth of a New Age. December 1955-December 1956* (Berkeley: University of California Press, 1997)

jailed at Philippi, beaten at Thessalonica, mobbed at Ephesus, and depressed at Athens. And yet I am still going. I came away from each of these experiences more persuaded than ever before that "neither death, nor life, nor angels, nor principalities, nor things present, nor things to come . . . shall separate us from the love of God, which is in Christ Jesus our Lord."* I still believe that standing up for the truth of God is the greatest thing in the world. This is the end of life. The end of life is not to be happy. The end of life is not to achieve pleasure and avoid pain. The end of life is to do the will of God, come what may.

I must bring my writing to a close now. Timothy is waiting to deliver this letter, and I must take leave for another church. But just before leaving, I must say to you, as I said to the church at Corinth, that I still believe that love is the most durable power in the world. Over the centuries, men have sought to discover the highest good. This has been the chief quest of ethical philosophy. This was one of the big questions of Greek philosophy. The Epicureans and the Stoics sought to answer it; Plato and Aristotle sought to answer it. What is the summum bonum of life? I think I have an answer, America. I think I have discovered the highest good. It is love. This principle stands at the center of the cosmos. As John says, "God is love." He who loves is a participant in the being of God. He who hates does not know God.†

So, American Christians, you may master the intricacies of the English language. You may possess all of the eloquence of articulate speech. But even if you "speak with the tongues of man and angels,

---

* Rom. 8:38–39, KJV.

† 1 John 4:16, KJV.

and have not love, you are become as sounding brass, or a tinkling cymbal."*

You may have the gift of prophecy and understanding all mysteries.[†] You may be able to break into the storehouse of nature and bring out many insights that men never dreamed were there. You may ascend to the heights of academic achievement, so that you will have all knowledge. You may boast of your great institutions of learning and the boundless extent of your degrees. But all of this amounts to absolutely nothing devoid of love.

But even more, Americans, you may give your goods to feed the poor. You may give great gifts to charity. You may tower high in philanthropy. But if you have not love, it means nothing. You may even give your body to be burned, and die the death of a martyr. Your spilt blood may be a symbol of honor for generations yet unborn, and thousands may praise you as history's supreme hero. But even so, if you have not love, your blood was spilt in vain.[†] You must come to see that it is possible for a man to be self-centered in his self-denial and self-righteous in his self-sacrifice. He may be generous in order to feed his ego and pious in order to feed his pride. Man has the tragic capacity to relegate a heightening virtue to a tragic vice. Without love, benevolence becomes egotism, and martyrdom becomes spiritual pride.

So the greatest of all virtues is love. It is here that we find the true meaning of the Christian faith. This is at bottom the meaning of the cross. The great event on Calvary signifies more than a

---

* Cf. 1 Cor. 13:1.

† Cf. 1 Cor. 13:2.

‡ 1 Cor. 13:3

meaningless drama that took place on the stage of history. It is a telescope through which we look out into the long vista of eternity and see the love of God breaking forth into time. It is an eternal reminder to a power-drunk generation that love is [the] most durable power in the world, and that it is at bottom the heartbeat of the moral cosmos. Only through achieving this love can you expect to matriculate into the university of eternal life.

I must say good-bye now. I hope this letter will find you strong in the faith. It is probable that I will not get to see you in America, but I will meet you in God's eternity. And now unto him who is able to keep us from falling, and lift us from the fatigue of despair to the buoyancy of hope, from the midnight of desperation to the daybreak of joy, to him be power and authority, forever and ever. Amen.*

---

* Cf. Jude 24–25.

Facing the Challenge of a New Age

EXCERPT FROM SPEECH AT FIRST ANNUAL INSTITUTE ON
NONVIOLENCE AND SOCIAL CHANGE WITH THE THEME
"FREEDOM AND DIGNITY THROUGH LOVE," ORGANIZED
BY THE MONTGOMERY IMPROVEMENT ASSOCIATION

Montgomery, Alabama

**"The urgency of the hour calls for leaders of wise judgment
and sound integrity—leaders not in love with money but
in love with justice; leaders not in love with publicity, but
in love with humanity."**

This event marked the anniversary of the formation of the Montgomery
Improvement Association. Back in the first days of the association's
founding, King had been asked to serve as the organization's president
and therefore became the spokesperson for the Montgomery Bus
Boycott. Several weeks before this speech, the Supreme Court had
handed down its decision that the Alabama State and Montgomery
city laws were unconstitutional, thus vindicating the Montgomery Improvement Association.

In his speech, excerpted here, King evoked many of his themes
concerning love, specifically agape—the love between God and hu-
mans. He also spoke to the challenges of modern man in keeping a
moral focus as advances in technology bewilder and dazzle us.

• • •

[Excerpt]

. . . Another thing that we must do in speeding up the coming of the new age is to develop intelligent, courageous, and dedicated leadership. This is one of the pressing needs of the hour. In this period of transition and growing social change, there is a dire need for leaders who are calm and yet positive; leaders who avoid the extremes of "hotheadedness" and "Uncle Tomism." The urgency of the hour calls for leaders of wise judgment and sound integrity—leaders not in love with money but in love with justice; leaders not in love with publicity but in love with humanity; leaders who can subject their particular egos to the greatness of the cause . . .

Nonviolence and Racial Justice

EXCERPT FROM ARTICLE IN *CHRISTIAN CENTURY*

"At the center of nonviolence stands the principle of love. . . . Along the way of life, someone must have sense enough and morality enough to cut off the chain of hate."

The weekly publication *Christian Century* had been supportive of the Montgomery Bus Boycott. But overall, religious leaders of the racial justice movement were frustrated at the lack of deep support from the white Christian community.

In September 1956, organizer and civil rights activist Bayard Rustin, seventeen years King's senior, encouraged him to submit an article to *Christian Century* to persuade its readers that opposing segregation was not just a political choice but a moral one. He enclosed a copy of his own writing as an example for King. Two months later, King submitted his piece.

The selection here is an excerpt from that article. In the piece's beginning, King considered why the issue of race had risen to dominant interest in the culture, pointing to the 1954 Supreme Court decision outlawing segregation in schools, the increased sense of self-worth among Black people, and the clear hostility of southern legislatures toward Black citizens. Local cultures not only had intimidated Black people but had in practice created an environment in which Black people were afraid to exert what rights they had. In 1957, for example, only 20 percent of Black Americans were registered to vote.

In this article, King repeated themes of earlier sermons but built upon them, while considering love as a tactical weapon.

[Excerpt]

. . . The basic question which confronts the world's oppressed is: How is the struggle against the forces of injustice to be waged? There are two possible answers. One is resort to the all too prevalent method of physical violence and corroding hatred. The danger of this method is its futility. Violence solves no social problems; it merely creates new and more complicated ones. Through the vistas of time a voice still cries to every potential Peter, "Put up your sword!"* The shores of history are white with the bleached bones of nations and communities that failed to follow this command. If the American Negro and other victims of oppression succumb to the temptation of using violence in the struggle for justice, unborn generations will live in a desolate night of bitterness, and their chief legacy will be an endless reign of chaos.

Alternative to Violence

The alternative to violence is nonviolent resistance. This method was made famous in our generation by Mohandas K. Gandhi, who used it to free India from the domination of the British empire. Five

---

* Cf. John 18:11.

points can be made concerning nonviolence as a method in bringing about better racial conditions.

First, this is not a method for cowards; it *does* resist. The nonviolent resister is just as strongly opposed to the evil against which he protests as is the person who uses violence. His method is passive or nonaggressive in the sense that he is not physically aggressive toward his opponent. But his mind and emotions are always active, constantly seeking to persuade the opponent that he is mistaken. This method is passive physically but strongly active spiritually; it is nonaggressive physically but dynamically aggressive spiritually.

A second point is that nonviolent resistance does not seek to defeat or humiliate the opponent, but to win his friendship and understanding. The nonviolent resister must often express his protest through noncooperation or boycotts, but he realizes that noncooperation and boycotts are not ends themselves; they are merely means to awaken a sense of moral shame in the opponent. The end is redemption and reconciliation. The aftermath of nonviolence is the creation of the beloved community, while the aftermath of violence is tragic bitterness.

A third characteristic of this method is that the attack is directed against forces of evil rather than against persons who are caught in those forces. It is evil we are seeking to defeat, not the persons victimized by evil. Those of us who struggle against racial injustice must come to see that the basic tension is not between races. As I like to say to the people in Montgomery, Alabama: "The tension in this city is not between white people and Negro people. The tension is at bottom between justice and injustice, between the forces of light and the forces of darkness. And if there is a victory it will be a victory not merely for 50,000 Negroes, but a victory for justice and the forces of light. We are out to defeat injustice and not white persons who may happen to be injust."

A fourth point that must be brought out concerning nonviolent resistance is that it avoids not only external physical violence but also internal violence of spirit. At the center of nonviolence stands the principle of love. In struggling for human dignity the oppressed people of the world must not allow themselves to become bitter or indulge in hate campaigns. To retaliate with hate and bitterness would do nothing but intensify the hate in the world. Along the way of life, someone must have sense enough and morality enough to cut off the chain of hate. This can be done only by projecting the ethics of love to the center of our lives.

The Meaning of "Love"

In speaking of love at this point, we are not referring to some sentimental emotion. It would be nonsense to urge men to love their oppressors in an affectionate sense. "Love" in this connection means understanding good will. There are three words for love in the Greek New Testament.* First, there is eros. In Platonic philosophy eros meant the yearning of the soul for the realm of the divine. It has come now to mean a sort of aesthetic or romantic love. Second, there is philia. It meant intimate affectionateness between friends. Philia denotes a sort of reciprocal love: the person loves because he is loved. When we speak of loving those who oppose us we refer to neither eros nor philia; we speak of a love which is expressed in the Greek word agape. Agape means nothing sentimental or basically affectionate; it means understanding, redeeming good will for all

---

* While the Greek language has three words for love, "eros" does not appear in the Greek New Testament.

men, an overflowing love which seeks nothing in return. It is the love of God working in the lives of men. When we love on the agape level we love men not because we like them, not because their attitudes and ways appeal to us, but because God loves them. Here we rise to the position of loving the person who does the evil deed while hating the deed he does.*

Finally, the method of nonviolence is based on the conviction that the universe is on the side of justice. It is this deep faith in the future that causes the nonviolent resister to accept suffering without retaliation. He knows that in his struggle for justice he has cosmic companionship. This belief that God is on the side of truth and justice comes down to us from the long tradition of our Christian faith. There is something at the very center of our faith which reminds us that Good Friday may reign for a day, but ultimately it must give way to the triumphant beat of the Easter drums. Evil may so shape events that Caesar will occupy a palace and Christ a cross, but one day that same Christ will rise up and split history into A.D. and B.C., so that even the life of Caesar must be dated by his name. So in Montgomery we can walk and never get weary, because we know that there will be a great camp meeting in the promised land of freedom and justice.†

This, in brief, is the method of nonviolent resistance. It is a method

---

* Cf. Harry Emerson Fosdick, *On Being Fit to Live With: Sermons on Post-War Christianity* (New York: Harper & Brothers, 1946), pp. 16–17.

† In a similar discussion in *Stride Toward Freedom* (New York: Ballantine Books, 1960), King included an additional element of nonviolence: "The nonviolent resister is willing to accept violence if necessary, but never to inflict it. He does not seek to dodge jail. . . . Suffering, the nonviolent resister realizes, has tremendous educational and transforming possibilities" (p. 103).

that challenges all people struggling for justice and freedom. God grant that we wage the struggle with dignity and discipline. May all who suffer oppression in this world reject the self-defeating method of retaliatory violence and choose the method that seeks to redeem. Through using this method wisely and courageously we will emerge from the bleak and desolate midnight of man's inhumanity to man into the bright daybreak of freedom and justice.

The Power of Nonviolence

EXCERPT FROM A SPEECH AT THE UNIVERSITY
OF CALIFORNIA, BERKELEY

Berkeley, California

"Nonviolent resistance is also an internal matter. It not only avoids external violence or external physical violence but also internal violence of spirit. And so at the center of our movement stood the philosophy of love."

King had traveled to Berkeley to talk to the University of California students at the invitation of the Interfraternity Council. Approximately seven thousand students stood in the sunshine to listen to him.

At the time, the president of South Vietnam had just visited the United States and was hailed as a hero for wiping out thousands of Communists in his country. The US was almost entirely funding his war, and US forces had been deployed in the hundreds. Student agitation against the war had begun to mount. Meanwhile, President Dwight D. Eisenhower had proposed pending civil rights legislation that would push further to create equal rights and make intimidation based on race unlawful.

What makes this short excerpt particularly interesting is King's idea that love is almost an inoculation against the psychological wounds of being attacked for standing up for justice.

• • •

[Excerpt]

. . . Another basic thing we had to get over is that nonviolent resistance is also an internal matter. It not only avoids external violence or external physical violence but also internal violence of spirit. And so at the center of our movement stood the philosophy of love. The attitude that the only way to ultimately change humanity and make for the society that we all long for is to keep love at the center of our lives. . . .

Conquering Self-Centeredness

SERMON DELIVERED AT DEXTER AVENUE BAPTIST CHURCH
Montgomery, Alabama

This sermon is included in full because it is one of King's most detailed analyses of self-love and its downfalls. By this time, King had become nationally famous. He had appeared on the cover of *Time* magazine and had delivered his first national address, at the Lincoln Memorial, urging lawmakers to "give us the ballot."

I want to make two or three announcements as quickly as possible so that we can move on with our worship service and not stay here too long in the midst of extreme heat. Unfortunately, we do not have an air-conditioned church, so we find ourselves suffering the consequences. And I will try to keep that in mind this morning and make our services as brief as possible.

You will notice on your bulletin that Deacon [S. D.] Turner, who was a deacon in this church for many, many years, passed this past week. And the funeral will be held tomorrow morning at eleven o'clock at the Ross-Clayton Chapel, the funeral home there, the chapel at the funeral home. Now I'm urging each member to respond by being present at the funeral tomorrow. Especially, I am asking the choir to be there, as many of you as possibly can, and all of the deacons. I would like to ask the deacons to serve as the pallbearers.

As you probably know, Brother Turner does not have any relatives. I understand that he has a son but we have no way of getting in touch with him. He hasn't heard. I remember when I visited him, so often he mentioned the son, but the son had not, he had not heard from his son for more than twenty or thirty years. So we don't know how to get in touch with his son. So I had to do the arranging of the funeral. And I want to urge every deacon of this church to be present tomorrow and to serve as pallbearers. I hope you will get that word around to the deacons who are not here this morning. That is, at eleven o'clock tomorrow morning at the chapel of the Ross-Clayton Funeral Home. And as many members as possible, as can come out, we're expecting you and also the choir. For Brother Turner served here many, many years. Most of you do not know him because he has been ill for about fourteen years. He's been out at Fraternal Hospital, where he passed the other day. So that is probably why you do not know him. But he was an active deacon here until the time that he went into the hospital and has been there ever since.

The financial statement will be out after the morning worship. You can receive copies. And I would like to say that I noticed several members are behind in their pledges for some reason. I don't know why that is, but I would like to urge you to catch up in your pledges, for our responsibilities are the same. We have a budget to carry out in the summer months, just as in any other period of the year. And I'm urging you to do that and to bring those pledges up before too long, so that we can face the many responsibilities that we have ahead in our church.

[*Here King continues his announcements and welcomes visitors to the service.*]

Will the ushers come forward now for the morning offering? Let us prepare to give liberally with open hearts and open spirits for the causes ahead. I said just a few minutes ago that many of our members are behind in their pledges for some reason, and I hope you will not get too far behind, that you will keep up. Because this is of vital importance, in order to be sure that our budget balances at all times. Let us remember that as the ushers come forward now.

O God, our Heavenly Father, we thank Thee for life and we thank Thee for health. We thank Thee for the ability to work and to live in this society. Help us to realize that as we make our money that we owe a portion of it to Thee. And help us to give it with open hearts and spirits, realizing that as we give, we give for the ongoing of Thy kingdom here on earth. Amen. [*recording interrupted*]

> Blessed thou!
> O words with heavenly comfort fraught!
> Whate'er I do, whate'er I do, where'er I be,
> Still 'tis God's hands that leadeth me!
> He leadeth me, He leadeth me,
> By His own hands He leadeth me.
> His faithful follower, I will be,
> For by His hand He leadeth me.*

Let us sing stanzas one, two, and three. [*Congregation sings "He Leadeth Me."*]

I want to continue the series of sermons this morning that I started several weeks ago, the series dealing with problems of personality integration. This morning our subject is "conquering self-centeredness." "Conquering self-centeredness." I probably will not have time to do justice to this many-sided subject because of the

---

* King is reciting from J. H. Gilmore's hymn "He Leadeth Me" (1862).

heat. And I don't want to preach too long. But for the moments left, I at least want to suggest certain ways to conquer self-centeredness and at least place the subject before you so that you can go out and add the meat and try, in some way, to make it meaningful and practical in your everyday lives.

We turn to the New Testament for our text this morning, a very familiar passage, a passage that I read in the morning lesson. It's found throughout the synoptic Gospels, Matthew, Mark, and Luke: "He that findeth his life, shall lose it: and he that loseth his life for my sake, shall find it."*

An individual has not begun to live until he can rise above the narrow horizons of his particular individualistic concerns to the broader concerns of all humanity. And this is one of the big problems of life, that so many people never quite get to the point of rising above self. And so they end up the tragic victims of self-centeredness. They end up the victims of distorted and disrupted personality.

Life has its beginning and its maturity comes into being when an individual rises above self to something greater. Few individuals learn this, and so they go through life merely existing and never living. Now you see signs all along in your everyday life with individuals who are the victims of self-centeredness. They are the people who live an eternal "I." They do not have the capacity to project the "I" into the "Thou."† They do not have the mental equipment for an eternal, dangerous, and sometimes costly altruism. They live a life of perpetual egotism. And they are the victims all around of

---

* Matthew, Mark, and Luke are referred to as the "synoptic Gospels" because they possess commonalities that the fourth Gospel, John, does not. Cf. Matt. 10:39, Matt. 16:25, Mark 8:35, Luke 9:24, and Luke 17:33.

† See Martin Buber, *I and Thou* (Edinburgh: T. & T. Clark, 1937).

the egocentric predicament. They start out, the minute you talk with them, talking about what they can do, what they have done. They're the people who will tell you, before you talk with them five minutes, where they have been and who they know. They're the people who can tell you in a few seconds how many degrees they have and where they went to school and how much money they have. We meet these people every day. And so this is not a foreign subject. It is not something far off. It is a problem that meets us in everyday life. We meet it in ourselves, we meet [it] in other selves: the problem of self-centeredness.

Now, we can say to a certain extent that persons in this situation are persons who have really never grown up. They are still children, at a point. For you see, a child is inevitably, necessarily egocentric. He is a bundle of his own sensations, clamoring to be cared for. And, to be sure, he has his own social context. He belongs to his mother, but he cares for her only because he wants to be fed and protected. He does not care for his mother for her sake, but he cares for his mother for his own sake. And so a child is inevitably egocentric, inevitably self-centered. And that is why Dr. [William Henry] Burnham says that during the first six or seven years of development, the ego is dominant within the child. And both in behavior and in attitudes, a child is a victim of self-centeredness.* This is a part of the early

---

* King adopted this passage from Harry Emerson Fosdick, *On Being a Real Person* (New York: Harper & Brothers, 1943), p. 80: "From one point of view this may be regarded as failure to grow up. An infant is necessarily egocentric. He is a bundle of his own sensations, clamoring to be taken care of. To be sure, he has vital social relationships; he belongs to his mother, but all he wants her for is food and protection. He does not care for her nor try to understand her *for her sake*; he wants her, and later everyone else within his reach, solely for his own sake. Self-centeredness is the inevitable attitude of early childhood. Says Dr. William Burnham: 'The first

development of a little child. When people become mature, they are to rise above this. I look at my little daughter every day, and she wants certain things, and when she wants them, she wants them. And she almost cries out, "I want what I want when I want it." She is not concerned about what I think about it or what Mrs. King thinks about it. She wants it. She's a child, and that's very natural and normal for a child. She is inevitably self-centered because she's a child.

But when one matures, when one rises above the early years of childhood, he begins to love people for their own sake. He turns himself to higher loyalties. He gives himself to something outside of himself. He gives himself to causes that he lives for and sometimes will even die for. He comes to the point that now he can rise above his individualistic concerns, and he understands then what Jesus meant when he says, "He who finds his life shall lose it; he who loses his life for my sake shall find it."* In other words, he who finds his ego shall lose his ego, but he who loseth his ego for my sake shall find it. And so you see people who are apparently selfish; it isn't merely an ethical issue but it is a psychological issue.† They

---

period up to the age of seven or eight is one in which the ego is dominant. Both the child's behavior and the child's thinking are alike egocentric. It is the child's business to be selfish at this period'" (Fosdick's quotation is from William Henry Burnham's *The Wholesome Personality* [New York: D. Appleton, 1932], p. 49).

* Fosdick, *On Being a Real Person*, pp. 80–81: "For a real person, maturely developed, is not egocentric. He has objective interests; he cares for other people for their sakes; he discovers causes and values for which he lives and might even die.... His enduring satisfactions are found in letting himself go for aims outside himself, and as Jesus said, he finds life by losing it."

† On page 96 of Fosdick's *On Being a Real Person*, King underlined the following lines: "In them Jesus' basic principle is shown to be not alone great ethics but sound psychology—only he who loses life saves it, only he who expends life keeps it, only he who invests life enriches it."

are the victims of arrested development, and they are still children. They haven't grown up. And like a modern novelist says about one of his characters, "Edith is a little country, bounded on the east and the west, on the north and the south, by Edith."* And so many people are little countries, bounded all around by themselves, and they never quite get out of themselves. And these are the persons who are victimized with arrested development.

Now the consequences, the disruptive effects of such self-centeredness, such egocentric desires, are tragic. And we see these every day. At first, it leads to frustration and disillusionment and unhappiness at many points. For usually when people are self-centered, they are self-centered because they are seeking attention, they want to be admired and this is the way they set out to do it. But in the process, because of their self-centeredness, they are not admired; they are mawkish, and people don't want to be bothered with them. And so the very thing they seek, they never get. And they end up frustrated and unhappy and disillusioned.†

I'm sure you have seen people in life who are so desirous of gaining attention that if they cannot have and gain attention through normal channels, through normal social channels, they will gain

---

* Fosdick, *On Being a Real Person*, p. 81: "Moralists censure them as selfish, but beneath the ethical is a psychological problem—they are specimens of arrested development. Says a contemporary novelist about one of her characters: 'Edith was a little country bounded on the north, south, east, and west by Edith.'" Fosdick quoted novelist Martha Ostenso, "Gardenias in Her Hair," *Pictorial Review* 38 (September 1937): 84.

† Fosdick, *On Being a Real Person*, pp. 81–82: "The disruptive effects of such egocentricity are serious. Like anybody else, the self-centered person wants to be appreciated; indeed like a spoiled child, he insists on it all the more ravenously, the more self-centered he is; but his egocentricity in any social group makes admiration difficult. . . . The egocentrics, therefore, are habitually baffled, frustrated, and unhappy."

it through antisocial means. There are those people who are so desirous of gaining attention that if everybody says, "Yes," they automatically say, "No," in order to be seen and to be heard. They are so self-centered that they must gain attention and they must be seen in order to survive. They want to be admired and in their quest for admiration, they don't gain it and in their failure to gain it, they become frustrated and bewildered and disillusioned.

Also, it leads to extreme sensitiveness. The individual who is self-centered, the individual who is egocentric, ends up being very sensitive, a very touchy person. And that is one of the tragic effects of a self-centered attitude, that it leads to a very sensitive and touchy response toward the universe. These are the people you have to handle with kid gloves because they are touchy, they are sensitive. And they are sensitive because they are self-centered. They are too absorbed in self and anything gets them off, anything makes them angry. Anything makes them feel that people are looking over them because of a tragic self-centeredness. That even leads to the point that the individual is not capable of facing trouble and the hard moments of life. One can become so self-centered, so egocentric that when the hard and difficult moments of life come, he cannot face them because he's too centered in himself. These are the people who cannot face disappointments. These are the people who cannot face being defeated. These are the people who cannot face being criticized. These are the people who cannot face these many experiences of life which inevitably come because they are too centered in themselves. In time, somebody criticizes them, [in] time somebody says something about them that they don't like too well, [in] time they are disappointed, [in] time they are defeated, even in a little game, they end up brokenhearted. They can't stand up under it because they are centered in self.

Then, finally, it can become so morbid that it rises to ominous proportions and leads to a tragic sense of persecution. There are persons who come to the point that they are so self-centered that they end up with a persecution complex, and the end result is insanity. They end up thinking that the universe stands against them, that everybody is against them. They are turning around within themselves. They are little solar systems within themselves, and they can't see beyond that. And as a result of their failure to get out of self, they end up with a persecution complex and sometimes madness and insanity. These are some of the effects of self-centeredness.

Now one will inevitably raise the question: How then do we conquer self-centeredness? How do we get away from this thing that we call self-centeredness? How can we live in this universe with a balance and with a type of perspective that keeps us going smoothly and we are not too absorbed in self? How do we do it? Let me make two or three suggestions, and I can assure you that these suggestions will not at all solve the problem. For you will have to solve it, in many points, for yourself. But at least these things, I hope, will give you some guidance.

I think one of the best ways to face this problem of self-centeredness is to discover some cause and some purpose, some loyalty outside of yourself and give yourself to that something. The best way to handle it is not to suppress the ego but to extend the ego into objectively meaningful channels.[*] And so many people are unhappy because they aren't doing anything. They're self-centered

---

[*] On page 91 of Fosdick's *On Being a Real Person*, King underlined the following: "They can, and do, and if they are to be mature they must, get out of themselves, not by suppressing their egos but by extending them." In the right-hand margin, King wrote: "We get out of ourselves, not by suppressing our egoes, but by extending them. One must expand his ego into an extended self."

because they aren't doing anything. They haven't given themselves to anything, and they just move around in their little circles. One of the ways to rise above this self-centeredness is to move away from self and objectify yourself in something outside of yourself. Find some great cause and some great purpose, some loyalty to which you can give yourself and become so absorbed in that something that you give your life to it. Men and women have done this throughout all of the generations. And they have found that necessary ego satisfaction that life presents and that one desires through projecting self in something outside of self. As I said, you don't solve the problem by trying to trample over the ego altogether. That doesn't solve the problem. For you will always have the ego, and the ego has certain desires, certain desires for significance. The three great psychoanalysts of this age, of this century, pointed out that there are certain basic desires that human beings have and that they long for and that they seek at any cost. And so for Freud the basic desire was to be loved. Jung would say that the basic desire is to be secure. But then Adler comes along and says the basic desire of human nature is to feel important and a sense of significance.* And I think of all of those, probably—certainly all are significant but the one that Adler mentions is probably even more significant than any: that all human beings have a desire to belong and to feel significant and important.†

And the way to solve this problem is not to drown out the ego but to find your sense of importance in something outside of the self.

---

* Alfred Adler (1870–1937) was an Austrian psychotherapist.

† Fosdick, *On Being a Real Person*, p. 97: "Of the three major figures in modern psychiatry, Freud may roughly be represented as saying that man wants most of all to be loved; Jung that he wants most of all to feel secure; Adler that he wants most of all to feel significant. Leaving the question of priority open, that last desire is insistent in all of us. Every man wants to feel that he counts."

And you are then able to live because you have given your life to something outside and something that is meaningful, objectified. You rise above this self-absorption to something outside. We look through history. We see that biography is a running commentary of this. We see a Wilberforce.* We see him somehow satisfying his desire by absorbing his life in the slave trade, those who are victims of the slave trade. We see a Florence Nightingale.† We see her finding meaning and finding a sense of belonging by giving herself to a great cause, to the unnursed wounded. We see an Albert Schweitzer who looks at men in dark Africa who have been the victims of colonialism and imperialism and there he gives his life to that. He objectifies himself in this great cause. And then we can even find Jesus totally objectifying himself when he cries out, "Ye have done it unto the least of these my brethren, ye have done it unto me."‡

This is the way to go through life with a balance, with the proper perspective, because you've given yourself to something greater than self. Sometimes it's friends, sometimes it's family, sometimes it's a great cause, it's a great loyalty, but give yourself to that something, and life becomes meaningful. I've seen people who discovered a great meaning in their jobs, and they became so absorbed in that that they didn't have time to become self-centered. They

---

* William Wilberforce (1759–1833) was a British politician who worked for the abolition of slavery.

† Florence Nightingale (1820–1910) directed British nursing services in Turkey during the Crimean War. In London, she founded the world's first training school for nurses in 1860.

‡ Cf. Matt. 25:40. Fosdick, *On Being a Real Person*, p. 91: "Wilberforce can identify himself with the victims of the slave trade, Florence Nightingale with the unnursed wounded in a war, and Jesus can carry this objectification of himself so far that he says, 'Inasmuch as ye have done it unto one of the least of these my brethren, ye have done it unto me.'"

loved their job. And the great prayer that anyone could pray at that point is: "O God, help me to love my job as this individual loves his or hers. O God, help me to give my self to my work and to my job and to my allegiance as this individual does." And this is the way out. And I think this is what [Ralph Waldo] Emerson meant when he said: "O, see how the masses of men worry themselves into nameless graves, while here and there, some great unselfish soul forgets himself into immortality." And this becomes a point of balance when you can forget yourself into immortality. You're not so absorbed in self, but you are absorbed in something beyond self.

And there is another way to rise above self-centeredness, and that is by having the proper inner attitude toward your position or toward your status in life or whatever it is. You conquer self-centeredness by coming to the point of seeing that you are where you are today because somebody helped you to get there. And so many people, you see, live a self-centered, egocentric life because they have the attitude that they are responsible for everything and for their position in life. For everything they do in life, they feel, somehow, that they are responsible and solely responsible for it.

An individual gets away from this type of self-centeredness when he pauses enough to see that no matter what he does in life, he does that because somebody helped him to do it. And he then gains the type of perspective and the type of balance which keeps him from becoming self-centered. He comes to see that somebody stands in the background, often doing a little job in a big way, making it possible for him to do what he's doing. Can you believe that? That no matter where you stand, no matter how much popularity you have, no matter how much education you have, no matter how much money you have, you have it because somebody in this universe helped you to get it. And when you see that, you can't be arrogant, you can't be supercilious. You discover that you have your position because of the events of history and because of individuals in the background making it possible for you to stand there.

Would you allow me to share a personal experience with you this morning? And I say it only because I think it has bearing on this message. One of the problems that I have to face and even fight every day is this problem of self-centeredness, this tendency that can so easily come to my life now that I'm something special, that I'm something important. Living over the past year, I can hardly go into any city or any town in this nation where I'm not lavished with hospitality by peoples of all races and of all creeds. I can hardly go anywhere to speak in this nation where hundreds and thousands of people are not turned away because of lack of space. And then after speaking, I often have to be rushed out to get away from the crowd rushing for autographs. I can hardly walk the street in any city of this nation where I'm not confronted with people running up the street, "Isn't this Reverend King of Alabama?" Living under this it's easy, it's a dangerous tendency that I will come to feel that I'm something special, that I stand somewhere in this universe because of my ingenuity, and that I'm important, that I can walk around life with a type of arrogance because of an importance that I have. And one of the prayers that I pray to God every day is: "O God, help me to see myself in my true perspective. Help me, O God, to see that I'm just a symbol of a movement. Help me to see that I'm the victim of what the Germans call a zeitgeist and that something was getting ready to happen in history; history was ready for it. And that a boycott would have taken place in Montgomery, Alabama, if I had never come to Alabama. Help me to realize that I'm where I am because of the forces of history and because of the fifty thousand Negroes of Alabama who will never get their names in the papers and in the headline. O God, help me to see that where I stand today, I stand because others helped me to stand there and because the forces of history projected me there. And this moment would have come in history even if M. L. King had never been born." And when we come to see that, we stand with a humility. This is the prayer I pray to God every day: "Lord help me to see M. L. King as M. L. King in his true perspective." Because if I don't see that, I will become the biggest fool in America.

And I think that's why Jesus looked at a man one day and called him a fool.* He was standing around talking about his barns. And he said, "I'm going to tear down my barns and build greater barns and I'm just going to say to my soul, 'Eat, drink and be merry.'" Jesus looked at that man and called him a fool. And Jesus called him a fool because he didn't have sense enough to realize that he stood where he was in terms of his barns and in terms of his wealth because somebody in the background helped him to get there. We never get anywhere in this world without the forces of history and individual persons in the background helping us to get there.

We think of Marian Anderson.† We think of this great person who stands on the stage of history, with all of the prestige and all of the fame that can come to an individual. Let us never forget that Marian Anderson, that great contralto, is there today because somebody in the background helped her to get there. Because there was that mother who was willing to work days and nights until her eyebrows were all but parched and her hands all but scorched in order that her daughter could get her training and an education. There

---

* Luke 12:16–20.

† Marian Anderson (1897–1993) was an internationally acclaimed African American opera singer.

were the people in Union Baptist Church in Philadelphia, Pennsylvania, the choir that she was singing in, who said, "You have it and go ahead and we are going to stand with you." And that is why Marian Anderson is great today because she recognizes that. One day, somebody said to Miss Anderson, "Miss Anderson, what has been the happiest moment in your life?" She said: "It was not the moment that I stood before the critics of the world and that I sang with the Philharmonic Orchestra of New York and the critics were lavish with their praise. Not the moment that I sang before the kings and queens of Europe. Not the moment that I sang before Sibelius of Finland and he said, 'My roof is too low for such a voice.' Not even the moment when the great Toscanini said that I possess a voice that only comes once in a century.* The greatest moment in my life was the moment that I could say, 'Mother, you may stop working now.'"

Marian Anderson discovered that she stands today in a position of fame and of prestige because somebody in the background helped her to get there. And only by seeing this can we rise out. If you have the privilege of a fine education, well, you have it because somebody made it possible. If you have the privilege to gain wealth and a bit of the world's goods, well, you have it because somebody made it possible. So don't boast. Don't be arrogant. You, at that moment, rise out of your self-centeredness to the type of living that makes you an integrated personality.

Finally, the proper religious faith gives you this type of balance and this type of perspective that I'm talking about. This, you see, is something of the genius of great religion, that on the one hand, it gives man a sense of belonging, and on the other hand, it gives him a

---

* Jean Sibelius (1865–1957) was a Finnish composer. Arturo Toscanini (1867–1957) was an Italian conductor who led the New York Philharmonic from 1928 to 1936.

sense of dependence on something higher. So he realizes that there is something beyond in which he lives and moves and even moves and gains his being.* This is what great religion does for him.

You know, Greek mythology used to talk about the goddess of Nemesis, and this was one of the functions of the goddess of Nemesis. The goddess of Nemesis kept everything on a common level. If you got too low, beat down, and you didn't feel that you were quite up to par, you felt a sense of inadequacy and a sense of inferiority, this goddess would pull you up. And then, if you got too high for yourself, you felt too highly of yourself, you felt too exalted, this goddess would do what the older people used to say: "Pull you a buttonhole lower." And everything was kept on a common level. And there needs to be something in your life of a goddess of Nemesis which pulls you down when you get too high and pulls you up when you feel the sense of inadequacy, and that is what religion at its best does. It keeps you to the point that you don't feel like you are too low and you don't feel like you are too high but you'll maintain that type of balance. And you come to see that you're an adjective, not a noun. It is only God that is a noun. You are a dependent clause, not an independent clause. You come to see through great religion, somehow, there is only one being in this universe that can say "I am" unconditionally. We turn over to Genesis and we read of God saying, "I am that I am," and that's the only being that can say that.† But man is a child of God, and he must always say, "I am, because of." And when you come to see that, you see that your existence is adjectival; it is dependent on something else. Your existence is dependent on the existence of a higher power, and you can't walk

---

* Cf. Acts 17:28.

† This verse is actually Exod. 3:14, KJV.

around the universe with arrogance. You can't walk about the universe with a haughty spirit because you know that there is a God in this universe that you are dependent on.

And I'm so glad that the new science did something to dampen our arrogant spirits. For a long time, man felt that he was the center of the universe, and all of his science had given him that. All of the days in the past he came up under what was known as the geocentric theory: the earth was the center of the universe, and everything revolved around the earth. Then came Copernicus and Galileo and others, said that the sun is the center; the heliocentric theory came into being. And that reminded us somehow that we are dependent on something. We are not just at the center of this universe. We are only at the center to the extent that we give ourselves and our allegiance to God Almighty.

And I'm so glad that the new science came into being to dampen our arrogance. It says to us that our earthly planet is a dependent planet; it is a small planet in the orbits of this universe. The sun is the center of this universe, that man must look beyond himself to discover his significance. And that does something to each of us so that we can see when we have faith in God that we have nothing to boast about, we have nothing to be arrogant about, but we live with a humility that keeps us going.

The other day, I went out to Kilby prison to pray with some of the men on death row. And it's always a very tragic experience, not so much a tragic experience as a sort of sad experience to look at men who have committed great crimes, and now they are standing in a little cell with nothing much there, just in a little cell between four walls. And they can't see much, and they're just waiting for the day of their death and the day of their ultimate doom. And I went to pray with some of these men. And I never can forget as I walked away from there after praying and walked out of all of these bars, I couldn't walk out with arrogance. I couldn't walk out with the feeling that I'm not like these men. I couldn't walk out with the attitude of the Pharisee, "I thank Thee, God, that I'm not like other men."* But as I walked out of that door, something was ringing in my heart saying, "But for the grace of God, you would be here."† As I look at drunkard men walking the streets of Montgomery and of other cities every day, I find myself saying, "But by the grace of God, you too would be a drunkard." As I look at those who have lost balance of themselves and those who are giving their lives to a tragic life of pleasure and throwing away everything they have in riotous living, I find myself saying, "But by the grace of God, I too would be here." And when you see that point, you cannot be arrogant. But you walk through life with a humility that takes away the self-centeredness that makes you a disintegrated personality. And you begin to sing:

> Amazing grace! How sweet the sound
> That saves a wretch like me!
> I once was lost, but now I'm found,
> Was blind, but now I see.
>
> Through many dangers, toils, and snares,
> I have already come;
> 'Twas grace that brought me safe thus far,
> And grace will lead me home.‡

---

* Cf. Luke 18:11.

† Cf. I Cor. 15:10.

‡ These are the first and third verses of the Christian hymn "Amazing Grace."

And when you take this attitude, you go into the room of your life and take down the mirrors because you cannot any longer see yourself. But the mirrors somehow are transformed into windows, and you look out into the objective world and see that you are what you are because of somebody else. You are what you are because of the grace of the Almighty God. He who seeks to find his ego will lose it. But he who loses his ego in some great cause, some great purpose, some great ideal, some great loyalty; he who discovers, somehow, that he stands where he stands because of the forces of history and because of other individuals; he who discovers that he stands where he stands because of the grace of God finds himself. He loses himself in that something but later finds himself. And this is the way, it seems to me, to the integrated personality.

O God, our gracious Heavenly Father, help us to rise out of our attitude of self-centeredness, out of our egotism. Help us to rise to the point of having faith in Thee and realizing that we are dependent on Thee. And when we realize this, O God, we will live life with a new meaning and with a new understanding and with a new integration. We ask Thee to grant all of these blessings in the name and spirit of Jesus. Amen.

Is there one this morning who will accept the Christ? I'm sure there is someone in this congregation who has not united with a church in Montgomery, someone in this congregation who has not united with a church in any city. And this morning I want to make a special call. I want to extend a special invitation to you. Who this morning will make the decision? Who this morning will accept the Christ? Who will come into this church and become a part of this Christian fellowship just as you are? This is the time now to make the decision. Let us turn to hymn number 162.

[*Speaking over congregational singing*] Is there one this morning who will make the decision? Is there another? And another? The recessional hymn is 371. Once more, let me say how very happy we are to have all of our visitors here this morning. And I will look forward to greeting you as you emerge from the sanctuary. Be sure, thank you very much [*King, who probably has been handed or told something by an unidentified person, thanks the person in mid-sentence of this address to the congregation.*], be sure to be back this evening for the Lord's Supper, that's at seven o'clock, just one hour. And I'm urging every member of this church to be here on time, the choir to be here and the deacons and all of the members. And we will be here just one hour. Will all of the members please do that? And those of you who have not had the right hand of fellowship, we are all urging you to be here for that purpose. Let us now turn to the recessional hymn 371. [*Congregation sings the first and second verses of "I Love to Tell the Story."*]

Loving Your Enemies

SERMON AT DEXTER AVENUE BAPTIST CHURCH

Montgomery, Alabama

"When you rise to the level of love, of its great beauty and power, you seek only to defeat evil systems. Individuals who happen to be caught up in that system, you love, but you seek to defeat the system."

In this sermon, delivered at his home church in November 1957 and reproduced here in full, King expanded his references to the international scene. He had delivered a similar sermon at Howard University a week before at their convocation.

Global relations at the time felt volatile. Countries in Africa and Asia had begun asserting their independence, including Ghana and Taiwan. In January 1957, President Eisenhower had declared that any Middle Eastern country that felt threatened could appeal to the United States for support, a policy that became known as the Eisenhower Doctrine.

And then in October, the Soviets launched the first satellite, Sputnik 1, into Earth's orbit. This unexpected and astounding technological feat hinted at Russia's advanced military capability and rattled the world, particularly when combined with the terror of nuclear weapons. The United States entered the space race.

At home, Congress passed a watered-down version of Eisenhower's Civil Rights Act of 1957 in September, establishing a Civil Rights Commission.

I am forced to preach under something of a handicap this morning. In fact, I had the doctor before coming to church. And he said that it would be best for me to stay in the bed this morning. And I insisted that I would have to come to preach. So he allowed me to come out with one stipulation, and that is that I would not come in the pulpit until time to preach, and that after, that I would immediately go back home and get in the bed. So I'm going to try to follow his instructions from that point on.

I want to use as a subject from which to preach this morning a very familiar subject, and it is familiar to you because I have preached from this subject twice before to my knowing in this pulpit. I try to make it something of a custom or tradition to preach from this passage of scripture at least once a year, adding new insights that I develop along the way, out of new experiences as I give these messages. Although the content is, the basic content is the same, new insights and new experiences naturally make for new illustrations.

So I want to turn your attention to this subject: "Loving Your Enemies." It's so basic to me because it is a part of my basic philosophical and theological orientation: the whole idea of love, the whole philosophy of love. In the fifth chapter of the Gospel as recorded by Saint Matthew, we read these very arresting words flowing from the lips of our Lord and Master: "Ye have heard that it has been said, Thou shall love thy neighbor, and hate thine enemy. But I say unto you, Love your enemies, bless them that curse you, do good to them that hate you, and pray for them that despitefully use you; that ye may be the children of your Father which is in heaven."*

Certainly these are great words, words lifted to cosmic proportions. And over the centuries, many persons have argued that this is an extremely difficult command. Many would go so far as to say that it just isn't possible to move out into the actual practice of this glorious command. They would go on to say that this is just additional proof that Jesus was an impractical idealist who never quite came down to earth. So the arguments abound. But far from being an impractical idealist, Jesus has become the practical realist. The words of this text glitter in our eyes with a new urgency. Far from being the pious injunction of a utopian dreamer, this command is an absolute necessity for the survival of our civilization. Yes, it is love that will save our world and our civilization, love even for enemies.

Now let me hasten to say that Jesus was very serious when he gave this command; he wasn't playing. He realized that it's hard to love your enemies. He realized that it's difficult to love those persons who seek to defeat you, those persons who say evil things about you. He realized that it was painfully hard, pressingly hard. But he wasn't playing. And we cannot dismiss this passage as just another example of Oriental hyperbole, just a sort of exaggeration to get over the point. This is a basic philosophy of all that we hear coming from the lips of our Master. Because Jesus wasn't playing; because he was serious. We have the Christian and moral responsibility to seek to discover the meaning of these words, and to discover how we can live out this command, and why we should live by this command.

---

* Cf. Matt. 5:43–45.

Now first let us deal with this question, which is the practical question: How do you go about loving your enemies? I think the first thing is this: in order to love your enemies, you must begin by analyzing self. And I'm sure that seems strange to you, that I start out telling you this morning that you love your enemies by beginning with a look at self. It seems to me that that is the first and foremost way to come to an adequate discovery to the how of this situation. Now, I'm aware of the fact that some people will not like you, not because of something you have done to them, but they just won't like you. I'm quite aware of that. Some people aren't going to like the way you walk; some people aren't going to like the way you talk. Some people aren't going to like you because you can do your job better than they can do theirs. Some people aren't going to like you because other people like you, and because you're popular, and because you're well-liked, they aren't going to like you. Some people aren't going to like you because your hair is a little shorter than theirs or your hair is a little longer than theirs. Some people aren't going to like you because your skin is a little brighter than theirs; and others aren't going to like you because your skin is a little darker than theirs. So that some people aren't going to like you. They're going to dislike you, not because of something that you've done to them but because of various jealous reactions and other reactions that are so prevalent in human nature.

But after looking at these things and admitting these things, we must face the fact that an individual might dislike us because of something that we've done deep down in the past, some personality attribute that we possess, something that we've done deep down in the past and we've forgotten about it; but it was that something that aroused the hate response within the individual. That is why I say, begin with yourself. There might be something within you that arouses the tragic hate response in the other individual.

This is true in our international struggle. We look at the struggle, the ideological struggle between communism on the one hand and democracy on the other, and we see the struggle between America and Russia. Now, certainly, we can never give our allegiance to the Russian way of life, to the communistic way of life, because communism is based on an ethical relativism and a metaphysical materialism that no Christian can accept. When we look at the methods of communism, a philosophy where somehow the end justifies the means, we cannot accept that because we believe as Christians that the end is preexistent in the means. But in spite of all of the weaknesses and evils inherent in communism, we must at the same time see the weaknesses and evils within democracy.

Democracy is the greatest form of government to my mind that man has ever conceived, but the weakness is that we have never touched it. Isn't it true that we have often taken necessities from the masses to give luxuries to the classes? Isn't it true that we have often in our democracy trampled over individuals and races with the iron feet of oppression? Isn't it true that through our Western powers we have perpetuated colonialism and imperialism? And all of these things must be taken under consideration as we look at Russia. We must face the fact that the rhythmic beat of the deep rumblings of discontent from Asia and Africa is at bottom a revolt against the imperialism and colonialism perpetuated by Western civilization all these many years. The success of communism in the world today is due to the failure of democracy to live up to the noble ideals and principles inherent in its system.

And this is what Jesus means when he said: "How is it that you can see the mote in your brother's eye and not see the beam in your own eye?" Or, to put it in Moffatt's translation: "How is it that you see the splinter in your brother's eye and fail to see the plank in your own eye?"* And this is one of the tragedies of human nature. So we begin to love our enemies and love those persons that hate us whether in collective life or individual life by looking at ourselves.

A second thing that an individual must do in seeking to love his enemy is to discover the element of good in his enemy, and every time you begin to hate that person and think of hating that person, realize that there is some good there and look at those good points which will overbalance the bad points. I've said to you on many occasions that each of us is something of a schizophrenic personality. We're split up and divided against ourselves. And there is something of a civil war going on within all of our lives. There is a recalcitrant South of our soul revolting against the North of our soul. And there is this continual struggle within the very structure of every individual life. There is something within all of us that causes us to cry out with Ovid, the Latin poet, "I see and approve the better things of life, but the evil things I do."† There is something within all of us that causes us to cry out with Plato that the human personality is like a charioteer with two headstrong horses, each wanting to go in different directions.‡ There is something within each of us that causes us to cry out with Goethe, "There is enough stuff in me to make both a gentleman and a rogue." There is something within

---

* Cf. Matt. 7:3 and Luke 6:41; see also James Moffatt, *The Bible: A New Translation by James Moffatt* (New York: Harper & Brothers, 1922).

† Ovid, *Metamorphoses* 7.20: "I see and approve better things, but follow worse."

‡ Plato, *Phaedrus*, part 2.

each of us that causes us to cry out with Apostle Paul: "I see and approve the better things of life, but the evil things I do."*

So somehow the "isness" of our present nature is out of harmony with the eternal "oughtness" that forever confronts us. And this simply means this: that within the best of us, there is some evil, and within the worst of us, there is some good. When we come to see this, we take a different attitude toward individuals. The person who hates you most has some good in him; even the nation that hates you most has some good in it; even the race that hates you most has some good in it. And when you come to the point that you look in the face of every man and see deep down within him what religion calls "the image of God," you begin to love him in spite of. No matter what he does, you see God's image there. There is an element of goodness that he can never slough off. Discover the element of good in your enemy. And as you seek to hate him, find the center of goodness and place your attention there and you will take a new attitude.

Another way that you love your enemy is this: when the opportunity presents itself for you to defeat your enemy, that is the time which you must not do it. There will come a time, in many instances, when the person who hates you most, the person who has misused you most, the person who has gossiped about you most, the person who has spread false rumors about you most—there will come a time when you will have an opportunity to defeat that person. It might be in terms of a recommendation for a job; it might be in terms of helping that person to make some move in life. That's the time you

---

* Here King mistakenly repeats his paraphrase of Ovid. In the Howard University version of this sermon, he quoted Paul: "The good that I would I do not, and the evil that I would not, that I do" (cf. Rom. 7:19).

must do it. That is the meaning of love. In the final analysis, love is not this sentimental something that we talk about. It's not merely an emotional something. Love is creative, understanding goodwill for all men. It is the refusal to defeat any individual. When you rise to the level of love, of its great beauty and power, you seek only to defeat evil systems. Individuals who happen to be caught up in that system, you love, but you seek to defeat the system.

The Greek language, as I've said so often before, is very powerful at this point. It comes to our aid beautifully in giving us the real meaning and depth of the whole philosophy of love. And I think it is quite apropos at this point, for you see the Greek language has three words for love, interestingly enough. It talks about love as eros. That's one word for love. Eros is a sort of aesthetic love. Plato talks about it a great deal in his Dialogues, a sort of yearning of the soul for the realm of the gods. And it's come to us to be a sort of romantic love, though it's a beautiful love. Everybody has experienced eros in all of its beauty when you find some individual that is attractive to you and that you pour out all of your like and your love on that individual. That is eros, you see, and it's a powerful, beautiful love that is given to us through all of the beauty of literature; we read about it.

Then the Greek language talks about philia, and that's another type of love that's also beautiful. It is a sort of intimate affection between personal friends. And this is the type of love that you have for those persons that you're friendly with, your intimate friends, or people that you call on the telephone and you go by to have dinner with, and your roommate in college and that type of thing. It's a sort of reciprocal love. On this level, you like a person because that person likes you. You love on this level because you are loved. You love on this level because there's something about the person you love that is likable to you. This too is a beautiful love. You can communicate with a person; you have certain things in common; you like to do things together. This is philia.

The Greek language comes out with another word for love. It is the word "agape," and agape is more than eros. Agape is more than philia. Agape is something of the understanding, creative, redemptive goodwill for all men. It is a love that seeks nothing in return. It is an overflowing love; it's what theologians would call the love of God working in the lives of men. And when you rise to love on this level, you begin to love men, not because they are likable, but because God loves them. You look at every man, and you love him because you know God loves him. And he might be the worst person you've ever seen.*

And this is what Jesus means, I think, in this very passage when he says, "Love your enemy." And it's significant that he does not say, "Like your enemy." Like is a sentimental something, an affectionate something. There are a lot of people that I find it difficult to like. I don't like what they do to me. I don't like what they say about me and other people. I don't like their attitudes. I don't like some of the things they're doing. I don't like them. But Jesus says love them. And love is greater than like. Love is understanding, redemptive goodwill for all men, so that you love everybody, because God loves them. You refuse to do anything that will defeat an individual because you have agape in your soul. And here you come to the point that you love the individual who does the evil deed, while hating the deed that the person does. This is what Jesus means when he says, "Love your enemy." This is the way to do

---

* Cf. Harry Emerson Fosdick, *On Being Fit to Live With: Sermons on Post-War Christianity* (New York: Harper & Brothers, 1946), pp. 6–7.

it. When the opportunity presents itself when you can defeat your enemy, you must not do it.

Now for the few moments left, let us move from the practical how to the theoretical why. It's not only necessary to know how to go about loving your enemies but also to go down into the question of why we should love our enemies. I think the first reason that we should love our enemies, and I think this was at the very center of Jesus's thinking, is this: that hate for hate only intensifies the existence of hate and evil in the universe. If I hit you and you hit me and I hit you back and you hit me back and so on, you see, that goes on ad infinitum. It just never ends. Somewhere somebody must have a little sense, and that's the strong person. The strong person is the person who can cut off the chain of hate, the chain of evil. And that is the tragedy of hate, that it doesn't cut it off. It only intensifies the existence of hate and evil in the universe. Somebody must have religion enough and morality enough to cut it off and inject within the very structure of the universe that strong and powerful element of love.

I think I mentioned before that sometime ago my brother and I were driving one evening to Chattanooga, Tennessee, from Atlanta. He was driving the car. And for some reason the drivers were very discourteous that night. They didn't dim their lights; hardly any driver that passed by dimmed his lights. And I remember very vividly, my brother A.D. looked over and in a tone of anger said: "I know what I'm going to do. The next car that comes along here and refuses to dim the lights, I'm going to fail to dim mine and pour them on in all of their power." And I looked at him right quick and said: "Oh no, don't do that. There'd be too much light on this highway, and it will end up in mutual destruction for all. Somebody got to have some sense on this highway."

Somebody must have sense enough to dim the lights, and that is the trouble, isn't it? That as all of the civilizations of the world move up the highway of history, so many civilizations, having looked at other civilizations that refused to dim the lights; they decided to refuse to dim theirs. And Toynbee tells that out of the twenty-two civilizations that have risen up, all but about seven have found themselves in the junk heap of destruction. It is because civilizations fail to have sense enough to dim the lights.* And if somebody doesn't have sense enough to turn on the dim and beautiful and powerful lights of love in this world, the whole of our civilization will be plunged into the abyss of destruction. And we will all end up destroyed because nobody had any sense on the highway of history. Somewhere somebody must have some sense. Men must see that force begets force, hate begets hate, toughness begets toughness. And it is all a descending spiral, ultimately ending in destruction for all and everybody. Somebody must have sense enough and morality enough to cut off the chain of hate and the chain of evil in the universe. And you do that by love.

There's another reason why you should love your enemies, and that is because hate distorts the personality of the hater. We usually think of what hate does for the individual hated or the individuals hated or the groups hated. But it is even more tragic, it is even more ruinous and injurious to the individual who hates. You just begin hating somebody, and you will begin to do irrational things. You can't see straight when you hate. You can't walk straight when

---

* Arnold Joseph Toynbee (1889–1975) was an English historian. In his Howard University sermon, King told the audience, "Oh, my friends, it may be that Western civilization will end up destroyed on the highway of history because we failed to dim our lights with the great light of love at the right time."

you hate. You can't stand upright. Your vision is distorted. There is nothing more tragic than to see an individual whose heart is filled with hate. He comes to the point that he becomes a pathological case. For the person who hates, you can stand up and see a person and that person can be beautiful, and you will call them ugly. For the person who hates, the beautiful becomes ugly and the ugly becomes beautiful. For the person who hates, the good becomes bad and the bad becomes good. For the person who hates, the true becomes false and the false becomes true. That's what hate does. You can't see right. The symbol of objectivity is lost. Hate destroys the very structure of the personality of the hater.

And this is why Jesus says hate, that you want to be integrated with yourself, and the way to be integrated with yourself is [to] be sure that you meet every situation of life with an abounding love. Never hate, because it ends up in tragic, neurotic responses.* Psychologists and psychiatrists are telling us today that the more we hate, the more we develop guilt feelings, and we begin to subconsciously repress or consciously suppress certain emotions, and they all stack up in our subconscious selves and make for tragic, neurotic responses. And may this not be the neuroses of many individuals as they confront life that that is an element of hate there. And modern psychology is calling on us now to love. But long before modern psychology came into being, the world's greatest psychologist who

---

* When King delivered this sermon at Howard University, he invoked a 1927 essay by African American sociologist E. Franklin Frazier, who wrote: "Southern white people afflicted with the Negro-complex show themselves incapable of performing certain social functions. They are, for instance, incapable of rendering just decisions when white and colored people are involved" (Frazier, "The Pathology of Race Prejudice," *Forum* 77 [June 1927]: 856–62).

walked around the hills of Galilee told us to love. He looked at men and said: "Love your enemies; don't hate anybody." It's not enough for us to hate your friends because—to, to love your friends—because when you start hating anybody, it destroys the very center of your creative response to life and the universe; so love everybody. Hate at any point is a cancer that gnaws away at the very vital center of your life and your existence. It is like eroding acid that eats away the best and the objective center of your life. So Jesus says love, because hate destroys the hater as well as the hated.

Now there is a final reason I think that Jesus says, "Love your enemies." It is this: that love has within it a redemptive power. And there is a power there that eventually transforms individuals. That's why Jesus says, "Love your enemies." Because if you hate your enemies, you have no way to redeem and to transform your enemies. But if you love your enemies, you will discover that at the very root of love is the power of redemption. You just keep loving people and keep loving them, even though they're mistreating you. Here's the person who is a neighbor, and this person is doing something wrong to you and all of that. Just keep being friendly to that person. Keep loving them. Don't do anything to embarrass them. Just keep loving them, and they can't stand it too long. Oh, they react in many ways in the beginning. They react with bitterness because they're mad because you love them like that. They react with guilt feelings, and sometimes they'll hate you a little more at that transition period, but just keep loving them. And by the power of your love, they will break down under the load. That's love, you see. It is redemptive, and this is why Jesus says love. There's something about love that builds up and is creative. There is something about hate that tears down and is destructive. "Love your enemies."

I think of one of the best examples of this. We all remember the great president of this United States, Abraham Lincoln—these United States rather. You remember when Abraham Lincoln was running for president of the United States, there was a man who ran all around the country talking about Lincoln. He said a lot of bad things about Lincoln, a lot of unkind things. And sometimes he would get to the point that he would even talk about his looks, saying, "You don't want a tall, lanky, ignorant man like this as the president of the United States." He went on and on and on and went around with that type of attitude and wrote about it. Finally, one day Abraham Lincoln was elected president of the United States. And if you read the great biography of Lincoln, if you read the great works about him, you will discover that as every president comes to the point, he came to the point of having to choose a Cabinet.* And then came the time for him to choose a secretary of war. He looked across the nation and decided to choose a man by the name of Mr. [Edwin M.] Stanton. And when Abraham Lincoln stood around his advisers and mentioned this fact, they said to him: "Mr. Lincoln, are you a fool? Do you know what Mr. Stanton has been saying about you? Do you know what he has done, tried to do to you? Do you know that he has tried to defeat you on every hand? Do you know that, Mr. Lincoln? Did you read all of those derogatory statements that he made about you?" Abraham Lincoln stood before the advisers around him and said: "Oh yes, I know about it. I read about it. I've heard him myself. But after looking over the country, I find that he is the best man for the job."

---

* King is likely referring to Benjamin Thomas's *Abraham Lincoln: A Biography* (New York: Alfred A. Knopf, 1952).

Mr. Stanton did become secretary of war, and a few months later,* Abraham Lincoln was assassinated. And if you go to Washington, you will discover that one of the greatest words or statements ever made about Abraham Lincoln was made [by] this man Stanton. And as Abraham Lincoln came to the end of his life, Stanton stood up and said: "Now he belongs to the ages." And he made a beautiful statement concerning the character and the stature of this man. If Abraham Lincoln had hated Stanton, if Abraham Lincoln had answered everything Stanton said, Abraham Lincoln would have not transformed and redeemed Stanton. Stanton would have gone to his grave hating Lincoln, and Lincoln would have gone to his grave hating Stanton. But through the power of love, Abraham Lincoln was able to redeem Stanton.

That's it. There is a power in love that our world has not discovered yet. Jesus discovered it centuries ago. Mahatma Gandhi of India discovered it a few years ago, but most men and most women never discover it. For they believe in hitting for hitting; they believe in an eye for an eye and a tooth for a tooth; they believe in hating for hating; but Jesus comes to us and says, "This isn't the way."

And oh this morning, as I think of the fact that our world is in transition now. Our whole world is facing a revolution. Our nation is facing a revolution, our nation. One of the things that concerns me most is that in the midst of the revolution of the world and the midst of the revolution of this nation, that we will discover the

---

* This is incorrect. Stanton became secretary of war in 1862, more than three years before Lincoln's assassination. King corrected this error in later deliveries of the sermon.

meaning of Jesus's words. History unfortunately leaves some people oppressed and some people oppressors. And there are three ways that individuals who are oppressed can deal with their oppression. One of them is to rise up against their oppressors with physical violence and corroding hatred. But oh this isn't the way. For the danger and the weakness of this method is its futility. Violence creates many more social problems than it solves. And I've said, in so many instances, that as the Negro, in particular, and colored peoples all over the world struggle for freedom, if they succumb to the temptation of using violence in their struggle, unborn generations will be the recipients of a long and desolate night of bitterness, and our chief legacy to the future will be an endless reign of meaningless chaos. Violence isn't the way.

Another way is to acquiesce and to give in, to resign yourself to the oppression. Some people do that. They discover the difficulties of the wilderness moving into the promised land, and they would rather go back to the despots of Egypt because it's difficult to get in the promised land. And so they resign themselves to the fate of oppression; they somehow acquiesce to this thing. But that too isn't the way because noncooperation with evil is as much a moral obligation as is cooperation with good.

But there is another way. And that is to organize mass nonviolent resistance based on the principle of love. It seems to me that this is the only way as our eyes look to the future. As we look out across the years and across the generations, let us develop and move right here. We must discover the power of love, the power, the redemptive power of love. And when we discover that, we will be able to make of this old world a new world. We will be able to make men better. Love is the only way. Jesus discovered that.

Not only did Jesus discover it, even great military leaders discover that. One day as Napoleon came toward the end of his career and looked back across the years—the great Napoleon that at a very early age had all but conquered the world. He was not stopped until he became, till he moved out to the battle of Leipzig and then to Waterloo. But that same Napoleon one day stood back and looked across the years and said: "Alexander, Caesar, Charlemagne, and I have built great empires. But upon what did they depend? They depended upon force. But long ago Jesus started an empire that depended on love, and even to this day millions will die for him."

Yes, I can see Jesus walking around the hills and the valleys of Palestine. And I can see him looking out at the Roman Empire with all of her fascinating and intricate military machinery. But in the midst of that, I can hear him saying: "I will not use this method. Neither will I hate the Roman Empire." [*Recording interrupted*] . . . just start marching.*

And I'm proud to stand here in Dexter this morning and say that that army is still marching. It grew up from a group of eleven or twelve men to more than 700 million today. Because of the power and influence of the personality of this Christ, he was able to split history into AD and BC. Because of his power, he was able to shake the hinges from the gates of the Roman Empire. And all around the world this morning, we can hear the glad echo of heaven ring: "Jesus shall reign wherever sun does his successive journeys run. His kingdom spreads from shore to shore, till moon shall wane and wax no more."†

---

* In his Howard University sermon, King said, "I am just going to use love as my ammunition, and I am going out and put on the breastplate of righteousness and the whole armor of God and just start marching."

† King is paraphrasing Isaac Watts's hymn "Jesus Shall Reign" (1719).

We can hear another chorus singing: "All hail the power of Jesus's name."

We can hear another chorus singing: "Hallelujah, hallelujah! He's King of Kings and Lord of Lords. Hallelujah, hallelujah!"

We can hear another choir singing: "In Christ there is no east or west. In Him no north or south, but one great fellowship of love throughout the whole wide world."* This is the only way.

And our civilization must discover that. Individuals must discover that as they deal with other individuals. There is a little tree planted on a little hill, and on that tree hangs the most influential character that ever came in this world. But never feel that that tree is a meaningless drama that took place on the stages of history. Oh no, it is a telescope through which we look out into the long vista of eternity, and see the love of God breaking forth into time. It is an eternal reminder to a power-drunk generation that love is the only way. It is an eternal reminder to a generation depending on nuclear and atomic energy, a generation depending on physical violence, that love is the only creative, redemptive, transforming power in the universe.

So this morning, as I look into your eyes, and into the eyes of all of my brothers in Alabama and all over America and over the world, I say to you, "I love you. I would rather die than hate you." And I'm foolish enough to believe that through the power of this love, somewhere men of the most recalcitrant bent will be transformed. And then we will be in God's kingdom. We will be able to matriculate into the university of eternal life because we had the power to love

---

* King refers to the traditional hymn "All Hail the Power of Jesus's Name," and quotes verses from the "Hallelujah Chorus" of George Frideric Handel's "Messiah" and from the Christian hymn "In Christ There Is No East or West."

our enemies, to bless those persons that cursed us, to even decide to be good to those persons who hated us, and we even prayed for those persons who despitefully used us.

Oh God, help us in our lives and in all of our attitudes, to work out this controlling force of love, this controlling power that can solve every problem that we confront in all areas. Oh, we talk about politics; we talk about the problems facing our atomic civilization. Grant that all men will come together and discover that as we solve the crisis and solve these problems—the international problems, the problems of atomic energy, the problems of nuclear energy, and yes, even the race problem—let us join together in a great fellowship of love and bow down at the feet of Jesus. Give us this strong determination. In the name and spirit of this Christ, we pray. Amen.

Nonviolence and Racial Justice

SPEECH AT FRIENDS GENERAL CONFERENCE GATHERING

Cape May, New Jersey

"Bomb our homes and spit upon our children, and we will still love you. Send your hooded perpetrators of violence into our communities after midnight hours, and take us out on some wayside road, and beat us and leave us half dead, and we will still love you. Go all over the nation with your propaganda and make it appear that we are not fit morally or culturally or otherwise for integration, and we will still love you. But we will wear you down by our capacity to suffer. . . . We will so appeal to your heart and your conscience that we will win you in the process . . . "

In June 1958, King addressed the national organization of Quakers, who had been supportive of the Montgomery Bus Boycott and were by creed committed to nonviolence. His speech is reproduced here in its entirety. King presented an earlier version of this speech in Chicago in February 1957.

It is impossible to look out into the wide arena of American life without noticing a real crisis in race relations. This crisis has been precipitated, on the one hand, by the determined resistance of reactionary elements in the South to the Supreme Court's decision outlawing segregation in the public schools. This resistance has often risen to ominous proportions. Many states have risen up in open defiance. The legislative halls of the South ring loud with such words as "interposition" and "nullification." The Ku Klux Klan is on the march again and that other so-called respectable White Citizens' Councils. Both of these organizations have as their basic aim to defeat and stand in the way of the implementation of the Supreme Court's decision on desegregation. They are determined to preserve segregation at any cost. So all of these forces have conjoined to make for massive resistance.

But interestingly enough, the crisis has been precipitated, on the other hand, by radical change in the Negro's evaluation of himself. There would be no crisis in race relations if the Negro continued to think of himself in inferior terms and patiently accepted injustice and exploitation. But it is at this very point that the change has come. Something happened to the Negro. Circumstances made it possible and necessary for him to travel more; with the coming of the automobile, the upheavals of two world wars, and a great depression, his rural plantation background gradually gave way to urban industrial life. His cultural life was gradually rising through the steady decline of crippling illiteracy. And even his economic life was rising through the growth of industry and other influences. Negro masses all over began to reevaluate themselves, and the Negro came to feel that he was somebody. His religion revealed to him that God loves all of His children and that all men are made in His image. And so he came to see that the important thing about a man is not his specificity but his fundamentum, not the texture of his hair or the color of his skin but the texture and quality of his soul.

Since the struggle [for freedom and human dignity] will continue, the question is this: How will the struggle for racial justice

105

be waged? What are the forces that will be at work? What is the method that will be used? What will the oppressed peoples of the world do in this struggle to achieve racial justice? There are several answers to this question, but I would like to deal with only two. One is that the oppressed peoples of the earth can resort to the all-too-prevalent method of physical violence and corroding hatred. We all know this method; we're familiar with it. It is something of the inseparable twin of Western materialism. It has even become the hallmark of its grandeur.

Now I cannot say that violence never wins any victories; it occasionally wins victories. Nations often receive their independence through the use of violence. But violence only achieves temporary victory; it never can achieve ultimate peace. It creates many more social problems than it solves. And violence ends up defeating itself. Therefore it is my firm conviction that if the Negro succumbs to the temptation of using violence in his struggle for justice, unborn generations will be the recipients of a long and desolate night of bitterness. And our chief legacy to the future will be an endless reign of meaningless chaos.

The other method that is open to oppressed people as they struggle for racial justice is the method of nonviolent resistance, made famous in our generation by Mohandas K. Gandhi of India, who used it effectively to free his people from political domination, the economic exploitation, and humiliation inflicted upon them by Britain. There are several things we can say about this method. First, it is not a method of cowardice, of stagnant passivity; it does resist. The nonviolent resister is just as opposed to the evil that he is resisting as the violent resister. He resists evil, but he resists it without violence. This method is strongly active. It is true that it is passive in the sense that the nonviolent resister is never physically aggressive toward the opponent, but the mind is always active, constantly seeking to persuade the opponent that he is wrong.

This method does not seek to defeat and humiliate the opponent but to win his friendship and understanding. Occasionally, the nonviolent resister will engage in boycotts and noncooperation. But noncooperation and boycotts are not ends within themselves; they are merely a means to awaken a sense of shame within the oppressor and to awaken his dozing conscience. The end is redemption; the end is reconciliation. And so the aftermath of nonviolence is the creation of the beloved community, while the aftermath of violence is bitterness. The method of nonviolence is directed at the forces of evil rather than at the individuals caught in the forces of evil. The nonviolent resister seeks to defeat evil systems rather than individuals who are victimized by the evil systems.

The nonviolent resister accepts suffering without retaliation. He willingly accepts suffering. The nonviolent resister realizes that unearned suffering is redemptive; he is willing to receive violence, but he never goes out as a perpetrator of violence. He comes to see that suffering does something to the sufferer as well as the inflicter of the suffering.

Somehow the Negro must come to the point that he can say to his white brothers who would use violence to prevent integration, "We will match your capacity to inflict suffering by our capacity to endure suffering. We will meet your physical force with soul force. We will not hate you, but we cannot in all good conscience obey your unjust laws. Do to us what you may, and we will still love you. Bomb our homes and spit upon our children, and we will still love you. Send your hooded perpetrators of violence into our communities after midnight hours, and take us out on some wayside road, and beat us and leave us half dead, and we will still love you. Go all over the nation with your propaganda and make it appear that we are not fit morally or culturally or otherwise for integration, and we will still love you. But we will wear you down by our capacity to suffer, and one day we will win our freedom, and we will not only win freedom for ourselves. We will so appeal to your heart and your conscience that we will win you in the process, and therefore our victory will be a double victory."

That is another basic thing about nonviolent resistance. The nonviolent resister not only avoids external physical violence, but he avoids internal violence of spirit. He not only refuses to shoot his opponent, but he refuses to hate him. The oppressed people of the world must not succumb to the temptation of becoming bitter or indulging in hate campaigns. We must somehow come to see that this leads us only deeper and deeper into the mire; to return hate for hate does nothing but intensify the existence of hate and evil in the universe. So somehow people in this universe must have sense enough and morality enough to return love for hate.

Now when I speak of love, I am not talking about some sentimental affectionate emotion. I'm talking about something much deeper. In the Greek language there are three words for love. The Greek, for instance, talks about eros, a sort of aesthetic love. Plato talks about it a great deal in his dialogues, a yearning of the soul for the realm of the divine. It has come to us as romantic love. Therefore we know about eros. We have lived with eros.

And the Greek language talks about philia, which is also a type of love we have experienced. It is an intimate affection between personal friends; it's a reciprocal love. On this level we love because we are loved; we love people because we like them, we have things in common. And so we all experience this type of love.

Then the Greek language comes out with another word for love; it calls it agape: creative, understanding, redemptive goodwill for all men. It is a spontaneous love which seeks nothing in return; it's an overflowing love. Theologians would say that it is the love of God working in the lives of men. When we rise to love on this level, we love men not because we like them, not because their ways appeal to us; we love them because God loves them. We come to the point that we love the person who does the evil deed while hating the deed the person does. And I believe that this is what Jesus meant when he said, "Love your enemies."

The nonviolent resister has faith in the future. He somehow believes that the universe is on the side of justice. So he goes about his way, struggling for man's humanity to man, struggling for justice, for the triumph of love, because of this faith in the future and this assurance that he has cosmic companionship as he struggles.

Call it what you may—whether it is Being Itself with Paul Tillich, or the Principle of Concretion with Whitehead, or whether it is a Process of Integration with Wieman, or whether it is a sort of impersonal Brahman with Hinduism, or whether it is a personal God with boundless power and infinite love—there is something in this universe that works in every moment to bring the disconnected aspects of reality into a harmonious whole. There is a power that seeks to bring low prodigious hilltops of evil and pull down gigantic mountains of injustice, and this is the faith, this is the hope that can keep us going amid the tension and the darkness of any moment of social transition. We come to see that the dark of the moral universe is long, but it bends toward justice. This is the faith and the hope that will keep us going.

The nonviolent resister sees within the universe something

at the core and the heartbeat of the moral cosmos that makes for togetherness. There is something in this universe which justifies James Russell Lowell in saying,

> Truth forever on the scaffold, Wrong forever on the throne,
> Yet that scaffold sways the future, and, behind the dim unknown,
> Standeth God within the shadow, keeping watch above his own.

So down in Montgomery, Alabama, we can walk and never get weary because we know there is a great camp meeting in the promised land of freedom and justice.

The problem of race is certainly the chief moral dilemma of our nation. We are faced now with the tremendous responsibility of solving this problem before it is too late. The state of the world today does not permit us the luxury of an anemic democracy, and the clock of destiny is ticking out. We must solve this problem before it is too late. We must go out once more and urge all men of goodwill to get to work, urge all the agencies of our nation, the federal government, white liberals of the North, white moderates of the South, organized labor, the church and all religious bodies, and the Negro himself. And all these agencies must come together to work hard now to bring about the fulfillment of the dream of our democracy. Social progress does not roll in on the wheels of inevitability. It comes only through persistent work and the tireless efforts of dedicated individuals. Without this persistent work, time itself becomes the ally of the insurgent and primitive forces of irrational emotionalism and social stagnation. I think of the great work that has been done by the Society of Friends. It gives all of us who struggle for justice new hope, and I simply say to you this evening:

continue in that struggle, continue with that same determination, continue with that same faith in the future.

Modern psychology has a word that is used probably more than any other word in modern psychology. It is the word "maladjusted." All of us are desirous of living the well-adjusted life. I know I am, and we must be concerned about living a well-adjusted life in order to avoid neurotic and schizophrenic personalities. But I say to you, as I come to my close, that there are certain things within our social order to which I am proud to be maladjusted, and I call upon you to be maladjusted to all of these things. I never intend to become adjusted to segregation and discrimination. I never intend to adjust myself to the viciousness of mob rule. I never intend to adjust myself to economic conditions which take necessities from the masses to give luxuries to the classes. I never intend to adjust myself to the madness of militarism and the self-defeating effects of physical violence.

I call upon you to be maladjusted to each of these things. It may be that the salvation of our world lies in the hands of the maladjusted. So let us be maladjusted. As maladjusted as the prophet Amos, who in the midst of the injustices of his day could cry out in words that echo across the generations, "Let judgment run down like waters, and righteousness like a mighty stream." As maladjusted as Abraham Lincoln, who had the vision to see that this nation could not exist half slave and half free. As maladjusted as Thomas Jefferson, who in the midst of an age amazingly adjusted to slavery could cry out in words lifted to cosmic proportions, "All men are created equal, [and] . . . are endowed by their Creator with certain unalienable rights, [and] . . . among these are life, liberty, and the pursuit of happiness." As maladjusted as Jesus of Nazareth, who could look at the men of his generation and cry out, "Love your enemies, bless them that curse you, pray for them that despitefully use you."

Through such maladjustment we will be able to emerge from the bleak and desolate midnight of man's inhumanity to man into the bright and glittering daybreak of freedom and justice. This is what stands ahead. We've made progress, and it is great progress that we must make if we are to fulfill the dreams of our democracy, the dreams of Christianity, the dreams of the great religions of the world.

I close by quoting the words of an old Negro slave preacher who didn't have his grammar quite right. But he uttered words with profound meaning. The words were in the form of a prayer: "Lord, we ain't what we want to be, we ain't what we ought to be, we ain't what we gonna be, but thank God, we ain't what we was." And so tonight I say, "We ain't what we ought to be, but thank God we ain't what we was." And let us continue, my friends, going on and on toward that great city where all men will live together as brothers in respected dignity and worth of all human personality. This will be a great day, a day, figuratively speaking, when the "morning stars will sing together, and the sons of God will shout for joy."

Palm Sunday Sermon on Mohandas K. Gandhi

SERMON AT DEXTER AVENUE BAPTIST CHURCH
Montgomery, Alabama

"Here was a man of nonviolence, falling at the hand of a man of violence. Here was a man of love, falling at the hands of a man of hate. This seems the way of history."

For two months, King had not preached at his home church because of travel that took him from Europe to India, Lebanon, Jerusalem, and Egypt. But he returned to preach on Palm Sunday, which is celebrated the week before Easter. Palm Sunday marks Jesus's triumphant return to Jerusalem before he endures betrayals both petty and profound, his arrest and his crucifixion in the days of the following week.

The sermon is included here in full because of Gandhi's importance to King as an example of a leader who put love at the center of his existence and managed to create massive change for his people. Back in 1950, King had questioned if a "love your enemies" approach could work beyond personal relationships, but a lecture by Mordecai Johnson, the president of Howard University, changed his mind, and he began his studies of Gandhi's life.

King delivered a variation of the oratory as his first sermon as co-pastor with his father at Ebenezer Baptist Church in Atlanta. The sermon was titled "Follow the Way of Love" and was included in his book *The Measure of a Man* (Philadelphia: Christian Education Press, 1959).

To the cross and its significance in human experience.

This is the time in the year when we think of the love of God breaking forth into time out of eternity. This is the time of the year when we come to see that the most powerful forces in the universe are not those forces of military might but those forces of spiritual might. And as we sing together this great hymn of our church, the Christian church, hymn number 191, let us think about it again:

> When I survey the wondrous cross,
> On which the prince of glory died,
> I count my richest gains but loss
> And pour contempt on all my pride.

A beautiful hymn. I think if there is any hymn of the Christian church that I would call a favorite hymn, it is this one. And then it goes on to say, in that last stanza:

> Were the whole realm of nature mine,
> That was a present far too small.
> Love so amazing, so divine,
> Demands my life, my all and my all.*

---

* King is paraphrasing Isaac Watts's hymn "When I Survey the Wondrous Cross" (1707).

We think about Christ and the cross in the days ahead as he walks through Jerusalem and he's carried from Jerusalem to Calvary Hill, where he is crucified. Let us think of this wondrous cross.

[*Congregation sings "When I Survey the Wondrous Cross."*]

This, as you know, is what has traditionally been known in the Christian church as Palm Sunday. And ordinarily the preacher is expected to preach a sermon on the Lordship or the Kingship of Christ—the triumphal entry, or something that relates to this great event as Jesus entered Jerusalem, for it was after this that Jesus was crucified. And I remember, the other day, at about seven or eight days ago, standing on the Mount of Olives and looking across just a few feet and noticing that gate that still stands there in Jerusalem, and through which Christ passed into Jerusalem, into the old city.* The ruins of that gate stand there, and one feels the sense of Christ's mission as he looks at the gate. And he looks at Jerusalem, and he sees what could take place in such a setting. And you notice there also the spot where the temple stood, and it was here that Jesus passed and he went into the temple and ran the money-changers out.†

And so that, if I talked about that this morning, I could talk about it not only from what the Bible says but from personal experience, firsthand experience. But I beg of you to indulge me this morning to talk about the life of a man who lived in India. And I think I'm justified in doing this because I believe this man, more than anybody else in the modern world, caught the spirit of Jesus Christ and lived it more completely in his life. His name was Gandhi, Mohandas K.

---

* For more on King's travels in the Middle East, see "A Walk Through the Holy Land" (page 136 in this book).

† Cf. Mark 11:15.

Gandhi. And after he lived a few years, the poet Tagore, who lived in India, gave him another name: "Mahatma," the great soul.* And we know him as Mahatma Gandhi.

I would like to use a double text for what I have to say this morning; both of them are found in the Gospel as recorded by Saint John. One [is] found in the tenth chapter, and the sixteenth verse, and it reads, "I have other sheep, which are not of this fold." "I have other sheep, which are not of this fold." And then the other one is found in the fourteenth chapter of John, in the twelfth verse. It reads, "Verily, verily, I say unto you, he that believeth on me, the works that I do, shall he do also. And greater works than these shall he do because I go unto my Father."

I want you to notice these two passages of scripture. On the one hand, "I have other sheep that are not of this fold." I think Jesus is saying here in substance that "I have followers who are not in this inner circle." He's saying in substance that "I have people dedicated and following my ways who have not become attached to the institution surrounding my name. I have other sheep that are not of this fold. And my influence is not limited to the institutional Christian church." I think this is what Jesus would say if he were living today concerning this passage, that "I have people who are following me who've never joined the Christian church as an institution."

And then that other passage, I think Jesus was saying this—it's a strange thing, and I used to wonder what Jesus meant when he

---

* Indian nationalist and poet Rabindranath Tagore (1861–1941) won the Nobel Prize for Literature in 1913. It is believed that he was the first to address Gandhi as Mahatma. See *The Collected Works of Mahatma Gandhi*, vol. 15, August 1918–July 1919 (Delhi: Publications Division, Ministry of Information and Broadcasting, Government of India, 1965), pp. 495–96.

said, "There will be people who will do greater things than I did."* And I have thought about the glory and honor surrounding the life of Christ, and I thought about the fact that he represented the absolute revelation of God. And I've thought about the fact that in his life, he represented all of the glory of eternity coming into time. And how would it be possible for anybody to do greater works than Christ? How would it be possible for anybody even to match him, or even to approximate his work?

But I've come to see what Christ meant. Christ meant that in his life he would only touch a few people. And in his lifetime—and if you study the life of Christ, and if you know your Bible, you realize that Christ never traveled outside of Palestine, and his influence in his own lifetime was limited to a small group of people. He never had more than twelve followers in his lifetime; others heard about him and others came to see him, but he never had but twelve real followers, and three of them turned out to be not too good. But he pictured the day that his spirit and his influence would go beyond the borders of Palestine, and that men would catch his message and carry it over the world, and that men all over the world would grasp the truth of his gospel. And they would be able to do things that he couldn't do. They [would] be able to travel places that he couldn't travel. And they would be able to convert people that he couldn't convert in his lifetime. And this is what he meant when he said, "Greater works shall ye do, for an Apostle Paul will catch my work."

And I remember just last Tuesday morning standing on that beautiful hill called the Acropolis in Athens. And there, standing around the Parthenon, as it stands still in all of its beautiful

---

* Cf. John 1:50.

and impressive proportions, although it has been torn somewhat through wars, but it still stands there. And right across from the Acropolis you see Mars Hill. And I remember when our guide said, "That's the hill where the Apostle Paul preached."*

Now when you think of the fact that Athens is a long ways from Jerusalem, for we traveled right over Damascus where Paul was converted, and Damascus is at least five hours by flight from Athens. And you think about the fact that Paul had caught this message and carried it beyond the Damascus Road all over the world, and he had gone as far as Greece, as far as Athens, to preach the gospel of Jesus Christ. This is what Jesus meant that "somebody will catch my message, and they would be able to carry it in places that I couldn't carry it, and they would be able to do things in their lives that I couldn't do."

And I believe these two passages of scripture apply more uniquely to the life and work of Mahatma Gandhi than to any other individual in the history of the world. For here was a man who was not a Christian in terms of being a member of the Christian church but who was a Christian. And it is one of the strange ironies of the modern world that the greatest Christian of the twentieth century was not a member of the Christian church. And the second thing is that this man took the message of Jesus Christ and was able to do even greater works than Jesus did in his lifetime. Jesus himself predicted this: "Ye shall do even greater works."†

---

* Cf. Acts 17:22.

† King may have been influenced by missionary E. Stanley Jones's book on the life of Gandhi: "One of the most Christlike men in history was not called a Christian at all. . . . God uses many instruments, and he has used Mahatma Gandhi to help Christianize unchristian Christianity" (Jones, *Mahatma Gandhi: An Interpretation* [New York: Abingdon-Cokesbury Press, 1948], p. 77). King owned and annotated a copy of Jones's book.

Now let us look at the life, as briefly as possible, the life of this man and his work, and see just what it gives us, and what this life reveals to us in terms of the struggles ahead. I would say the first thing that we must see about this life is that Mahatma Gandhi was able to achieve for his people independence [*Congregation: Yes*] through nonviolent means. I think you should underscore this. He was able to achieve for his people independence from the domination of the British Empire without lifting one gun or without uttering one curse word. He did it with the spirit of Jesus Christ in his heart and the love of God, and this was all he had. He had no weapons. He had no army, in terms of military might. And yet he was able to achieve independence from the largest empire in the history of this world without picking up a gun or without any ammunition.

Gandhi was born in India in a little place called Porbandar, down almost in central India. And he had seen the conditions of this country. India had been under the domination of the British Empire for many years. And under the domination of the British Empire, the people of India suffered all types of exploitation. And you think about the fact that while Britain was in India, that out of a population of four hundred million people, more than three hundred and sixty-five million of these people made less than fifty dollars a year. And more than half of this had to be spent for taxes.

Gandhi looked at all of this. He looked at his people as they lived in ghettos and hovels and as they lived out on the streets, many of them. And even today, after being exploited so many years, they haven't been able to solve those problems. For we landed in Bombay, India, and I never will forget it, that night. We got up early in the morning to take a plane for Delhi. And as we rode out to the airport we looked out on the street and saw people sleeping out on the sidewalks and out in the streets, and everywhere we went to. Walk through the train station, and you can't hardly get to the train, because people are sleeping on the platforms of the train station. No homes to live in. In Bombay, India, where they have a population of three million people, five hundred thousand of these people sleep on the streets at night. Nowhere to sleep, no homes to live in, making no more than fifteen or twenty dollars a year or even less than that.

And this was the exploitation that Mahatma Gandhi noticed years ago. And even more than that, these people were humiliated and embarrassed and segregated in their own land. There were places that the Indian people could not even go in their own land. The British had come in there and set up clubs and other places and even hotels where Indians couldn't even enter in their own land. Gandhi looked at all of this, and as a young lawyer, after he had just left England and gotten his law, received his law training, he went over to South Africa. And there he saw in South Africa [that] Indians were even exploited there.*

And one day he was taking a train to Pretoria, and he had first-class accommodations on that train. And when they came to took up the tickets, they noticed that he was an Indian, that he had a brown face, and they told him to get out and move on to the third-class accommodation, that he wasn't supposed to be there with any first-class accommodation. And Gandhi that day refused to move, and they threw him off the train. And there, in that cold station that night, he stayed all night, and he started meditating on his plight and the plight of his people. And he decided from

* Gandhi was called to the bar in London in 1891 and traveled to South Africa two years later.

that point on that he would never submit himself to injustice or to exploitation.

It was there on the next day that he called a meeting of all of the Indians in South Africa, in that particular region of South Africa, and told them what had happened, and told them what was happening to them every day, and said that "we must do something about it. We must organize ourselves to rid our community, the South African community, and also the Indian community back home, of the domination and the exploitation of foreign powers."*

But Mahatma Gandhi came to something else in that moment. As he started organizing his forces in South Africa, he read the Sermon on the Mount.† He later read the works of the American poet Thoreau. And he later read the Russian author Tolstoy. And he found something in all of this that gave him insights. Started reading in the Bible, "turn the other cheek," "resist evil with good," "blessed are the meek, for they shall inherit the earth."‡ And all of these things inspired him to no end. He read Thoreau as he said that no just man can submit to anything evil, even if it means standing up and being disobedient to the laws of the state. And so this he combined into a new method, and he said to his people, "Now, it's possible to resist evil; this is your first responsibility; never adjust to evil, resist it. But if you can resist it without resorting to violence or

---

* Gandhi describes these events in his autobiography, *Gandhi's Autobiography: The Story of My Experiments with Truth* (Washington, DC: Public Affairs Press, 1948), part 2, chaps. 8–12.

† Cf. Matt. 5–7.

‡ Cf. Matt. 5:39, Rom. 12:21, and Matt. 5:5. In his autobiography, Gandhi recalled reading the Bible while a student in England (Gandhi, *Gandhi's Autobiography*, pp. 91–93).

to hate, you can stand up against it and still love the individuals that carry on the evil system that you are resisting."*

And a few years later, after he won a victory in South Africa, he went back to India. And there his people called on him, called on his leadership, to organize them and get ready for the trials ahead, and he did just that. He went back, and in 1917 he started his first campaign in India.† And throughout his long struggle there, he followed the way of nonviolent resistance. Never uttered a curse word, mark you. He never owned an instrument of violence. And he had nothing but love and understanding goodwill in his heart for the people who were seeking to defeat him and who were exploiting and humiliating his people.

And then came that day when he said to the people of India, "I'm going to leave this community." He had set up in a place called Ahmedabad, and there was the Sabarmati Ashram. He lived there with a group of people; his ashram was a place of quiet and meditation where the people lived together. And one day he said to those people, "I'm going to leave this place, and I will not return until India has received her independence." And this was in 1930. And he had so organized the whole of India then; people had left their jobs.

---

* Gandhi suggested that Thoreau's impact on him had been overstated: "The statement that I had derived my idea of civil disobedience from the writings of Thoreau is wrong. The resistance to authority in South Africa was well advanced before I got the essay of Thoreau on civil disobedience" (Gandhi to Kodanda Rao, September 10, 1935, in *The Collected Works of Mahatma Gandhi*, vol. 61, April 25–September 30, 1935 [Delhi: Publications Division, Ministry of Information and Broadcasting, Government of India, 1975], p. 401).

† Gandhi returned to India in 1915 and in 1917 began his first protest movement on behalf of exploited indigo farmers in Champaran, Bihar. The campaign, which consisted of rent strikes, work boycotts, and community development, led to the signing of the Champaran Agrarian Act (1918).

People with tremendous and powerful law practices had left their jobs. The president of India was a lawyer who had made almost a million rupees—a million dollars—and he left it, turned it all over to the movement. The father, the president of, the prime minister of India, Mr. [Motilal] Nehru, left his law practice to get in the freedom movement with Gandhi, and he had organized the whole of India.*

And you have read of the Salt March, which was a very significant thing in the Indian struggle. And this demonstrates how Gandhi used this method of nonviolence and how he would mobilize his people and galvanize the whole of the nation to bring about victory. In India, the British people had come to the point where they were charging the Indian people a tax on all of the salt, and they would not allow them even to make their own salt from all of the salt seas around the country. They couldn't touch it; it was against the law. And Gandhi got all of the people of India to see the injustice of this. And he decided one day that they would march from Ahmedabad down to a place called Dandi.

We had the privilege of spending a day or so at Ahmedabad at that Sabarmati Ashram, and we stood there at the point where Gandhi started his long walk of 218 miles. And he started there walking with eighty people. And gradually the number grew to a million, and it grew to millions and millions. And finally, they kept walking and walking until they reached the little village of Dandi. And there, Gandhi went on and reached down in the river, or in the sea rather, and brought up a little salt in his hand to demonstrate and

---

* In his autobiography, Jawaharlal Nehru describes his father's immersion into the freedom movement: "Noncooperation meant his withdrawing from his legal practice; it meant a total break with his past life and a new fashioning of it—not an easy matter when one is on the eve of one's sixtieth birthday" (Nehru, *Toward Freedom: The Autobiography of Jawaharlal Nehru* [New York: John Day Co., 1941], p. 66).

dramatize the fact that they were breaking this law in protest against the injustices they had faced all over the years with these salt laws.

And Gandhi said to his people, "If you are hit, don't hit back; even if they shoot at you, don't shoot back; if they curse you, don't curse back, (*Yes, Yes*) but just keep moving. Some of us might have to die before we get there; some of us might be thrown in jail before we get there, but let us just keep moving." And they kept moving, and they walked and walked, and millions of them had gotten together when they finally reached that point. And the British Empire knew, then, that this little man had mobilized the people of India to the point that they could never defeat them. And they realized, at that very point, that this was the beginning of the end of the British Empire as far as India was concerned.

He was able to mobilize and galvanize more people than, in his lifetime, than any other person in the history of this world. And just with a little love in his heart and understanding goodwill and a refusal to cooperate with an evil law, he was able to break the backbone of the British Empire. And this, I think, is one of the most significant things that has ever happened in the history of the world, and more than three hundred and ninety million people achieved their freedom. And they achieved it nonviolently when a man refused to follow the way of hate, and he refused to follow the way of violence, and only decided to follow the way of love and understanding goodwill and refused to cooperate with any system of evil.

And the significant thing is that when you follow this way, when the battle is almost over, a new friendship and reconciliation exists between the people who have been the oppressors and the oppressed. There is no greater friendship anywhere in the world today than between the Indian people and the British people. If you ask the Indian people today who they love more, what people, whether

they love Americans more, British more, they will say to you immediately that they love the British people more.

The night we had dinner with Prime Minister Nehru, the person who sat at that dinner table with us, as a guest of the prime
minister at that time, was Lady Mountbatten with her daughter,
the wife of Lord Mountbatten, who was the viceroy of India when
it received its independence.* And they're marvelous and great and
lasting friends. There is a lasting friendship there. And this is only
because Gandhi followed the way of love and nonviolence, refusing to hate and refusing to follow the way of violence. And a new
friendship exists. The aftermath of violence is always bitterness; the
aftermath of nonviolence is the creation of the beloved community
so that when the battle is over, it's over, and a new love and a new
understanding and a new relationship comes into being between
the oppressed and the oppressor.

This little man, one of the greatest conquerors that the world
has ever known. Somebody said that when Mahatma Gandhi was
coming over to England for the roundtable conference in 1932, a
group of people stood there waiting.† And somebody pointed out,
and while they were waiting somebody said, "You see around that
cliff? That was where Julius Caesar came, the way he came in when
he invaded Britain years ago." And then somebody pointed over to
another place and said, "That was the way William the Conqueror
came in. They invaded years ago in the Battle of Hastings." Then

---

* Louis Mountbatten (1900–1979) was the last viceroy of India. His wife, Edwina
Mountbatten (1901–1960), and their daughter Pamela (1929–) attended the
February 10 dinner with Nehru and the Kings.

† Between 1930 and 1932, three roundtable conferences were held in London to
consider a future constitution for India. Gandhi represented the Indian National
Congress at the second roundtable in 1931.

somebody else looked over and said, "There is another conqueror coming in. In just a few minutes the third and greatest conqueror that has ever come into Great Britain." And strangely enough, this little man came in with no armies, no guards around him, no military might, no beautiful clothes, just loincloth, but this man proved to be the greatest conqueror that the British Empire ever faced. He was able to achieve, through love and nonviolence, the independence of his people and break the backbone of the British Empire. "Ye shall do greater works than I have done." And this is exemplified in the life of Mahatma Gandhi.

Let me rush on to say a second thing: Here is a man who achieved in his life absolute self-discipline. Absolute self-discipline. So that in his life there was no gulf between the private and the public; there was no gulf in his life between the "is" and the "oughts." Here was a man who had absolved the "isness" of his being and the "oughtness" of his being. And this was one of the greatest accomplishments in his life. Gandhi used to say to his people, "I have no secrets. My life is an open book." And he lived that every day. He achieved in his life absolute self-discipline.

He started out as a young lawyer. He went to South Africa, and he became a thriving, promising lawyer making more than thirty thousand dollars a year. And then he came to see that he had a task ahead to free his people. And he vowed poverty, decided to do away with all of the money that he had made, and he went back to India and started wearing the very clothes that all of these disinherited masses of people of India had been wearing. He had been a popular young man in England, worn all of the beautiful clothes and his wife the beautiful saris of India with all of its silk beauty, but then he came to that point of saying to his wife, "You've got to drop this." And he started wearing what was called the dhoti, loincloth, the same thing that these masses of people wore. He did it, identified himself with them absolutely.

And he had no income; he had nothing in this world, not even a piece of property. This man achieved in his life absolute self-discipline to the point of renouncing the world. And when he died, the only thing that he owned was a pair of glasses, a pair of sandals, a loincloth, some false teeth, and some little monkeys who saw no evil, who said no evil, and who somehow didn't see any evil. This is all he had. And if you ask people in India today why was it that Mahatma Gandhi was able to do what he did in India, they would say they followed him because of his absolute sincerity and his absolute dedication. Here was a man who achieved in his life this bridging of the gulf between the "ought" and the "is." He achieved in his life absolute self-discipline.

And there is a final thing Mahatma Gandhi was able to do. He had the amazing capacity, the amazing capacity for internal criticism. Most others have the amazing capacity for external criticism. We can always see the evil in others; we can always see the evil in our oppressors. But Gandhi had the amazing capacity to see not only the splinter in his opponent's eye but also the planks in his own eye and the eye of his people.* He had the amazing capacity for self-criticism. And this was true in his individual life; it was true in his family life; and it was true in his people's life. He not only criticized the British Empire, but he criticized his own people when they needed it, and he criticized himself when he needed it.

And whenever he made a mistake, he confessed it publicly. Here was a man who would say to his people, "I'm not perfect. I'm not infallible. I don't want you to start a religion around me. I'm not

---

* Cf. Luke 6:41–42.

a god." And I'm convinced that today there would be a religion around Gandhi if Gandhi had not insisted all through his life that "I don't want a religion around me because I'm too human. I'm too fallible. Never think that I'm infallible."

And any time he made a mistake, even in his personal life or even in decisions that he made in the independence struggle, he came out in the public and said, "I made a mistake." In 1922, when he had started one of his first campaigns of nonviolence and some of the people started getting violent, some of the Indian people started getting violent, and they killed twenty some, twenty-eight of the British people in this struggle. And in the midst of this struggle, Gandhi came to the forefront of the scene and called the campaign off. And he stood up before the Indian people and before the British people and said, "I made a Himalayan blunder. I thought my people were ready; I thought they were disciplined for this task."* And people around Gandhi were angry with him. Even Prime Minister Nehru says in *Toward Freedom* that he was angry. His father was angry. All of these people who had left their hundreds and thousands of dollars to follow Gandhi and his movement were angry when he called this movement off.† But he called it off because, as he said, "I've made a blunder." And he never hesitated to acknowledge before the public when he made a mistake. And he always went back and said, "I made a mistake. I'm going back to rethink it; I'm going back to meditate over it. And I'll be coming

---

* Gandhi admitted to making a "Himalayan miscalculation" in organizing a protest movement against the English repression of Indian civil liberties in 1919 (Gandhi, *Gandhi's Autobiography*, p. 469). Three years later, Gandhi halted a noncooperation movement after an Indian mob killed twenty-two British officials in Chauri Chaura, Uttar Pradesh.

† Nehru, *Toward Freedom*, pp. 79–80.

back. Don't think the struggle is over; don't think I'm retreating from this thing permanently and ultimately. I'm just taking a temporary retreat because I made a mistake."

But not only that, he confessed the errors and the mistakes of his family. Even when his son, one of his sons, went wrong he wrote in his paper about it.[*] And his wife committed an act once that was sinful to him. He had pledged himself to poverty, and he would never use any of the money that came in for his personal benefit. And one day his wife, feeling the need for some of that money that had come in, decided to use it. And Gandhi discovered it, and he wrote in his paper that his wife had committed a grave sin.[†] He didn't mind letting the world know it. Here was a man who confessed his errors publicly and didn't mind if you saw him fail. He saw his own shortcomings, the shortcomings of his family, and then he saw the shortcomings of his own people.

We went in some little villages, and in these villages we saw hundreds of people sleeping on the ground. They didn't have any beds to sleep in. We looked in these same villages; there was no running water there, nothing to wash with. We looked in these villages, and we saw people there in their little huts and in their little rooms, and the cow, their little cow, or their calves slept in the same room with them. If they had a few chickens, the chickens slept in the same room with them. We looked at these people, and they had nothing that we would consider convenient, none of the comforts of life.

---

[*] Gandhi was responding to allegations that his eldest son, Harilal, operated a fraudulent business (*Young India*, June 18, 1925, in *The Collected Works of Mahatma Gandhi*, vol. 27, May–July 1925 [Delhi: Publications Division, Ministry of Information and Broadcasting, Government of India, 1968], pp. 259–62).

[†] Gandhi reflected on this incident in his autobiography (pp. 219–22).

Here they are, sleeping in the same room with the beast of the field. This is all they had. Pretty soon we discovered that these people were the untouchables.

Now you know in India you have what is known as the caste system, and that existed for years. And there were those people who were the outcasts, some seventy million of them. They were called untouchables. And these were the people who were exploited, and they were trampled over even by the Indian people themselves. And Gandhi looked at this system. Gandhi couldn't stand this system, and he looked at his people, and he said, "Now, you have selected me and you've asked me to free you from the political domination and the economic exploitation inflicted upon you by Britain. And here you are trampling over and exploiting seventy million of your brothers." And he decided that he would not ever adjust to that system and that he would speak against it and stand up against it the rest of his life.

And you read, back in his early life, the first thing he did when he went to India was to adopt an untouchable girl as his daughter.* And his wife thought he was going crazy because she was a member of one of the high castes. And she said, "What in the world are you doing adopting an untouchable? We are not supposed to touch these people." And he said, "I am going to have this young lady as my daughter." And he brought her into his ashram, and she lived there, and she lives in India today. And he demonstrated in his own life that untouchability had to go. And one of the greatest

* Gandhi adopted Lakshmi Dafda Sharma (1914–) in October 1920. Lakshmi and her parents, Dudabhai and Danibehn Dafda, became residents of the Satyagraha Ashram near Ahmedabad in September 1915 at Gandhi's invitation.

tasks ever performed by Mahatma Gandhi was against untouchability.

One day he stood before his people and said, "You are exploiting these untouchables. Even though we are fighting with all that we have in our bodies and our souls to break loose from the bondage of the British Empire, we are exploiting these people, and we're taking from them their selfhood and their self-respect." And he said, "We will not even allow these people to go into temple." They couldn't go in the temple and worship God like other people. They could not draw water like other people, and there were certain streets they couldn't even walk on.

And he looked at all of this. One day he said, "Beginning on the twenty-first of September at twelve o'clock, I will refuse to eat. And I will not eat any more until the leaders of the caste system will come to me with the leaders of the untouchables and say that there will be an end to untouchability. And I will not eat any more until the Hindu temples of India will open their doors to the untouchables." And he refused to eat. And days passed. Nothing happened. Finally, when Gandhi was about to breathe his last, breathe his last breath and his body—it was all but gone and he had lost many pounds. A group came to him. A group from the untouchables and a group from the Brahman caste came to him and signed a statement saying that we will no longer adhere to the caste system and to untouchability. And the priests of the temple came to him and said now the temple will be open unto the untouchables. And that afternoon, untouchables from all over India went into the temples, and all of these thousands and millions of people put their arms around the Brahmans and peoples of other castes. Hundreds and millions of people who had never touched each other for two thousand years were now singing and praising God together. And this was the great contribution that Mahatma Gandhi brought about.*

And today in India, untouchability is a crime punishable by the law. And if anybody practices untouchability, he can be put in prison for as long as three years. And as one political leader said to me, "You cannot find in India one hundred people today who would sign the public statement endorsing untouchability." Here was a man who had the amazing capacity for internal criticism to the point that he saw the shortcomings of his own people. And he was just as firm against doing something about that as he was about doing away with the exploitation of the British Empire. And this is what makes him one of the great men of history.

And the final thing that I would like to say to you this morning is that the world doesn't like people like Gandhi. That's strange, isn't it? They don't like people like Christ. They don't like people like Abraham Lincoln. They kill them. And this man, who had done all of that for India, this man who had given his life and who had mobilized and galvanized four hundred million people for independence so that in 1947 India received its independence, and he became the father of that nation. This same man because he decided that he would not rest until he saw the Muslims and the Hindus together; they had been fighting among themselves, they had been in riots among themselves, and he wanted to see this straight. And one of his own fellow Hindus felt that he was a little too favorable toward the Muslims, felt that he was giving in a little too much toward the Muslims.

And one afternoon, when he was at Birla House, living there with one of the big industrialists for a few days in Delhi, he walked

---

* King describes Gandhi's September 1932 fast, which was triggered by the British government's announcement of separate electorates for the untouchables.

out to his evening prayer meeting.* Every evening he had a prayer meeting where hundreds of people came, and he prayed with them. And on his way out there that afternoon, one of his fellow Hindus shot him. And here was a man of nonviolence, falling at the hand of a man of violence. Here was a man of love, falling at the hands of a man of hate.† This seems the way of history.

And isn't it significant that he died on the same day that Christ died; it was on a Friday. This is the story of history. But thank God it never stops here. Thank God Good Friday is never the end. And the man who shot Gandhi only shot him into the hearts of humanity. And just as when Abraham Lincoln was shot—mark you, for the same reason that Mahatma Gandhi was shot, that is, the attempt to heal the wounds of a divided nation. When the great leader Abraham Lincoln was shot, Secretary Stanton stood by the body of this leader and said, "Now he belongs to the ages." And that same thing can be said about Mahatma Gandhi now.‡ He belongs to the ages, and he belongs especially to this age, an age drifting once more to its doom.§ And he has revealed to us that we must learn to go another way.

For in a day when Sputniks and Explorers are dashing through outer space and guided ballistic missiles are carving highways of death through the stratosphere, no nation can win a war. Today it

---

* Gandhi frequently stayed at the home of G. D. Birla in New Delhi.

† Gandhi was murdered on January 30, 1948, by Nathuram Vinayak Godse, a member of the Rashtriya Swayamsevak Sangh, a Hindu nationalist organization. Godse was later hanged with a coconspirator.

‡ King used this same description in his March 9, 1959, "Farewell Statement for All India Radio." *The Papers of Martin Luther King, Jr. Volume V: Threshold of A New Decade. January 1959–December 1960* (Berkeley: University of California Press, 2005).

§ Jones, *Mahatma Gandhi: An Interpretation*, p. 159: "So Mahatma Gandhi is God's appeal to this age—an age drifting again to its doom."

is no longer a choice between violence and nonviolence; it is either nonviolence or nonexistence. It may not be that Mahatma Gandhi is God's appeal to this age, an age drifting to its doom. And that warning and that appeal is always in the form of a warning: "He who lives by the sword will perish by the sword."* Jesus said it years ago. Whenever men follow that and see that way, new horizons begin to emerge, and a new world unfolds. Who today will follow Christ in his way and follow it so much that we'll be able to do greater things even than he did because we will be able to bring about the peace of the world and mobilize hundreds and thousands of men to follow the way of Christ?

I close by quoting the words of John Oxenham:

> To every man there openeth a way, and ways, and a way
> The high soul climbs the high way, and the low soul gropes
> the low,
> And in between on the misty flats, the rest drift to and fro.
> But to every man—to every nation, to every civilization—there
> openeth a high and a low way.
> Every soul decideth which way it shall go.†

And God grant that we shall choose the high way, even if it will mean assassination, even if it will mean crucifixion, for by going

---

* Cf. Matt. 26:52.

† King is paraphrasing Oxenham's "The Ways," which was published in a collection of poems entitled *All's Well!* (New York: George H. Doran, 1916), p. 91. Allan Knight Chalmers, a professor of preaching and applied Christianity at Boston University and an acquaintance of King's, quoted Oxenham's verse in two of his books: *The Constant Fire* (New York: Charles Scribner's Sons, 1944), p. 104; and *High Wind at Noon* (New York: Charles Scribner's Sons, 1948), pp. 76–77.

this way we will discover that death would be only the beginning of our influence.

"I have other sheep," says Jesus, "which are not of this fold. And if you will believe in me and follow my way, you will be even, you will be able to do even greater works than I did in my lifetime."

O God, our gracious Heavenly Father, we thank Thee for the fact that you have inspired men and women in all nations and in all cultures. We call you different names: some call Thee Allah; some call you Elohim; some call you Jehovah; some call you Brahma; and some call you the unmoved Mover; some call you the Architectonic Good. But we know that these are all names for one and the same God, and we know you are one.

And grant, O God, that we will follow Thee and become so committed to Thy way and Thy kingdom that we will be able to establish in our lives and in this world a brotherhood. We will be able to establish here a kingdom of understanding, where men will live together as brothers and respect the dignity and worth of all human personality.

In the name and spirit of Jesus we pray. Amen. [*organ plays*]

We open the doors of the church now. Is there one who will accept the Christ this morning just as you are? Who will make that decision as we stand and sing together? One hundred and sixty-two. [*Congregation sings "Just As I Am."*]

Let us remain standing now for the recessional hymn. We are grateful to God for these persons who have come to unite with the church. I might mention, just before leaving, that this afternoon the baby contest which is sponsored by the August club [*recording interrupted*]

A Walk Through the Holy Land

EASTER SUNDAY SERMON AT DEXTER AVENUE BAPTIST CHURCH

Montgomery, Alabama

"[The cross] tells us not only about the courage and the commitment, the moral commitment, of Jesus Christ, but it tells us about the love of God himself, the length to which God is willing to go to restore broken communities."

A week after King's sermon on Gandhi, he delivered this sermon, included here in full, at Dexter Avenue Baptist Church in celebration of Easter Sunday.

It was on a beautiful afternoon a few weeks ago that we journeyed from our hotel in Beirut, Lebanon, to the airport to take a plane for Jerusalem. Lebanon is that beautiful country in the Middle East that we remember from biblical times, for occasionally we read about the cedars of Lebanon. And Beirut is that beautiful city that sits elevated on a hill overlooking the mighty Mediterranean Sea. Pretty soon we were in the air passing through places like Damascus. There again you remember Damascus, you remember it in modern days as the capital of the little country of Syria. But you remember Damascus as an ancient city, for it was on the Damascus road that the apostle Paul was converted. You remember as he stood one day before King

Agrippa, he said, "It was at noon day, oh King, that I saw a light, a light that outshines the radiance, the brilliance of the sun."* And after seeing that light and gaining a new vision, he was transformed from Saul the persecutor to Paul the Christian and became one of the great Christian saints of all generations.

After about two hours in the air we were notified to fasten our seat belts—we were beginning to descend, the descent for the airport in Jerusalem. Now, I must say that when you say "landing in Jerusalem," you must qualify what you are saying and tell what part of Jerusalem. That is because men have not solved their social problems, and we're still banned because in their Jerusalem, that ancient holy city has been divided and split up and partitioned. And before you can enter one side of the city, it must be clear that you will not enter the other because one side is Jerusalem, Israel, the other side is Jerusalem, Jordan. Because of the Arab-Israeli conflict, this city has been divided. And if on your visa it is revealed that you are going into any Arab nation, you can only go to Israel without being able to ever go back to an Arab country in the life of your passport; the hate is intensified. And so this was a strange feeling to go to the ancient city of God and see the tragedies of man's hate and his evil, which causes him to fight and live in conflict.

But we were going to Jerusalem, Jordan. And it is in this section of Jerusalem that all of the ancient sites, on the whole, are preserved. Those sacred, holy sites. We landed there, in Jerusalem, Jordan, and in a few moments, we had checked in [at] our hotel, which was a YMCA hotel. Pretty soon we discovered, after checking in, that many other people were there from all over the world, many people from the United States, who were on tour through the world from

---

* Cf. Acts 26:13.

various sections of the world. This is always one of the interesting things about traveling, that you learn to know people. You meet people of all races and of all cultures, and you tend to be lifted above provincialism, and chauvinism, and what the sociologists call ethnocentrism. You come to see a unity in mankind. If I had my way, I would recommend that all of the students who can afford it to go to college five years; they would study in that college four years, and they would use their tuition one year and their board and what have you to travel abroad. I think this is the greatest education that can ever come to an individual. I think if more of our white brothers in the South had traveled a little more, many of our problems would be solved today. So often we live in our little shells because we've never risen above the province. We've never risen above sectionalism. And so it was a great pleasure to meet people, various sections of the world, various sections of our own nation.

The next morning we rose early because we knew that this was the day that we would start our pilgrimage around this holy city, and this was the day that we would tour Jerusalem itself. The next day we were to go to Hebron. There stands abound the points where Abraham stood. There we would see the tomb of Abraham, Isaac, and Jacob, and Sarah, and others. And from there we moved to Bethlehem, that city, "oh little town of Bethlehem," we hear Phillips Brooks talking about it. We sing about it. We talk about "yet in the dark streets shineth the everlasting light." We think about it as that city where "the hopes and fears of all the years met in thee tonight."* And that city where the wise men decided to leave because an event

---

* Episcopalian minister and abolitionist Phillips Brooks (1835–1893) wrote the hymn "O Little Town of Bethlehem" in 1868, recalling his visit to the Holy Land three years earlier. King is paraphrasing lines from the opening stanza of the hymn.

was taking place, and they went to see it and be a part of it.* We were to stand there to see this spot and this place where our Christ was born. And to see the little inn, which is still preserved, where there was no room, no room for Christ, crowded out.† When one looks at that, he cannot help but think of the fact that this is the long story of human history. We crowd him out by being preoccupied with other things. It doesn't mean that we are preoccupied with bad things either. So often the choice in life is not between the bad and the good; it's between the good and the better. And so often we fail to make way for the better because we are bogged down in the good. Those were not bad people in that inn that night. They were good people, I'm sure, and they had noble purposes for being there; and the innkeeper was good, but they didn't have room for the better. This is so often the tragedy of life. And this came back as we stood there.

A day later we were to journey into Samaria. There, I think about the ancient days when the Jews had no dealings with the Samaritans. We looked up in Mount Gerizim, where the temple of the Samaritans used to exist, and we attended a service one afternoon. There are only two hundred and thirty Samaritans left in the whole world, and they live right around that little ancient shore there. And there we went and saw those people, and they had preserved there in their little temple an ancient document known as the Pentateuch, the first five books of the Bible. And it is supposed to be the most ancient document in the world. And these five books of the Bible—Genesis, Exodus, Leviticus, Numbers, and Deuteronomy—we had a privilege, the privilege to see that, written in its old Hebrew.

---

* Cf. Matt. 2:9–12.

† Cf. Luke 2:6–7.

Then we were to go later to Jericho and to see that great city. And to think of the Jericho road that Jesus had talked about, that winding road. And when you travel on that road you can see why a man could easily be robbed on that road. Jesus told a parable about it one day.* And then you see the walls of Jericho, which have recently been excavated. And you think about the walls of Jericho, and you think about Joshua, and you think about Joshua fighting the battle of Jericho.† And then around Jericho you go to the Dead Sea and also the river of Jordan. And all of these things were in store for us.

And we stood in the holy city, but this day we would only go around the city of Jerusalem. Our guide came early that morning immediately after we had eaten breakfast. We'd started out, and interestingly enough, our first stop that morning was a mountain, a mountain that we've all heard about called the Mount of Olives. We've heard about that mountain in our Bible; we've read about [it]. And every night, every first Sunday night when we have communion, we read about it. Well, you remember it says that after the last supper they had sung a hymn, and they went out into the Mount of Olives.‡ This was a significant mountain in the life of Christ. It has many interesting connotations. And you can stand there on the Mount of Olives and look over the whole of Jerusalem. Exalted that high, elevated that high, and you can look all around and see the old city and the new city. There we stood there on the Mount of Olives with all of its sacred meaning. Just below that mount at the bottom you see a little garden. It is known as the garden of Gethsemane,

---

* Cf. Luke 10:30–37.

† Cf. Josh. 4:13–24.

‡ Cf. Matt. 26:30–31.

and it's still preserved there with beautiful flowers; it's a beautiful garden.

But there is something about that garden that we must always remember. It is the garden where Christ agonized with his own soul.* It is the garden where Christ uttered a statement which reveals that he was amazingly human. He didn't want to die, for we read that he said, "Father, if Thy be willing, let this cup pass from me."† This is a painful, difficult cup. But then we see there the meaning of religion and all of its profound meaning, the transformation that comes about when you love God and when you know him. We hear him in that same garden, saying a few minutes later, "Not my will but Thy will be done."‡ It was the same garden. And there is something else that you must remember about this garden. It was the garden where Jesus faced the most lonesome moments of his life. It was the garden where his three friends deceived him and were not concerned enough about him to stay awake while he was there praying. We read in the scripture that they went to sleep not concerned.§ Isn't it tragic and dark in life when even those people that we have confidence in and that we believe in and we call our friends fail to understand us? And in the most difficult moments of life they leave us going the road alone. This is the story of life, though. So Gethsemane is not only a spot on the map. Gethsemane is an experience in the heart and the soul. Gethsemane is something that we

---

* King's Palm Sunday sermon two years earlier had focused on Jesus's experience in the garden (King, "Garden of Gethsemane," sermon delivered at Dexter Avenue Baptist Church, Montgomery, AL, April 14, 1957).

† Cf. Matt. 26:39.

‡ Cf. Matt. 26:42.

§ Cf. Matt. 26:43–45.

go through every day. For whenever our friends deceive us, we face Gethsemane. Whenever we face great moral decisions in life and we find that we must stand there and people turn their backs on us and they think we are crazy, we are facing Gethsemane. Gethsemane is a story that comes to all of us in life. We looked at this garden, and all of these thoughts came back.

Just over from Gethsemane we saw a gate. And our guide said to us that this is the gate where Jesus entered Jerusalem. This is the gate where Jesus made the triumphal entry. We read about this. We read about the triumphant entry that day when Jesus came into Jerusalem. He came by way of the Mount of Olives, by the way, and entered that holy city, that city where so many things stood in terms of the long history of Judaism. That city that had stoned its prophets, that city that had crucified men because they stood up for right. This is the city that Jesus entered, and he entered through that gate. Why did he enter in this triumphant entry? We don't know. Some scholars said that this was the moment that Jesus decided to let the secret out; the messianic secret had been a secret for a long time, and now he would let men know that he was Messiah. Others would say that Jesus was not doing this himself, but his followers were doing it. Those that he had let in on the, allowed to know the secret, would now let men know it, and so they were the ones who precipitated the triumphant entry. Others would say that this was the day of the Feast of Tabernacles. And it so often happened that on that day there were great parades and great crowds. And so it happened that Jesus entered on the day of the Feast of Tabernacles, and the people decided that they wanted to honor this great prophet as he entered the city on the day of the Feast of Tabernacles.[*]

---

[*] Cf. Luke 19:28–38.

Maybe there is some truth in all three of these theories. But at least there is something more basic than all of this and that was that Jesus entered Jerusalem as a different kind of king. He didn't enter as David with great military power and great military might or as Saul with all of the military power. [*word inaudible*] Not even as Solomon with all of his wealth. But he entered on a lowly ass, which revealed that this was a new kind of king, not the same type of king that had come in the past but a king who had another type of kingdom. And so his escort would be not spear but palm. And he would enter by the voices of little children, not by the shouts of soldiers. A new kind of kingdom and a new kind of king.

And he entered this gate, and we walked around and through there and pretty soon, about fifty feet from the gate, we came to a spot and the guide said, "This is where the old temple stood, the Temple of Jerusalem." You remember that temple fell in 70 AD. The Roman Empire came to stop an uprising in Palestine, and they destroyed the temple. But the spot is still reserved, and there is a big stone in the middle of that point where all of the sacrifices used to take place on the altar. This was the temple where Jesus entered as soon as he got to Jerusalem a few hours and ran the money-changers out of the temple.* This was where Jesus made his profound mistake. And what was his profound mistake? His profound mistake was that he went beyond the realm of talking about what he believed but he was willing to act about it. And he was willing to act on truth, and the world considers that a mistake.

We looked at this temple; then we started walking the ancient streets of Jerusalem. And you cannot walk those little narrow streets in that old city, as you move through the gate of Damascus and the

---

* Cf. Luke 19:45–48.

gate of Corinth, without getting a real sense of history and the ancient qualities of that old city. We walked those narrow streets, and then finally that afternoon we came to another point. This was the point known as Pilate's judgment hall. In Jerusalem today all of the sacred points are enclosed, you see; they have churches around them now. Helena, the mother of Constantine, back in the fourth century went to Jerusalem. After finding all of these sacred points of the death and the life of Jesus and the Resurrection of Jesus, she had churches erected there. And so you will find a church erected around every sacred point in Jerusalem. And we stood there where the church stands now, that point known as Pilate's judgment hall. This was where Jesus was tried. This was where Jesus faced, on the outside, a crowd crying, "Crucify him."* This is where Jesus had to stand before a man who knew that he had no faults but who, willing to content the people, decided to crucify him. And one cannot leave that point without weeping for Pilate, for here is a man who sacrificed truth on the altar of his self-interest. Here was a man who crucified justice on the cross of his egotism.

Then you leave that point, which is the judgment hall, and you start a new walk. It is known as the Via Dolorosa. This is the way of sorrow. And it is the way Jesus walked from the judgment hall on to the cross. You walk there—it's about a mile—from that point up to Golgotha, the place of the skull, or Calvary. This is the walk that is a noble walk. It is a walk that does something to the soul because you know that as you walk there, you're walking the way of sorrow that Christ walked. And they have, as you walk along the way, spots. They call them stations—station one, station two—

---

* Cf. John 19:6–15.

and there are fourteen stations between the judgment hall of Pilate and the place where Jesus was brought and crucified. And at every station, some significant event occurred, something happened. At one station Jesus stumbled; at another station Jesus fell; at another station he got up; at another station somebody came to help him along the way. And I will remember the experience that came when the guide said, "At this station Jesus stumbled and fell with that heavy cross on his shoulder." This was the tradition, you see, for when a person was crucified they made them carry the cross themselves. This was heavy, and Jesus had broken down under the load, and he'd fallen.

And I started thinking of something that I heard my friend Archibald Carey say some time ago.* The thing that I thought about at that moment was the fact that when Jesus fell and stumbled under that cross it was a Black man that picked it up for him and said, "I will help you," and took it on up to Calvary. And I think we know today there is a struggle, a desperate struggle, going on in this world. Two-thirds of the people of the world are colored people. They have been dominated politically, exploited economically, trampled over, and humiliated. There is a struggle on the part of these people today to gain freedom and human dignity. And I think one day God will remember that it was a Black man that helped His son in the darkest and most desolate moment of his life. It was a Black man who picked up that cross for him and who took that cross on up to Calvary. God will remember this. And in all of our struggles for peace and security, freedom and human dignity, one day God will

* Archibald Carey (1868–1931) was pastor of Quinn Chapel AME Church in Chicago.

145

remember that it was a Black man who aided his only begotten son in the darkest hour of his life.*

You keep walking on that way, that way of sorrow, that way of trials and tribulations, and you finally come to that church known as the Church of the Holy Sepulchre. And it's here, it is here within that church that you find the point where Jesus was crucified. It is here that you come to the cross of Jesus the Christ. Now certainly the cross that stands there today is not the same cross that Jesus was crucified on, but you forget that for the moment. You begin to feel the fact that you are around the spot where he was crucified. I never will forget the experience that came to me. And I stood before that cross and before the point, something within began to well up. There was a captivating quality there, there was something that overwhelmed me, and before I knew it, I was on my knees praying at that point. And before I knew it, I was weeping. This was a great world-shaking, transfiguring experience. And I remember we were with some other people and I, after that, went back to the hotel. And I left Coretta and the other people and said I was going in to the hotel, and I went on back alone. I walked back that same way and went back to the hotel alone and tried to meditate on the meaning of that cross and the meaning of the experience that I just had. And I started thinking in a way that I'd never thought before of the meaning of the cross.

And as I meditated on that cross, these things came to my mind. As I tried to calculate in my own mind and in my own limited way the meaning of this cross, these things came to my mind. That first, Jesus didn't have to go to this cross. He voluntarily did something

---

* King is referring to Simon of Cyrene, who was commanded by Pilate's soldiers to carry Jesus's cross (cf. Matt. 27:32).

that nobody could demand him to do. Nobody could ever demand that he sacrifice his life in a way like this. And he didn't have to do it. He could have recanted, and everything could have been all right. He could have gone back on the back side with the Mount of Olives and gone on back to Galilee, forgotten about the whole thing, and everything would have been all right. But here was a man who had the amazing capacity to be obedient to unenforceable obligations. I think this is what the cross says to us this morning. If there is any one thing that I would like for you to leave with this morning and that is that a man is not a man until he is obedient to the unenforceable.

There are three groups of people in the world. They are the lawless people on the one hand—people who break laws, people who are in our prisons, people who never follow the codes of society, whether they are written laws or customs. These are the lawless people. Then you have a second group—the law-abiding people whose standards of conduct come mainly from without. Their standards come from the man-made law, the law written on the book, or the customs and mores of society. So many people fit into this category. I would suspect that most of us here this morning would fit into this category. We are not lawless people; we are law-abiding. We follow what the law says, and we follow what the law without says; we are certainly true to the customs and mores of our community. There is a third group—those people who are committed to an inner law, those people who have an interior criteria of conduct. And this is the difference. These are the people who have an inner [*word inaudible*]. These are the people who are obedient to the unenforceable. These are the people who are obedient to something that the law without could never demand and could never write for you to do. These are the people who, in the words of, those beautiful words that Shakespeare said about Desdemona: "They hold it something of a vice in their goodness not to do more than is required.* These are the people who change history and who make history. They come occasionally.

It might be a Socrates who talks to his friend Crito, who tells him that he can leave and everything can be all right and he need not face the tragedy of the hemlock. Socrates looks back and says to him, "I must stand on what I consider to be right and true, even if it brings death to me."† And now he said at the end of the *Apology*, "I go to life and, you—I go to death, and you go to life. Which of us goes to the better life, nobody knows but God. But I go because I believe finally in truth."‡

It might be a Martin Luther who stands before the officials of the Catholic Church. They tried to get him to recant and take back everything that he said about the corruption in the system of indulgences, about the Ninety-Five Theses that he tacked on the door of Wittenberg. And he stands before them and said, "Here I stand. I can do none other, so help me God."

It might be a Jesus of Nazareth who can leave and go back to Nazareth and become merely an insignificant character in history but who said to himself, "Oh no, I cannot follow this way. I must be true to what I know is truth and what I know is right. What I know will eventually be a part of the structure of the universe." And this is what the cross says to us this morning: greatness in life comes when we are obedient to the unenforceable.

---

* William Shakespeare, *Othello*, act 2, scene 3.

† Plato, *Crito*.

‡ Plato, *Apology*.

A great nation is a nation that has citizens who are obedient not only to the laws written on the books but people who are obedient to those unenforceable laws. Great family, beautiful home life built not on the enforceable, on the unenforceable. Ultimately, there is a quality that can't be enforced. Whether a man is faithful to his wife or whether a wife is faithful to the husband is not enforceable. Ultimately, the individual must be obedient to the unenforceable. Whether a man will support his children and be true to them is unenforceable. The law can say you must support your children, but the law can't make you love your children. The law cannot make you give as much time to your children as you should. The law cannot keep you from going into endless activities and endless social functions while you neglect your children. The law can't make you stop doing that. Ultimately it is obedience to the unenforceable. And whenever a man rises to this point, he rises to the greatness of Jesus Christ on the cross.

This is what the cross says to me more than anything else—that we find a man who had the amazing capacity to be obedient to unenforceable obligation. And this is what he meant in his life, he lived it in his life. You remember he said, "Go the second mile. If they compel you to go the first, go the second."* Now what was Jesus saying? He said it again, "If men ask you to forgive them, don't stop seven times; forgive seventy times seven."† Maybe they can require you to forgive seven times. But what he's saying is this—that the privilege of generosity begins when the requirement of the law ends. Jesus said this, and this is what he is doing on the cross. The cross

* Cf. Matt. 5:41.
† Cf. Matt. 18:21–22.

is a climax of all that he had lived and expressed in his life. Going the second mile means merely being obedient to the unenforceable. This was the one thing that that cross said to me.

But it said something else to me which had great meaning as I thought about it. The cross is an eternal expression of the length to which God is willing to go to restore a broken community. Now this, I think is very vital. It tells us not only about the courage and the commitment, the moral commitment, of Jesus Christ, but it tells us about the love of God himself, the length to which God is willing to go to restore broken communities. Through our sins, through our evil, and through our wickedness, we've broken up communities. We've torn up society. Families are divided; homes are divided; cultures are divided; nations are divided; generations are divided; civilizations are divided. Jesus experienced this in his day. He knew that, and God looked out, he looked back at Israel, and he knew that Israel had been a naughty child. She had gone whoring after other gods. She had brought about division in the very center of her being. And what is the cross but God's way of saying to a wayward child, "I still love you, and I am willing to go any length, including sacrificing the life of my only begotten son, in order to redeem you. And in order to come and to say to you that if you will see within that suffering Christ on the cross my power, you will be able to be transformed. And you will be redeemed." That cross is an expression of the eternal love of God our Father.

There is a final point. The cross is not only an expression of the love of God and the courage and moral commitment of Jesus Christ who is obedient to the unenforceable. But I started thinking of the fact; as we stood at that cross, there was a little walk, maybe about sixty or seventy-five feet. They said to us that this is the tomb where

Jesus was buried. Strangely enough, it was a borrowed tomb.* Borrowed tomb—he didn't have anything; he didn't have any money. He didn't have anywhere to lay his head.† Even when he died on a cross, one of the most ignominious deaths that we can ever point to in history, he had to be buried in a borrowed grave. We stood in there. But that guide began to talk, and he became eloquent when he talked about it. He said, "But I want you to know that this tomb is empty. He is not there now. This is just a symbol of where he was, but he isn't there now." And oh, that cross to me is a demonstration of something. It is triumph, isn't it? It is not only tragedy, but it is triumph. It is a revelation of the power of God to ultimately win out over all of the forces of evil.

Whatever you believe about the Resurrection this morning isn't important. The form that you believe in, that isn't the important thing. The fact that the revelation, Resurrection is something that nobody can refute, that is the important thing. Some people felt, the disciples felt, that it was a physical resurrection, that the physical body got up. Then Paul came on the scene, who had been trained in Greek philosophy, who knew a little about Greek philosophy and had read a little, probably, of Plato and others who believed in the immortality of the soul, and he tried to synthesize the Greek doctrine of the immortality of the soul with the Jewish-Hebrew doctrine of resurrection. And he talked, as you remember and you read it, about a spiritual body. A spiritual body. Whatever form, that isn't important right now. The important thing is that that Resurrection did occur. Important thing is that that grave was

---

* Cf. Matt. 27:59–60.

† Cf. Matt. 8:20.

empty. Important thing is the fact that Jesus had given himself to certain eternal truths and eternal principles that nobody could crucify and escape. So all of the nails in the world could never pierce this truth. All of the crosses of the world could never block this love. All of the graves in the world could never bury this goodness. Jesus had given himself to certain universal principles. And so today the Jesus and the God that we worship are inescapable.

We can talk this morning about the inescapable Christ. We can get by and for all of the world he lives today. He lives today in society; he lives today in our lives; he lives today in the world. And this is our hope. This is what keeps us going. There is something in the cross that is not only an element of tragedy; there is an element of triumph within that cross. So you can go out this morning with new hope, new hope for the future. No matter how dark it gets, realize that God ultimately transforms Good Friday into Easter.

Some years ago, somebody asked William Howard Taft, "What about the League of Nations?" He said most good things in this world get crucified, eventually placed in a tomb.* There's always the third day. Isn't that true? That League of Nations that was one day crucified, today, [*gap in tape*] has been resurrected in the United Nations. Woodrow Wilson probably died unhappy and frustrated because men didn't have the vision to see it.† They didn't have the vision to follow it. But today there's the United Nations, which is nothing but the old League of Nations on a broader scale. And be-

---

* William Howard Taft (1857–1930) was the twenty-seventh president of the United States (1909–1913). In 1921, Taft was appointed chief justice of the US Supreme Court.

† In 1920, President Woodrow Wilson (1856–1924) failed in his efforts to gain Senate approval for US membership in the League of Nations. He died four years later. The United States joined the United Nations in 1945.

fore there can ever be peace in this world, we must turn to an instrument like the United Nations and disarm the whole world and develop a world police power so that no nation will possess atomic and hydrogen bombs for destruction. This is our hope, isn't it? It was buried one day, but now it has been resurrected. Years ago, back in 1896, doctrine was crucified, the doctrine of righteousness, the doctrine of treating men as equals. The doctrine of integration, it was crucified. There was a man by the name of Justice [John Marshall] Harlan who was crucified along with it, I guess. He was condemned because he gave a dissenting vote when they set forth the *Plessy v. Ferguson* decision.* But thank God there came May 17, 1954, and it was resurrected.† Given in a unanimous decision by the Supreme Court of the United [States], here was a minority opinion in 1896 which became a majority opinion in 1954. What is this saying? The cross reveals to us that ultimately the impractical idealists of yesterday become the practical realists of today. The cross reveals to us that what was a minority opinion yesterday becomes a majority opinion tomorrow, and the world forgets that it ever trampled over it because it rises up with new truth and new meaning and new beauty. This is what the cross tells us. It brings hope to us.

And so this morning, let us not be disillusioned. Let us not lose faith. So often we've been crucified. We've been buried in numerous graves—the grave of economic insecurity, the grave of exploitation, the grave of oppression. We've watched justice trampled over and

---

* The Supreme Court's 1896 *Plessy v. Ferguson* (163 U.S. 537) decision upheld a Louisiana law mandating separate but equal accommodations for Blacks and whites on intrastate railroads.

† In 1954, in *Brown v. Board of Education* (347 U.S. 483), the Supreme Court unanimously reversed the doctrine of "separate but equal" and declared racial segregation in public schools unconstitutional.

truth crucified. But I'm here to tell you this morning, Easter reminds us that it won't be like that all the way. It reminds us that God has a light that can shine amid all of the darkness. And he can bring all of the light of day out of the darkness of the midnight.

I close with this little experience some weeks ago, about four Sundays ago. Mrs. King and I journeyed down to a city in India called Trivandrum. It is a city in the last state, the southernmost point of the country of India. And then we went from Trivandrum on down to a point known as Cape Comorin. This is the point where the land of India ends and the vast and rolling waters of the ocean have their beginning. It is one of the most beautiful points in all the world. The point where three great bodies of water meet together in all of their majestic splendor: the Bay of Bengal, the Arabian Sea, the Indian Ocean.

I remember that afternoon how we went out there and we took a seat on a rock that slightly protruded itself out into the waters, out into the ocean. We looked at the waves of these great bodies of water as they unfolded in almost rhythmic procession. Then we looked at the beautiful skies, all of their radiant beauty. Then we looked over at the sun; as it stood like a great cosmic ball of fire, it started setting. And you know at the setting of the sun you see that glowing fusion of colors so characteristic of the setting of the sun. We watched it. It went down. We were sitting there on that rock as the waves were beating upon it, looking at the sun. And that sun started going down and down, and it looked like it was sinking in the very ocean itself. Finally, it had passed away so that we couldn't see any more of the sun. It started getting a little dark and hazy about. Then, right at that moment, I turned around, and I said to Coretta, "But look, there is another light." It was the light of the moon over there in the East. And this was an interesting thing; this is, as I said, one of the most beautiful points in all the world. And this happened to be one of those days when the moon was full. And this is one of the few points in all the world that you can see the setting of the sun and the emergence of the moon simultaneously. And I looked at that, and something came to my mind that I had to share it, Coretta and Dr. Reddick and the other people who were accompanying us around at that point. I said to myself there is something in this that is an analogy to life.

So often we come to those points when it gets dark. It seems that the light of life is out. The sunlight of day moves out of our being and out the rest of our faith. We get disillusioned and confused and give up in despair. But if we will only look around, we will discover that God has another light. And when we discover that, we need never walk in darkness. I've seen this so often in my own personal experience. For when it was dark and tragedy around, seemed that the light of day had gone out, darkness all around and sunlight passing away, I got enough strength in my being to turn around and only to discover that God had another light. This would be a tragic universe if God had only one light. But I came to see in a way that I'd never seen it before, that God has another light, a light that can guide you through the darkness of any midnight. Are you disillusioned this morning? Are you confused about life? Have you been disappointed? Have your highest dreams and hopes been buried? You about to give up in despair? I say to you, "Don't give up, because God has another light, and it is the light that can shine amid the darkness of a thousand midnights." This is what the cross tells us. It reminds us that when men put the sunlight out, that God has the light of the moon. And no matter how dark it gets, God is still around with all of his power. They put the light out on Good Friday, but God brought it back on on Easter morning. They've put the light out so many times in history. I've seen empires and kings and rulers put it out. But God has another light. Go into the valleys, through the hedges, and into the highways and tell men that God has another light. You can turn the light off, but he has another light to turn on. And then you will discover that He even turns that light on that went out again.

For I started thinking finally that that light which went down in India, went up in Montgomery, Alabama. The minute that the light was going out in India, the light of the sun is getting up in Montgomery because there is twelve hours difference in the time. And even that same light that will get up in Montgomery and go down, will be getting up in India again. You don't block God's lights. He manipulates and controls them. And we never need walk in darkness because God has a light for the night and a light for the day, and he controls both. This is our hope. This is what the Resurrection tells us. This is what Easter tells us. And this is what I found as I walked around that holy land and stood around that cross.

Be obedient, not only to the external written law but to that law written in your heart, obedient to the unenforceable. Not only that, be grateful to God for his love. And even then, you can't repay it. Because when you survey that wondrous cross on which the prince of glory died, there is something that reminds you that your greatest gain you must count as loss and pour contempt on all your pride. And then even after that you find yourself saying, "Were the whole realm of nature mine, that were a present far too small. Love so amazing, so divine, demands my life, my all, and my all.* But not only that. Know that God has the universe in His hands. And because of that, segregation will die one day. Because of that, all of

---

* King is paraphrasing the last stanza of Isaac Watts's hymn "When I Survey the Wondrous Cross" (1707).

the lands of Africa will be free one day. Several years ago, forty years ago, only two of them were free—that was Liberia and Ethiopia. Today eight of them have been added, and in 1960 some more will be added—Nigeria, Togoland, the Cameroons, and Somalia.* And then I predict that fifteen years from now, all of them will be free, and there will not be a colonial power existing anywhere in this world. Why is all of that? It is because God holds the reins of the universe in His hands, and when the light goes out at one hour, it comes on at another with the power of His being. And this is the hope that can keep us going and keep us from getting frustrated as we walk along the way of life. Let us pray. O God our gracious [*recording interrupted*]

---

* In addition to the four King mentions, thirteen other African nations gained their independence in 1960: Benin, Burkina Faso, Central African Republic, Chad, Congo, Ivory Coast, Democratic Republic of the Congo, Gabon, Madagascar, Mali, Mauritania, Niger, and Senegal.

Speech at the Youth March for Integrated Schools

EXCERPT FROM SPEECH AT THE WASHINGTON MONUMENT

Washington, DC

"Become a dedicated fighter for civil rights. . . . It will give you that rare sense of nobility that can only spring from love and selflessly helping your fellow man."

King addressed twenty-six thousand high school and college students who had traveled from around the nation to march in support of the 1954 Supreme Court decision to desegregate schools. In his speech, excerpted here, he spoke of the hope he felt seeing a sea of white and Black faces and about what the future might hold.

[Excerpt]

... As June approaches, with its graduation ceremonies and speeches, a thought suggests itself. You will hear much about careers, security, and prosperity. I will leave the discussion of such matters to your deans, your principals, and your valedictorians. But I do have a graduation thought to pass along to you. Whatever career you may choose for yourself—doctor, lawyer, teacher—let me propose an avocation to be pursued along with it. Become a dedicated fighter for civil rights. Make it a central part of your life.

It will make you a better doctor, a better lawyer, a better teacher. It will enrich your spirit as nothing else possibly can. It will give you that rare sense of nobility that can only spring from love and selflessly helping your fellow man. Make a career of humanity. Commit yourself to the noble struggle for equal rights. You will make a greater person of yourself, a greater nation of your country, and a finer world to live in. . . .

The Three Dimensions of a Complete Life

SERMON AT UNITARIAN CHURCH OF GERMANTOWN

Philadelphia, Pennsylvania

"Before we can love other selves adequately, we must love our own selves properly."

In 1960, King, heartbroken to depart, left the Dexter Avenue Baptist Church in Montgomery to join his father as co-pastor of Ebenezer Baptist Church in Atlanta, Georgia, which would put him closer to the headquarters of the Southern Christian Leadership Conference. This sermon was the same one he delivered as his first sermon at Ebenezer after joining the pastorate; he delivered a shorter version in his audition to become pastor at Dexter Avenue Baptist Church.

Reverend [Max Franklin] Daskam and members and friends of this great church, ladies and gentlemen.* I need not pause to say how very delighted I am to be here today and to be with you and this community and to have the opportunity of sharing this great ecumenical pulpit. It is always a real pleasure to come back

---

* In a May 24 letter to Max Daskam, who had been pastor of the church since 1929, Maude Ballou relayed King's consent to preach. Daskam first invited King on March 24, 1959.

to Philadelphia and this area. I never feel like a stranger when I return because I lived in this community some three years, and I was a student in theological seminary.* At that time I met many, many people in this area, and I feel that I have some real genuine friends in Philadelphia. So it is always a rewarding experience to come back to this area. And it is a great pleasure to be in this pulpit, and I want to express my personal appreciation to Reverend Daskam for extending the invitation.

And this morning I would like to have you think with me on the subject "The Three Dimensions of a Complete Life." The three dimensions of a complete life. Many, many centuries ago a man by the name of John was in prison out on a lonely obscure island called Patmos. While in this situation, John imagined that he saw the new Jerusalem descending out of heaven from God. One of the greatest glories of this new city of God that John saw was its completeness. It was not partial and one-sided, but it was complete in all three of its dimensions. So in describing the city in the sixteenth chapter of the book of Revelation, John says this: "The length and the height and the breadth of it are equal."† In other words, of this new city of God, this city of ideal humanity is not an unbalanced entity, but it is complete on all sides. And John is saying something quite significant here. [For] so many of us, the book of Revelation is a difficult book, puzzling to decode. We see it as something of an enigma wrapped in mystery. And I guess the book of Revelation is a difficult book, shrouded with impenetrable mysteries, if we accept everything in the book as a record of actual historical

---

* King attended nearby Crozer Theological Seminary near Chester, Pennsylvania, from 1948 until 1951.

† Cf. Rev. 21:16.

occurrences. But if we will look beneath the peculiar jargon of the author, what theologians call the prevailing apocalyptic symbolism, we will find there many eternal truths which forever confront us, and one such truth is the truth of this text. For what John is really saying is this: that life at its best and life as it should be is three-dimensional; it's complete on all sides. So there are three dimensions of any complete life, for which we can certainly give the words of this text: length, breadth, and height.*

The length of life, as we shall use it here, is not its longevity, its duration, not how long it lasts, but it is a push, the push of a life forward to achieve its personal ends and ambitions. It is the inward concern for one's own welfare. The breadth of life is the outward concern for the welfare of others. The height of life is the upward reach for God. So these are the three dimensions. On one hand, we find the individual person; on the other hand, we find other persons; at the top we find the supreme infinite person. These three must work together; they must be concatenated in an individual life if that life is to be complete, for the complete life is the three-dimensional life.

Now, let us think, first, of the length of life, and this is that dimension of life, as I've said, in which the individual is concerned with developing his inner powers. In a sense this is the selfish dimension

---

* Phillips Brooks, *Selected Sermons*, ed. William Scarlett (New York: E. P. Dutton, 1949), p. 195: "St. John in his great vision sees the mystic city, 'the holy Jerusalem,' descending out of heaven from God. It is the picture of glorified humanity, of humanity as it shall be when it is brought to its completeness by being thoroughly filled with God. And one of the glories of the city which he saw was its symmetry. Our cities, our developments and presentations of human life, are partial and one-sided. This city out of heaven was symmetrical. In all its three dimensions it was complete. Neither was sacrificed to the other. 'The length and the breadth and the height of it are equal.'"

of life. There is such a thing as rational, healthy, and moral self-interest. If an individual is not concerned about himself, he cannot really be concerned about other selves. Some years ago a brilliant Jewish rabbi, the late Joshua Liebman, wrote a book entitled *Peace of Mind*. And he has a chapter in that book entitled "Love Thyself Properly."* What he says in that chapter in substance is this: that before we can love other selves adequately, we must love our own selves properly. And many people have been plunged into the abyss of emotional fatalism because they didn't love themselves properly. So we have a legitimate obligation: be concerned about ourselves. We have a legitimate obligation to set out in life to see what we are made for, to find that center of creativity, for there is within all of us a center of creativity seeking to break forth, and we have the responsibility of discovering this, discovering that life's work.

Then once we discover what we are made for, what we are called to do in life, we must set out to do it with all of the strength and all of the power that we can muster up. Individuals should seek to do his life's work so well that the living, the dead, or the unborn couldn't do it better. He must see it as something with cosmic significance; no matter how small it happens to be, or no matter how insignificant we tend to feel it is, we must come to see that it has great significance, that it is for the upbuilding of humanity. So to carry it to one extreme, if it falls one's lot to be a street sweeper, he should at that moment seek to sweep streets like Michelangelo carved marble, like Raphael painted pictures. He should seek to sweep streets like Beethoven composed the music or like Shakespeare wrote poetry. He should seek to sweep streets so well that

---

* Joshua Loth Liebman, *Peace of Mind* (New York: Simon and Schuster, 1946), pp. 38–58.

all the hosts of heaven and earth will have to pause and say, "Here lived a great street sweeper, and he swept his job well."* And I think this is what Douglas Malloch meant when he said, "If you can't be a pine on the top of the hill, be a shrub in the valley—but be the best little shrub on the side of the rill; be a bush if you can't be a tree. If you can't be a highway just be a trail, if you can't be the sun be a star, for it isn't by size that you win or you fail—be the best of whatever you are."† This power to discover what you are made for, this onward push to the end of personal achievement, the length of a man's life.

We must not stop here. It's dangerous to stop with the length of life. Some people never get beyond this first dimension of life. They're often brilliant people. They develop their inner powers. They do extraordinarily well in their fields of endeavor. They live life as if nobody else lived in the world but themselves. Other people become mere means by which they climb to their personal ends or their personal ambitions. Their love is only a utilitarian love. There is nothing more tragic in life to find an individual bogged down in the length of life, devoid of the breadth.

The breadth of life is that outward concern for the welfare of others. I should submit to you this morning that unless an individual can rise above the narrow confines of his individualistic concerns to the broader concerns of all humanity, he hasn't even

---

* In an earlier speech, King attributed this quotation to Morehouse College president Benjamin Mays. See King, "Facing the Challenge of a New Age," address delivered at NAACP Emancipation Day Rally, January 1, 1957, in *Papers*, 4:79.

† King is paraphrasing Douglas Malloch's poem "Be the Best of Whatever You Are" (1926).

started living.* You remember a man went to Jesus one day to raise some serious questions; he was interested about life and all of its eternal meaning. Finally he got around to the question, "Who is my neighbor?"† Now it could've very easily ended up in a sort of philosophical debate, in an abstract discussion. Jesus immediately pulled that question out of midair and placed it on a dangerous curve between Jerusalem and Jericho. He talked about a certain man that fell among thieves. Three men passed, you remember. One was a Levite; one was a priest. And they passed by on the other side; they didn't stop to help the man. And finally a man of another race came by. The Samaritan, you remember. He stopped; he administered first aid; he helped the man in need. Jesus implied that this Samaritan was good, that he was great, because he had the capacity to project the I into the Thou.

Now, when we read this parable, we tend to use our imagination a great deal. I know I do when I read it. We begin to wonder why the priest didn't stop and why the Levite didn't stop. Now, there are many reasons when we begin to use our imagination about it. It's possible that they were busy and they were in a big hurry because they had some ecclesiastical meeting to attend. That's a

---

* Brooks, *Selected Sermons*, p. 196: "The Breadth of a life, on the other hand, is its outreach laterally, if we may say so. It is the constantly diffusive tendency which is always drawing a man outward into sympathy with other men. And the Height of a life is its reach upward towards God; its sense of childhood; its consciousness of the Divine Life over it with which it tries to live in love, communion, and obedience. These are the three dimensions of a life,—its length and breadth and height,— without the due development of all of which no life becomes complete."

† This question was asked of Jesus, who replied with the Parable of the Good Samaritan (see Luke 10:29).

possibility. And so they just didn't have time; they had to be there on time; they didn't want to be late; they considered the duties of ecclesiastical concerns more important. Now, there is also a possibility that they were going down to Jericho to organize the Jericho Road Improvement Association. That's another, a real possibility.

Well, you know there is another possibility that I often think about when I think about this parable. It's really possible that those men were afraid. You know, the Jericho road is a dangerous road. A few months ago Mrs. King and I were in Jerusalem, and we rented a car and drove down the Jericho road from Jerusalem to Jericho.* And I said to her as we went around this road—it's a meandering, curvy road—and I said I can easily see why Jesus used this as a setting for the parable because there is something dangerous about this road, and it's conducive for robbery. Here is Jerusalem, some twenty-six hundred feet above sea level, and here is Jericho, some one thousand feet below sea level, and you go that distance within about fifteen or sixteen miles. Mountainous, dangerous, meandering road, and so it is possible that the priest and the Levite had a little fear. The robbers could have still been around, and they could have raised this question. Maybe they are still around; or maybe the man on the ground is faking, and he's just trying to get us over there to end up robbing us in the long run. So may it not be that the first question that the priest raised or the first question that the Levite raised was this: "If I stop to help this man, what will happen to me?" Then the Good Samaritan came by, and in the very nature of his concern reversed the question: "If I do not stop to help this man, what will happen to

---

* In an Easter Sunday sermon at Dexter Avenue Baptist Church in 1959, King recalled his recent visit to Jericho. See "A Walk Through the Holy Land" (page 136 in this book).

him?'" And so he was a great man because he had the mental equipment for a dangerous altruism. He was a great man because he not only ascended to the heights of economic security but because he could condescend to the depths of human need. He was a great man because he discovered in his own life that he who would be greatest among you must be your servant.[†]

Now this text has a great deal of bearing, this whole question of the breadth of life has a great deal of bearing on the crisis which we face in race relations in our own nation. I am absolutely convinced that the problems which we face today in the Southland grow out of the fact that too many of our white brothers are concerned merely about the length of life rather than the breadth of life, concerned about their so-called way of life, concerned about perpetuating a preferred economic position, concerned about preserving a sort of political status and power, concerned about preserving a so-called social status. As we look to these problems, we find ourselves saying, if they would only add breadth to length, the other-regarding dimension to the self-regarding dimension, the jangling discords of the South would be transformed into a beautiful symphony of brotherhood.

We look at New Orleans today—what do we see there? We find hundreds, hundreds and thousands of people infiltrated with hatred. We find a legislative body using all of the fears and all of the emotions to keep the people confused.[‡] In many instances these

---

* Cf. Luke 10:30–37.

† Cf. Matt. 23:11.

‡ Judge J. Skelly Wright had ordered the New Orleans public schools to desegregate on November 14, 1960, prompting whites to mob city hall and withdraw children in large numbers from the local schools (Claude Sitton, "Pupils Integrate in New Orleans as Crowd Jeers," *New York Times*, November 15, 1960).

political leaders are concerned merely about perpetuating their political power. So we see many irresponsible leaders of states in the South using this issue merely to keep the people confused and arousing their fears just to get elected, concerned merely about the length of life, not the breadth. For you see in a real sense the system of segregation itself is wrong because it is based on the question of length and not breadth; it is exclusive and not inclusive. Segregation is wrong because it substitutes an I-it relationship for the I-Thou relationship.* Segregation is wrong because it relegates persons to the status of things. Segregation is wrong because it assumes that God made a mistake and stamped a badge of inferiority on certain people because of the color of their skin.† Therefore, all men of goodwill have a moral obligation to work assiduously to remove this cancerous disease from the body of our nation. It must be done not merely to meet the Communist challenge, although it will be diplomatically expedient to do it. It must be done not merely to appeal to Asian and African people, although it would be expedient to do it. In the final analysis segregation and discrimination must be removed from our nation because they are morally wrong. They stand in conflict with all of the noble principles of our Judeo-Christian heritage. They must be removed because they are wrong at the very core.

I don't want to give the impression that those individuals who are working to remove the system and those individuals who have been on the oppressed end of the old order must not themselves be concerned about breadth. But I realize that so often in history

---

* Cf. Martin Buber, *I and Thou* (Edinburgh: T. & T. Clark, 1937).

† King's discussion of the effects of segregation is similar to Benjamin E. Mays's treatment in a 1955 speech, "The Moral Aspects of Segregation."

when oppressed people rise up against their oppression, they are too concerned about length too often. It is my firm conviction those of us who have been on the oppressed end of the old order have as much responsibility to be concerned about breadth as anybody else. This is why I believe so firmly in nonviolence. Our aim must not be merely to achieve rights for Negroes or rights for colored people. We are concerned about this only, we will seek to rise from a position of disadvantage to one of advantage, thus subverting justice. The aim must never be to do that but to achieve democracy for everybody. And this is why I disagree so firmly with any philosophy of Black supremacy, for I am absolutely convinced that God is not interested merely in the freedom of Black men and brown men and yellow men. But God is interested in the freedom of the whole human race, the creation of a society where all men will live together as brothers and every man will respect the dignity and worth of all human personality. And a doctrine of white supremacy is concerned merely about the length of life, not the breadth of life. So the aim of the Negro [should] never be to defeat or humiliate the white man but to win his friendship and understanding.

As I said, the tension which we face in America today, not so much a tension between Black men and white men, but it's a tension between justice and injustice, a struggle between the forces of light and the forces of darkness. And, if there is a victory, it will be a victory not merely for seventeen or eighteen million Negroes. It will be a victory for democracy, a victory for justice, a victory for freedom. And this is why I admire so much these hundreds and thousands of students all across our Southland not merely because they are working for constructive ends but because they have decided to use means that have the element of breadth. For all of these months they have taken the deep groans and the passionate yearnings of the

Negro people and filtered them in their own souls, fashioned them into a creative protest, which is an epic known all over our nation. Yes, they have moved in a uniquely meaningful orbit, [*imparting?*] light and heat to distant satellite. And I am convinced that when the history books are written, the historians will have to record this movement as one of the most significant epics of our heritage, not merely because it seeks to bring about humanitarian ends, because it also has humanitarian means.

And not only does this text have bearing on our struggle in America in the area of race relations, but it has a great deal of bearing on the crisis in the world in international relations. This text says to us, in substance, that every nation must be concerned about every other nation. No nation can live in isolation today. We live in a world that is geographically one now. We have the job of making it spiritually one. A few months ago Mrs. King and I journeyed to that great country in the Far East known as India. I never will forget the experience; it was a most rewarding experience, one that I will remember as long as the chords of memory shall lengthen, experience of talking with the great leaders of government, meeting hundreds and thousands of people all over India, most rewarding experience. And I say to you this morning that there were those depressing moments. How can one avoid being depressed when he sees with his own eyes millions of people going to bed hungry at night? How can one avoid being moved and concerned when he sees with his own eyes millions of people sleeping on the sidewalks at night? In Calcutta alone more than a million people sleep on the sidewalk every night. In Bombay more than five hundred thousand people sleep on the sidewalk every night, no houses to go in, no beds to sleep in. How can one avoid being depressed [when] he discovers that out of India's population of four hundred million people, more than three hundred and fifty million of these people make an annual income of less than sixty dollars a year? Most of these people have never seen a doctor or a dentist. Many of these conditions exist because these people for many, many years were dominated politically, exploited economically, segregated and humiliated by foreign power.

As I watched these conditions, I found conditions, I found myself asking, can we in America stand idly by and not be concerned? I thought of the fact that we spend millions of dollars a day to store surplus food, and I started thinking to myself, I know where we can store this food free of charge—in the wrinkled stomachs of the hundreds and thousands and millions of people all over the world who are hungry. Maybe in America we spend too much of our money establishing military bases around the world rather than establishing bases of genuine concern and understanding. And all I'm saying is simply this: that all life is interrelated. Somehow we are tied in a single garment of destiny, caught in an inescapable network of mutuality, where what affects one directly affects all indirectly. As long as there is poverty in this world, you can never be totally rich, even if you have a billion dollars. As long as diseases are rampant and millions of people cannot expect to live more than thirty or thirty-two years, you can never be totally healthy, even if you just got a clean bill of health from Mayo Clinic or John[s] Hopkins Hospital. Strangely enough I can never be what I ought to be until you are what you ought to be, and you can never be what you ought to be until I am what I ought to be. This is the way the world is made; I didn't make it that way, but it's like that. And John Donne recorded it years ago and placed it in graphic terms: "No man is an island, entire of itself; every man is a piece of the continent, a part of the main." And then he goes on toward the end to say: "Any man's death diminishes me because I am involved in mankind. Therefore never send to know for whom the bell tolls; it tolls for thee."* Only by discovering this are we able to master the breadth of life.

Finally, there is another dimension. We must not stop with length and breadth. There is another dimension. Now some people never get beyond the first two. They are brilliant people, and in many instances they love humanity. They have active social concerns. They stop right there, so they seek to live life without a sky. They live only on the horizontal plane with no real concern for the vertical. Now I know that there are many reasons why people neglect this third dimension, this point of reaching up for the eternal God.† Some people, I'm sure, have honest reasons for, for not pursuing the ends of the third dimension. Some people have looked out into the world, and they have noticed evil in all of its glaring and colossal dimensions. That's something that the poet Keats called "the giant agony of the world."‡ They found themselves asking how is it that a good God who is at the same time an all-powerful God, how is it that such a God will allow all of this evil to exist in the world? And so they find themselves caught up in the problem of evil. Because of that they end up neglecting the third dimension.

And others who've gotten disgusted with organized religion and as a result of their disgust with organized religion, and those people who claim that they believe in God living contrary to all of the

---

* King is quoting lines from John Donne's "Meditation XVII" from *Meditations upon Emergent Occasions* (1624).

† Brooks, *Selected Sermons*, p. 202: "So much I say about the length and breadth of life. One other dimension still remains. The length and breadth and height of it are equal. The Height of life is its reach upward toward something distinctly greater than humanity.... The reaching of mankind towards God!"

‡ King is quoting from John Keats's *The Fall of Hyperion: A Dream* (1819).

demands of religion, they have decided that the third dimension is a waste of time. And we must admit that so often the church has been the arch conserver of the status quo. The church has too often been that institution that serves to crystallize the patterns of society through often evil patterns. How often in the church have we had a high blood pressure of creeds and an anemia of deeds? People looking out at that, seeing that the church has often gone out in society with no social consciousness, they've decided to neglect the third dimension. And then there are others who find it difficult to square their intellectual worldview to the sometimes unscientific dogmas of religion.

But I imagine that most people fit in another category all together. They are not theoretical atheists; they are practical atheists. They are not the people who deny the existence of God with their minds and their lips, but they are the people who deny God's existence with their lives. For some of these other people who have the theoretical doubts and honest doubts reveal a deeper commitment in so many instances because while they deny God's existence with their minds, they affirm God's existence in the bottom of their hearts and with their lives. But there is another type of atheism that is much more damaging. And so there are so many people that have neglected this third dimension just because they've become so involved in things [*gap in tape*] Greek civilization, unconsciously believing that only those things which we can see and touch, apply the five senses to, their existence.

But in spite of our theoretical denial, we still feel in life another order impinging upon us. In spite of our doubts, we go on in life having spiritual experiences that cannot be explained in materialistic terms. In spite of our inordinate worship of things, something keeps reminding us that the eternal things of the universe are never seen. We go out at night and look up at the beautiful stars as they bedeck the heavens like swinging lanterns of eternity; for the moment we think we see all. Then something comes to tell us, "Oh no." We can never see the law of gravitation that holds them there. We look at this beautiful church building, and we see the beautiful architecture, and we think for the moment we see all. Oh no. We can never see the mind of the architect who drew the blueprint; we can never see the love and the faith and the hope of the individuals who made it so. You look here this morning, and I know you're saying, "We see Martin Luther King." I hate to disappoint you. You merely see my body. You can never see my mind; you can never see my personality; you can never see the me that makes *me* me. So in a real sense everything that we see in life is something of a shadow cast by that which we do not see. Plato was right: "The visible is a shadow cast by the invisible."*

And so in spite of our denials we are still reminded of this, and may it not be that God is still around? And all of our new knowledge will not diminish his being one iota. All of our new developments can banish God neither from the microcosmic compass of the atom nor from the vast unfathomable ranges of interstellar space, living in a universe in which we are forced to measure stellar distance by light years, confronted with the illimitable expanse of the universe in which stars are five hundred million billion miles from the Earth, which heavenly bodies travel at incredible speed, and in which the ages of planets are reckoned in terms of billions of years. Modern man is forced to cry out with the solace of old: "When I behold the heavens, the work of Thy hands, the moon,

---

* King is referring to Plato's allegory of the cave, from *The Republic*: "The truth would be literally nothing but the shadows of the images" (514a–c, 521a–e).

the stars, and all that Thou hast created, what is man that Thou art mindful of him and the son of man that Thou remembereth him?"* And so it may well be that God is still around. So let us go out with a cultivation of the third dimension, for it can give life new meaning. It can give life new zest, and I can speak of this out of personal experience.

Over the last few years, circumstances have made it necessary for me to stand so often amid the surging [*moment?*] of life's restless sea.† Moments of frustration, the chilly winds of adversity all around, but there was always something deep down within that could keep me going, a strange feeling that you are not alone in this struggle, that the struggle for the good life is a struggle in which the individual has cosmic companionship. For so many times I have been able with my people to walk and never get weary because I am convinced that there is a great camp meeting in the promised land of God's universe.‡ Maybe Saint Augustine was right: we were made for God; we will be restless until we find rest in him.§

Love yourself if that means rational, healthy, and moral self-interest. You are commanded to do that; that is the length of life. Love your neighbor as you love yourself. You are commanded to do that; that is the breadth of life. But never forget there is a first and

---

* Cf. Ps. 8:3–4.

† King may have borrowed the phrase "restless sea" from Cecil F. Alexander's hymn "Jesus Calls Us" (1852): "Jesus calls us o'er the tumult of our life's wild, restless sea; day by day His sweet voice soundeth, saying, 'Christian, follow me.'"

‡ King is adapting the lyrics of the spiritual "There's a Great Camp Meeting": "Walk together children, Don't you get weary, Don't you get weary, There's a great camp meeting in the Promised Land."

§ *The Confessions of Saint Augustine*, 1.1: "Thou madest us for Thyself, and our heart is restless, until it repose in Thee."

even greater commandment: "Love the Lord thy God with all thy heart, and with all thy soul, and with all thy mind."* That is the height of life. When an individual does this, he lives a complete life. Thank God for John, who centuries ago caught vision of the New Jerusalem; and grant to those of us who are left to walk the streets and the highways of life will [sic] also catch vision of the New Jerusalem, decide to move toward that city of complete life in our individual lives, in our national lives, in which the length and the breadth and the height are equal.

Let us pray. Eternal God, our Father, we thank Thee for the insights of old, the insights of prophets and those who have lived near to Thee. Grant that as we continue to live, we will seek to develop all of those dimensions that will bring completeness to us. Grant somehow that we will learn to be concerned about ourselves, but at the same time give us that great concern for other selves. At the same time, help us to be concerned about Thee and to worship Thee in spirit and truth.† Grant that somehow we will come to the great conclusion that unless we have all three of these, we somehow live lives that are incomplete. Amen.

---

* Matt. 22:37, KJV.

† Cf. John 4:24.

Levels of Love

SERMON AT EBENEZER BAPTIST CHURCH

Atlanta, Georgia

"I talked with a white man in Albany, Georgia, the other day, and . . . he said, . . . 'I used to love the Negro, but I don't have the kind of love for them that I used to have.' . . . And I said to myself, 'You never did love Negroes (*That's right*) because your love was a conditional love. It was conditioned upon the Negro staying in his place, and the minute he stood up as a man and as somebody, you didn't love him anymore because your love was a utilitarian love that grew up from the dark days of slavery and then almost a hundred years of segregation.'"

This sermon, delivered in September 1962 and reproduced here in full, repeats ideas King had expressed previously but brings them together in one overview of love. In July of that year, he had been jailed for two weeks for participating in a prayer vigil in Albany, Georgia.

I hope that at this moment you will not utter a word unless that word is uttered to God. For the moment you will rise above the miasma and the hurly-burly of everyday life and center your vision on those eternal verities, those eternal values that should shape our destiny. Life is difficult. It is the road we travel, but in traveling this road we encounter rough places. At points it's a meandering road; it has its numerous curves; it has its hilly places; and we struggle to get over the hills. Sometimes it's painful; sometimes it's trying. But [*somehow?*] we have a faith, and we have a belief that even though the road of life is meandering and curvy and rough and difficult, we can make it if God guides us and leads us. We go on with that faith, and we can keep on keeping on. We can smile when others all around us are giving up in despair. Lead me. Guide me. Be with me as I journey the road of life.

May we open our hearts and spirits now as we listen to the words from the choir. [*Choir sings.*]

This morning I would like to continue the series of sermons that I'm preaching on love. I'll preach a sermon this morning that I preached in this pulpit some two years ago, but one that I've had a chance to give some more thought to.* And one that I hope will clear up some of the things that we have been discussing in the two previous sermons. You remember we started the series preaching from the subject "Loving Your Enemies." The second sermon in the series was "Love in Action," based on the prayer of Jesus Christ on the cross: "Father, forgive them; for they know not what they do."†

And I'd like to use as the subject this morning "Levels of Love," trying to bring out the meaning of the various types of love. Cer-

---

* This was also King's announced sermon topic for August 14, 1960 ("'Levels of Love' to Be Subject at Ebenezer," *Atlanta Daily World*, August 13, 1960).

† "Dr. King Jr. to Preach on 'Love Your Enemies' at Ebenezer Sunday," *Atlanta Daily World*, August 18, 1962; "'Love in Action,' King Jr.'s Topic at Ebenezer Sunday," *Atlanta Daily World*, September 1, 1962; Luke 23:34, KJV.

tainly, there is no word in the English language more familiar than the word "love." And yet in spite of our familiarity with the word, it is one of the most misunderstood words. In a sense it is an ambiguous term. And we often confuse when we begin to grapple with the meaning of love and when we attempt to define it. And I think a great deal of the confusion results from the fact that many people feel that love can be defined in one category, in one pattern, in one type. But in order to understand love and its meaning and its many sides, its qualities, we must understand that there are levels of love. And this is what I would like to set forth this morning as my thesis and try to give these various levels of love.

First, there is what I would refer to as utilitarian love. This is love at the lowest level. Here one loves another for his usefulness to him. The individual loves that person that he can use. A great deal of friendship is based on this, and this why it is meaningless pseudo-friendship, because it is based on this idea of using the object of love. [*Congregation: That's right*] There are some people who never get beyond the level of utilitarian love. They see other people as mere steps by which they can climb to their personal ends and ambitions, and the minute they discover that they can't use those persons, they disassociate themselves, they lose (*All right*) this affection that they once had for them. (*That's right*)

Now we can easily see what is wrong with this love. Number one—it is based on true selfishness, for in reality the person who engages in utilitarian love is merely loving himself (*That's right*) through somebody else. The second thing wrong with it is that it ends up depersonalizing persons. The great philosopher Immanuel Kant said, in what he called his categorical imperative, that "every man should so live that he treats every other man as an end and

never as a means.'"* Kant had something there because the minute you use a person as a means, you depersonalize that person,
and that person becomes merely an object. This is what we do for
things. We use things, and whenever you use somebody you, in
your own mind, thingify that person. A great Jewish philosopher
by the name of Martin Buber wrote a book entitled *I and Thou*,
and he says in that book that life at its best is always on the level
of "I and Thou," and whenever it degenerates to the level of "I and
It," it becomes dangerous and terrible.† Whenever we treat people
not as thous, whenever we treat a man not as a him, a woman not
as a her but as an it, we make them a thing, and this is the tragedy
of this level of love. This is the tragedy of racial segregation. In the
final analysis, segregation is wrong not merely because it makes for
physical inconveniences, not merely because it leaves the individuals who are segregated with inferior facilities, but segregation is
wrong, in the final analysis, because it substitutes an I-It relationship for the I-Thou relationship and relegates persons to the status
of things. This is utilitarian love. And the other thing wrong with
it is that it is always a conditional love, and love at its best is always
unconditional.

I talked with a white man in Albany, Georgia, the other day,
and when we got down in the conversation he said, "The thing
that worries me so much about this movement here is that it's creating so much tension, and we'd had such peaceful and harmo-

---

* "Accordingly the practical imperative will be as follows: So act as to treat
humanity, whether in thine own person or in that of any other, in every case as an
end withal, never as a means only" (Kant, *Fundamental Principles of the Metaphysic
of Morals*, trans. Thomas K. Abbott [Indianapolis: Bobbs-Merrill, 1949], p. 46).

† Martin Buber, *I and Thou* (Edinburgh: T. & T. Clark, 1937).

nious race relations." And then he went on to say, "I used to love the Negro, but I don't have the kind of love for them that I used to have. You know, used to give money to Negro churches. And even the man who worked for me, I would give him something every year extra; I'd give him a suit. But I just don't feel that way now. I don't love Negroes like I used to." And I said to myself, "You never did love Negroes (*That's right*) because your love was a conditional love. It was conditioned upon the Negro staying in his place, and the minute he stood up as a man and as somebody, you didn't love him anymore because your love was a utilitarian love that grew up from the dark days of slavery and then almost a hundred years of segregation." This is what the system has done, you see. (*Yes*) It makes for the crudest level of love. Utilitarian love is the lowest level of love.

Now there is another type of love which is real love, and we're moving on up now into genuine, meaningful, profound love. It is explained through the Greek word "eros." Plato used to use that word a great deal in his dialogues as a sort of yearning of the soul for the realm of the divine. But now we see it as romantic love, and there is something beautiful about romantic love. When it reaches its height, there is nothing more beautiful in all the world. A romantic love rises above utilitarian love in the sense that it does have a degree of altruism, for a person who really loves with romantic love will die for the object of his love. A person who is really engaged in true romantic love will do anything to satisfy the object of that love, the great love. We've read about it in all of the beauties of literature, whether in ancient or medieval days. We could read about it in a Romeo and Juliet, Antony and Cleopatra, Tristan and Isolde, beauty of romantic love. Edgar Allan Poe talks about it in his beautiful "Annabel Lee" with the love surrounded by the halo of eternity.* I've quoted for you before those great words of Shakespeare which explain the beauty of romantic love:

> Love is not love
> Which alters when it alteration finds,
> Or bends with the remover to remove.
> O no, it is an ever-fixèd mark
> That looks on tempests and is never shaken;
> It is the star to every wand'ring bark.†

Oh, it's a beautiful love. There is something about romantic love that lifts it above the crude level of utilitarian love.

But I must warn you that romantic love is not the highest love. And we must never forget this. With all of its beauty this can't be the highest form of love because it is basically selfish. This is often difficult to think about, but it is true. You love your lover because there is something about that person that attracts you. If you are a man, it may be the way she looks. It may be the way she talks. It may be her glowing femininity. It may be her intellectual qualities. It may be other physical qualities—something about her that attracts you. If you are a woman, it may be something about that man that attracts you, and even if you can't put it in words, you end up saying, "I don't quite know what it is, but I just know that he moves me." [*laughter*] This is the, this is romantic love. It's a selfish love. And so with all of its beauty, it can never be considered the highest quality of love.

---

* Edgar Allan Poe, "Annabel Lee" (1849).

† William Shakespeare, "Sonnet 116" (1609).

Well, there is another type of love, certainly on the same level of romantic love, and that is mother's love. (*That's right*) Oh, when life presents it in its beauty, it gives us something that we never forget, for there is nothing more beautiful than the loving care, the tender concern, and the patience (*That's right*) of a real mother. (*That's right*) This is a great love, and life would be ugly without it. Mother's love brings sunshine into dark places. (*Yes*) And there is something about it that never quite gives up. (*Amen, That's right*) The child may wander to some strange and dark far country, but there's always that mother who's there waiting (*Yes Lord*), and even her mind journeys to the far country. (*Yes Lord*) No matter what the mistake is, no matter how low the child sinks, if it's a real mother, she still loves him. (*Praise Him, Lord*) How beautiful it is. (*Oh yes*) It has been written about, too, in beautiful, glowing language. We've read about it. We've seen it in beautiful stories. It is a great love.

There is another level of love that I would like to mention this morning. But before mentioning that let me say that even mother's love can't be the highest. (*That's right*) We hate to hear that, I guess, but you see, a mother loves her child because it is her child. (*That's right*) And if she isn't careful, she can't quite love that other person's child like she loves her child. (*That's right*) Even mother's love has a degree of selfishness in it. (*Yes*)

Well, we move on up to another level of love that is explained in another Greek word, the word "philia," which is the sort of intimate affection between personal friends. This is friendship. In a sense it moves a little higher, not because the love itself is deeper, not because the person who is participating in the love is any more genuine of concern, but because its scope is broader, because it is more inclusive. You see, romantic love, at its best, is always between two individuals of opposite sex, but when we rise to friendship, a man can love a man, a woman can love a woman. Friendship becomes one of the most beautiful things in all the world. One can have five friends, ten friends, twenty friends, and jealousy does not creep in as the horizon broadens and as the group enlarges. (*That's right*) In romantic love, always, jealousy emerges when the one individual moves toward a love act with another individual, and rightly so. Then in friendship, which is not based on sex, which is not based on physical attraction, one has risen to another level of love where they stand side by side and become united because of a common interest in something beyond themselves. In romantic love, the individuals in love sit face to face absorbed in each other. In friendship the individuals sit side by side absorbed in some great concern and some great cause and some great issue beyond themselves, something they like to do together. It may be hunting. It may be going and swimming together. It may be discussing great ideas together. It may be in a great movement of freedom together. Friendship is beautiful. (*Yes Lord*) There is a beauty about it that will always stand. There is nothing more beautiful in all the world than to see real friendship, and there isn't much of it either. (*That's right*) You labor a long time to find a real genuine friend (*Yes Lord, Preach it*), somebody who's so close to you that they know your heartbeat. I must hasten to say that as we discuss these levels of love, we must remember that one can be involved in several levels simultaneously. A young lady who loves her husband is engaged in romantic love, but at the same time she will have some children later—she engages in mother's love, and if she's really a wonderful person, she's a good friend of her husband. So that one can engage in romantic love and mother's love and friendship simultaneously. This is a beautiful level.

But even friendship can't be the highest level of love because there is something about friendship that is selfish. You love people that you like. And it's hard to be friendly with Mr. [James O.] Eastland.* It's hard to be friendly with Mr. Marvin Griffin if you believe in democracy.† Friendship is always based on an affection for somebody that you like, and it's difficult to like Mr. Griffin. It's difficult to like Mr. Eastland because we don't like what they are doing. But this would be a terrible world if God hadn't provided us with something where we could love Mr. Griffin even though it's impossible for us to really like him. And friendship limits the circle even though it enlarges the circle over romantic and mother's love. It limits it because it says that the friend is the person who has mutual concerns and the person that you like to be with, that you like to talk with (*That's right*), that you like to deal with.

Well, there is a love that goes a little higher than that. We refer to that as humanitarian love. It gets a little higher because it gets a little broad and more inclusive. The individual rises to the point that he loves humanity. And he rises to the point of saying that within every man there is a divine spark. He rises to the point of saying that within every man there is something sacred and so all humanity must be loved. And so when one rises to love at this point, he does get a little higher because he is seriously attempting to love everybody. But it still can't be the highest point because it has a danger point. It is impersonal; it says I love this abstract something

---

* Senator James Oliver Eastland of Mississippi served in Congress in 1941 and from 1943 until 1978, using his power as chair of the Senate Judiciary Committee to block civil rights legislation.

† Marvin Griffin served as governor of Georgia from 1955 to 1959.

called humanity, which is never quite concretized in an individual. Dostoyevsky, the great Russian novelist, said once in one of his novels, "I love humanity in general so much that I don't love anybody in particular."* [*laughter*] So many people get to this point. It's so easy to love an abstraction called humanity and not love individual human beings. And how many people have been caught in that. (*That's right*) Think of the millions of dollars raised by many of the white churches in the South and all over America sent to Africa for the missionary effort because of a humanitarian love. And yet if the Africans who got that money came into their churches to worship on Sunday morning, they would kick them out. (*Yes, they would*) They love humanity in general, but they don't love Africans in particular. [*laughter*] (*That's right*) There is always this danger in humanitarian love—that it will not quite get there. The greatness of God's love is that His love is big enough to love everybody and is small enough to love even me. (*That's right*) And so humanitarian love can't be the highest.

Let me rush on to that point which is explained by the Greek word "agape." Agape is higher than all of the things I have talked about. Why is it higher? Because it is unmotivated; it is spontaneous; it is overflowing; it seeks nothing in return. It is not motivated by some quality in the object. Utilitarian love is motivated by a quality in the object, namely the object's usefulness to him. Romantic love is motivated by some quality in the object, maybe the beauty of the object or the quality that moves the individual. A mother's love is motivated by the fact that this is her child, something in the object

---

* Cf. Fyodor Dostoyevsky, *The Brothers Karamazov* (New York: Modern Library, 1937), p. 56: "But it has always happened that the more I detest men individually the more ardent becomes my love for humanity."

before her. Move on up to friendship, it is motivated by that quality of friendliness and that quality of concern that is mutual. Go on up to humanity, humanitarian love; it is motivated by something within the object, namely a divine spark, namely something sacred about human personality. But when we rise to agape, to Christian love, it is higher than *all* of this. It becomes the love of God operating in the human heart. (*Amen, Yes Lord*) The greatness of it is that you love every man, not for your sake but for his sake. And you love every man because God loves him. (*Amen, That's right*) And so it becomes all inclusive. The person may be ugly, or the person may be beautiful. The person may be tall, or the person may be short. The person may be light, or the person may be dark. The person may be rich, or the person may be poor. The person may be up and in; the person may be down and out. The person may be white; the person may be Black. The person may be Jew; the person may be Gentile. The person may be Catholic; the person may be Protestant. In other words, you come to the point of loving *every* man and [it] becomes an all-inclusive love. It is the love of God operating in the human heart. And it comes to the point that you even love the enemy.* (*Amen*) Christian love does something that no other love can do. It says that you love every man. You hate the deed that he does if he's your enemy and he's evil, but you love the person who does the evil deed.

And so this is the distinction that I want you to see this morning. And on all other levels we have a need love, but when we come to agape, we have a gift love. And so it is the love that includes everybody. And the only testing point for you to know whether you have real genuine love is that you love your enemy (*Yeah*), for

* Cf. Matt. 5:44.

if you fail to love your enemy, there is no way for you to fit into the category of Christian love. You test it by your ability to love your enemy.*

And so this is what we have before us as Christians. This is what God has left for us. He's left us a love. As He loved us, so let us love the brother. And therefore, I'm convinced this morning that love is the greatest power in all the world. Over the centuries men have asked about the highest good; they've wanted to know. All of the great philosophers have raised the question, "What is the summum bonum of life? What is the highest good?" Epicureans and the Stoics sought to answer it. Plato and Aristotle sought to answer it. What is that good that is productive and that produces every other good? And I am convinced this morning that it is love. God is light. God is love. And he who hates does not know God. But he who loves, at that moment, rises to a knowledge of God.†

And so you may be able to speak well, you may rise to the eloquence of articulate speech, but if you have not love, you are become as sounding brass or the tinkling cymbal. (*Yes Lord*) You may have the gift of prophecy so that you can understand all mysteries. You may break into the storehouse of nature and bring out many insights that men never knew were there. You may have all knowledge so that you build great universities. You may have endless degrees. But if you have not love it means nothing. Yes, you may give your gifts and your goods to feed the poor. You may rise high in philanthropy, but if you have not love, your gifts have been given in vain.

---

* King is drawing upon Harry Emerson Fosdick's discussion of agape in *On Being Fit to Live With: Sermons on Post-War Christianity* (New York: Harper & Brothers, 1946), pp. 6–7.

† Cf. 1 John 4:7–8.

Yes, you may give your body to be burned, (*All right*) and you may die the death of a martyr. You may have your blood spilt, and it will become a symbol of honor for generations yet unborn. But if you have not love, your blood was spilt in vain.* (*All right*) We must come to see that it is possible to be self-centered in our self-sacrifice and self-righteous in our self-denial. We may be generous in order to feed our ego. We may be pious in order to feed our pride. And so without love, spiritual pride becomes a reality in our life, and even martyrdom becomes egotism.

Love is the greatest force in all the world. And this is why Jesus was great. He realized it in his life, and he took this force and split history into AD and BC so that all history has to sing about him and talk about him because he made love the center of his life. And what does the cross mean? It means that God's love shines before us through that cross in all of its dimensions. And so "when I survey the wondrous cross on which the Prince of Glory died, I count my richest gains but loss and pour contempt on all my pride. Were the whole realm of nature mine that were a present far too small. Love so amazing, so divine, demands my life, my all, and my all."† This is our legacy. This is what we have. And may we go on with a love in our hearts that will change us and change the lives of those who surround us. And we will make this old world a new world. And God's kingdom will be a reality.

We open the doors of the church now. Someone here this morning needs to accept the Christ. Someone needs to make a decision for Him. If you have the faith, He has the power. Who this morn-

---

* Cf. 1 Cor. 13:1–3.

† King is paraphrasing Isaac Watts's hymn "When I Survey the Wondrous Cross" (1707).

ing will come? Just as you are, will you come? Just as you are, will you come? And make this church not only a place to come as a regular attending person but a spiritual home. Who this morning will make that decision as we sing this great hymn, "Just as I Am?"* Wherever you are, will you accept Christ? By Christian experience baptism [*words inaudible*]. Wherever you are, you come this morning. God's love stands before us. God's love is always ready. He's calling you now. Make the church the center of your life, for here, we come to the mercy seat. Here, you learn the great realities of life. [*Congregation sings.*]

Now let us stand for the next stanza, and if you are there, we still bid you come wherever you are. Who will come this morning? Just as I am, wherever you are, will you come? Is there one who will accept Christ this morning?

Now let us sing that last stanza, and as we prepare to sing, I make this last plea. There is someone here this morning without a church home. There is someone here this morning standing between two opinions. There is someone here this morning who lives in Atlanta, who was a Christian back home, but who is not united with a church in this city. We give you this opportunity, in the name of Christ, to come as we sing this last stanza. This is the hour for you to decide. [*Congregation sings.*]

God bless you . . . [*recording interrupted*]

---

* King is referring to Charlotte Elliott's hymn "Just as I Am" (1836).

DECEMBER 27, 1962

The Ethical Demands for Integration

EXCERPT FROM SPEECH AT CHURCH CONFERENCE

Nashville, Tennessee

"A vigorous enforcement of civil rights laws will bring an end to segregated public facilities which are barriers to a truly desegregated society, but it cannot bring an end to fears, prejudice, pride, and irrationality, which are the barriers to a truly integrated society. Those dark and demonic responses will be removed only as men are possessed by the invisible, inner law which etches on their hearts the conviction that all men are brothers and that love is mankind's most potent weapon for personal and social transformation."

The speech excerpted here is a variation on King's earlier examinations of the limits of love and the need for legislation to augment it: "A law can't make a man love me, but it can keep him from lynching me."

Here King reached into more personal terrain: the hard-heartedness of people in general, underscoring the need for a moral conversion that goes beyond the law. Without saying the word "self-love," he referenced it. And he returned to the concept of the immutable laws of the universe, discussed in his very early "Rediscovering Lost Values" (see page 1).

• • •

[Excerpt]

The problem of race and color prejudice remains America's greatest moral dilemma. When one considers the impact it has upon our nation, internally and externally, its resolution might well determine our destiny. History has thrust upon our generation an indescribably important task—to complete a process of democratization which our nation has too long developed too slowly, but which is our most powerful weapon for world respect and emulation. How we deal with this crucial situation will determine our moral health as individuals, our cultural health as a region, our political health as a nation, and our prestige as a leader of the free world. The shape of the world today does not afford us the luxury of an anemic democracy. The price that America must pay for the continued oppression of the Negro is the price of its own destruction. The hour is late; the clock of destiny is ticking out; we must act now before it is too late. . . .

Desegregation Is "Enforceable" But Integration Is Not

I can summarize all that I have been saying by affirming that the demands of desegregation are enforceable demands while the demands of integration fall within the scope of unenforceable demands.

Some time ago Dr. Harry Emerson Fosdick made an impressive distinction between enforceable and unenforceable obligations. The former are regulated by the codes of society and the vigorous implementation of law-enforcement agencies. Breaking these obligations, spelled out on thousands of pages in law books, has filled numerous prisons. But unenforceable obligations are beyond the reach of the laws of society. They concern inner attitudes, genuine person-to-person relations, and expressions of compassion which law books cannot regulate and jails cannot rectify. Such obligations are met by one's commitment to an inner law, written on the heart. Man-made laws ensure justice, but a higher law produces love. No code of conduct ever compelled a father to love his children or a husband to show affection to his wife. The law court may force him to provide bread for the family, but it cannot make him provide the bread of love. A good father is obedient to the unenforceable.

Law Can Help

Let us never succumb to the temptation of believing that legislation and judicial decrees play only minor roles in solving this problem. Morality cannot be legislated, but behavior can be regulated. Judicial decrees may not change the heart, but they can restrain the heartless. The law cannot make an employer love an employee, but it can prevent him from refusing to hire me because of the color of my skin. The habits, if not the hearts, of people have been and are being altered everyday by legislative acts, judicial decisions, and executive orders. Let us not be misled by those who argue that segregation cannot be ended by the force of law.

But acknowledging this, we must admit that the ultimate solution to the race problem lies in the willingness of men to obey the unenforceable. Court orders and federal enforcement agencies are of inestimable value in achieving desegregation, but desegregation is only a partial, though necessary step toward the final goal which we seek to realize: genuine intergroup and interpersonal living. Desegregation will break down the legal barriers and bring men together physically, but something must touch the hearts and souls of men so that they will come together spiritually because it is natural and right. A vigorous enforcement of civil rights laws will bring an end to segregated public facilities which are barriers to a truly desegregated society, but it cannot bring an end to fears, prejudice, pride, and irrationality, which are the barriers to a truly integrated society. Those dark and demonic responses will be removed only as men are possessed by the invisible, inner law which etches on their hearts the conviction that all men are brothers and that love is mankind's most potent weapon for personal and social transformation. True integration will be achieved by true neighbors who are willingly obedient to unenforceable obligations.

The Discipline of Nonviolence

I cannot conclude without saying that integration places certain ethical demands upon those who have been on the oppressed end of the old order. Perhaps this is why it is my personal conviction that the most potent instrument the Negro community can use to gain total emancipation in America is that of nonviolent resistance. The evidence of the last few years supports my faith that through the use of nonviolence much can be done to raise the Negro to a sense of self-respect and human dignity. The Gandhian concept of noninjury parallels the Hebraic-Christian teaching of the sacredness of every human being.

In the context of the Negro's thrust for the full exercise of constitutional privilege, nonviolence has introduced the additive that has helped the Negro stand taller. When a library is declared to be desegregated, the presence and practice of nonviolence allows him to seek the use of the facilities without fear and apprehension. More than this, it has instilled in him the verve to challenge segregation and discrimination in whatever form it exists. Nonviolence in so many ways has given the Negro a new sense of "somebodyness." The impact of the nonviolent discipline has done a great deal toward creating in the mind of the Negro a new image of himself.

It has literally exalted the person of the Negro in the South in the face of daily confrontations that scream at him that he is inferior or less than because of the accident of his birth.

How Nonviolence Helps

Nonviolence helps the individuals to adhere to proper means and proper goals. The nonviolent technique is double-barreled; not only has the Negro developed a new image of himself employing its practices, but it has also thwarted the growth of bitterness. In a very large measure, nonviolence has helped to diminish long-repressed feelings of anger and frustration. In the course of respecting the discipline of the nonviolent way, the Negro has learned that he must respect the adversary who inflicts the system upon him and he develops the capacity to hate segregation but to love the segregationist. He learns in the midst of his determined efforts to destroy the system that has shackled him so long, that a commitment to nonviolence demands that he respect the personhood of his opponent. Thus, nonviolence exalts the personality of the segregator as well as the segregated. The common denominator of the flux of social change in the South is the growing awareness on the part of the respective opponents that mutually they confront the eternality of the basic worth of every member of the human family.

The Birmingham Pledge Card

Birmingham, Alabama

"WALK and TALK in the manner of love, for God is love."

In 1963, the Southern Christian Leadership Conference focused on creating change in Birmingham, Alabama, one of the most segregated cities in the United States. The plan was for college students from the North to bus down over the Easter weekend and participate in marches calling for integration.

Participants in the Birmingham boycotts and sit-ins were asked to fill out pledge cards, with their names, addresses, closest relative, and the activities they would volunteer to take on listed under the following commitments.

I hereby pledge myself—my person and body—to the nonviolent movement, therefore I will keep the following ten commandments!

1. MEDITATE daily on the teachings and life of Jesus.

2. REMEMBER always that the nonviolent movement in Birmingham seeks justice and reconciliation—not victory.

3. WALK and TALK in the manner of love, for God is love.

4. PRAY daily to be used by God in order that all men might be free.

5. SACRIFICE personal wishes in order that all men might be free.

6. OBSERVE with both friend and foe the ordinary rules of courtesy.

7. SEEK to perform regular service for others and for the world.

8. REFRAIN from the violence of fist, tongue, or heart.

9. STRIVE to be in good spiritual and bodily health.

10. FOLLOW the directions of the movement and of the captain on a demonstration.

Letter from Birmingham Jail

EXCERPT FROM OPEN LETTER WRITTEN IN BIRMINGHAM, ALABAMA

"I gradually gained a bit of satisfaction from being considered an extremist. Was not Jesus an extremist in love?"

King was arrested on Good Friday 1963 for ignoring an injunction against boycotts. He was placed in solitary confinement, where he wrote what he described as his longest open letter in response to eight liberal white clergymen who had penned their own open letter calling on King to stand down and let federal and local courts decide the issue of integration. They warned him that his actions would incite greater discord.

The letter excerpt reproduced here includes the material related to love. The earlier pages addressed why he chose to write at all, given that he had regularly been criticized and had chosen to ignore it. But he expressed frustration with the religious leaders who ignored the immorality of segregation. He clarified that he was invited by a local affiliate to join the nonviolent protest in his role as the president of the Southern Christian Leadership Conference. He then proceeded to take on the criticisms systematically.

A month later, on May 10, Birmingham agreed to desegregate fountains, lunch counters, restrooms, and fitting rooms.

• • •

[Excerpt]

. . . The Negro has many pent-up resentments and latent frustrations. He has to get them out. So let him march sometime; let him have his prayer pilgrimages to the city hall; understand why he must have sit-ins and freedom rides. If his repressed emotions do not come out in these nonviolent ways, they will come out in ominous expressions of violence. This is not a threat; it is a fact of history. So I have not said to my people, "Get rid of your discontent." But I have tried to say that this normal and healthy discontent can be channeled through the creative outlet of nonviolent direct action. Now this approach is being dismissed as extremist. I must admit that I was initially disappointed in being so categorized.

But as I continued to think about the matter, I gradually gained a bit of satisfaction from being considered an extremist. Was not Jesus an extremist in love?—"Love your enemies, bless them that curse you, pray for them that despitefully use you." Was not Amos an extremist for justice?—"Let justice roll down like waters and righteousness like a mighty stream." Was not Paul an extremist for the gospel of Jesus Christ?—"I bear in my body the marks of the Lord Jesus." Was not Martin Luther an extremist?—"Here I stand; I can do no other so help me God." Was not John Bunyan an extremist?—"I will stay in jail to the end of my days before I make a mockery of my conscience." Was not Abraham Lincoln an extremist?—"This nation cannot survive half slave and half free." Was not Thomas Jefferson an extremist?—"We hold these truths to be self-evident, that all men are created equal." So the question is not whether we will be extremist, but what kind of extremists we will be. Will we be extremists for hate, or will we be extremists for love? Will we be extremists for the preservation of injustice, or will we be extremists for the cause of justice?

[Excerpt]

... I had hoped that the white moderate would see this. Maybe I was too optimistic. Maybe I expected too much. I guess I should have realized that few members of a race that has oppressed another race can understand or appreciate the deep groans and passionate yearnings of those that have been oppressed, and still fewer have the vision to see that injustice must be rooted out by strong, persistent, and determined action. I am thankful, however, that some of our white brothers have grasped the meaning of this social revolution and committed themselves to it. They are still all too small in quantity, but they are big in quality....

[Excerpt]

... I have traveled the length and breadth of Alabama, Mississippi, and all the other southern states. On sweltering summer days and crisp autumn mornings I have looked at the South's beautiful churches with their lofty spires pointing heavenward. I have beheld the impressive outlines of her massive religious education buildings. Over and over I have found myself asking: "What kind of people worship here? Who is their God? Where were their voices when the lips of Governor [Ross] Barnett dripped with words of interposition and nullification? Where were they when Governor [George] Wallace gave a clarion call for defiance and hatred? Where were their voices of support when bruised and weary Negro men and women decided to rise from the dark dungeons of complacency to the bright hills of creative protest?"

Yes, these questions are still in my mind. In deep disappointment I have wept over the laxity of the church. But be assured that my tears have been tears of love. There can be no deep disappointment where there is not deep love. Yes, I love the church. How could I do otherwise? I am in the rather unique position of being the son, the grandson, and the great grandson of preachers. Yes, I see the church as the body of Christ. But, oh! How we have blemished and scarred that body through social neglect and through fear of being nonconformists. . . .

PUBLISHED JUNE 1963

Strength to Love

SELECTIONS FROM THE BOOK

"[Jesus] did not seek to overcome evil with evil. He overcame evil with good. Although crucified by hate, he responded with aggressive love."

Strength to Love was King's second book but the first to collect his philosophy. As such, *Strength to Love* was greeted with curiosity by the press, who saw it as a key to understanding the motivations of the charismatic leader. The book was largely well received. The *New York Times* called it "a compelling call." A reviewer in the *Detroit News* wrote, "Dr. King's methods keep the moral issue completely clear."

In the spring of 1963, King toured the country speaking to large crowds in Los Angeles (twenty-five thousand) and Chicago (ten thousand), essentially demanding equality *now*, a real program to address poverty and change conditions in US ghettos. Following the attention to his "Letter from Birmingham Jail," more people were joining his protest: Black Americans were organizing in their home cities and marching in large numbers, and white people were admitting to the essential moral argument for racial equality.

In late May, King began hoping for a national march to push President John F. Kennedy to create legislation backing up intentions with action. Activist Bayard Rustin had been harboring the idea of a national march for years. Two months after the publication of *Strength to Love*, King and a quarter million leaders and protesters would participate in the March on Washington, where King delivered his famous "I Have a Dream" speech.

Strength to Love is a collection of sermons reworked by King for print. He prepared much of the material in 1962 while locked in a filthy jail for fifteen days in Albany, Georgia, for holding a prayer vigil outside city hall. As King noted in his preface, he did not think sermons made for good reading. The original versions of several of the sermons are reproduced in this book, and here we are highlighting sections of his reworked versions that show an evolution of his concepts on love or that introduce a new idea.

We omitted chapters that were essentially identical to the originally preached sermon, such as "The Three Dimensions of a Complete Life" (page 160) and "Paul's Letter to American Christians" (page 43). Included here are King's complete preface and selected chapters. We include:

Chapter IV, "Love in Action," which shows how he expanded on the idea that not only is love the answer to our societal problems, but that soul blindness is a hindrance to love

Chapter V, "Loving Your Enemies," in full, in which King refines ideas included earlier in this book (p. 85) and exerts even more confidence in his expression

Chapter VI, "A Knock at Midnight," about how modern life leaves us feeling unloved

Chapter X, "Shattered Dreams," in full, which warns of what can happen to a person who gives up on love and hope

Chapter XIV, "Antidotes for Fear," in full, which explains God's role in granting peace and even sanity

An excerpt from the final chapter, Chapter XVII, "Pilgrimage to Nonviolence," which asserts that we are under the control of a loving purpose. King believed that love was the prerequisite for a strategy of nonviolence; without love as the foundation, the activist would be unable to persist and would absorb damage to their own soul. This sermon goes beyond the topic of love but is included because it clarifies his thoughts about God as a loving presence.

Preface

In these turbulent days of uncertainty the evils of war and of economic and racial injustice threaten the very survival of the human race. Indeed, we live in a day of grave crisis. The sermons in this volume have the present crisis as their background; and they have been selected for this volume because, in one way or another, they deal with the personal and collective problems that the crisis presents. In these sermons I have sought to bring the Christian message to bear on the social evils that cloud our day and the personal witness and discipline required. All of these sermons were originally written for my former parishioners in the Dexter Avenue Baptist Church of Montgomery, Alabama, and my present parishioners in the Ebenezer Baptist Church of Atlanta, Georgia. Many of the sermons were later preached to congregations throughout the nation.

All of these sermons were preached during or after the bus protest in Montgomery, Alabama, and I have drawn a number of illustrations from that particular movement, some of which were included in my book *Stride Toward Freedom.* Three of the sermons—"Love in Action," "Loving Your Enemies," and "Shattered Dreams"—were written while I was in Georgia jails. "Pilgrimage to Nonviolence" is a revision and updating of material which previously appeared in *The Christian Century* and *Stride Toward Freedom.* Although it is not a sermon, it has been included at the end of the volume at the specific urging of the publisher.

I have been rather reluctant to have a volume of sermons printed. My misgivings have grown out of the fact that a sermon is not an essay to be read but a discourse to be heard. It should be a convincing appeal to a listening congregation. Therefore, a sermon is directed toward the listening ear rather than the reading eye. While I have tried to rewrite these sermons for the eye, I am convinced that this venture could never be entirely successful. So even as this volume goes to press I have not altogether overcome my misgivings. But in deference to my former congregation, my present congregation, my close associates in the Southern Christian Leadership Conference, and my many friends across the nation who have asked for copies of individual sermons, I offer these discourses in the hope that a message may come to life for readers of these printed words.

I am happy to express my deep gratitude to many helpers. I am indebted to my close friend and Executive Assistant, Wyatt Tee Walker, a fine preacher in his own right, for reading the entire manuscript and offering valuable suggestions. I am also indebted to my teacher and friend, Samuel W. Williams, for helpful and stimulating suggestions. Charles L. Wallis gave valuable editorial assistance on the final manuscript. My thanks also go to my efficient secretary, Miss Dora E. McDonald, who constantly offered encouraging words and transferred my handwritten pages to typewritten copy. Most of all I must thank my devoted wife, Coretta, who has read the complete manuscript and given invaluable suggestions and inspiration. Her love and patience enabled her to be understanding in the face of my increased absence from her and our children while completing this volume.

Martin Luther King, Jr.

Love in Action

CHAPTER IV OF *STRENGTH TO LOVE*

"The moment of testing emerges. Christ, the innocent Son of God, is stretched in painful agony on an uplifted cross. What place is there for love and forgiveness now?"

Then said Jesus, Father, forgive them;
for they know not what they do.

LUKE 23:34

Few words in the New Testament more clearly and solemnly express the magnanimity of Jesus' spirit than that sublime utterance from the cross, "Father, forgive them; for they know not what they do." This is love at its best.

We shall not fully understand the great meaning of Jesus' prayer unless we first notice that the text opens with the word "then." The verse immediately preceding reads thus: "And when they were come to the place, which is called Calvary, there they crucified him, and the malefactors, one on the right hand, and the other on the left. Then said Jesus, Father, forgive them." *Then*—when he was being plunged into the abyss of nagging agony. *Then*—when man had stooped to his worst. *Then*—when he was dying, a most ignominious death. *Then*—when the wicked hands of the creature had dared to crucify the only begotten Son of the Creator. Then said Jesus, "Father, forgive them." That "then" might well have been otherwise. He could have said, "Father, get even with them," or "Father, let loose the mighty thunderbolts of righteous wrath and destroy them," or "Father, open the flood gates of justice and permit the staggering avalanche of retribution to pour upon them." But none of these was his response. Though subjected to inexpressible agony, suffering excruciating pain, and despised and rejected, nevertheless, he cried, "Father, forgive them."

Let us take note of two basic lessons to be gleaned from this text.

I

First, it is a marvelous expression of Jesus' ability to match words with actions. One of the great tragedies of life is that men seldom bridge the gulf between practice and profession, between doing and saying. A persistent schizophrenia leaves so many of us tragically divided against ourselves. On the one hand, we proudly profess certain sublime and noble principles, but on the other hand, we sadly practice the very antithesis of those principles. How often are our lives characterized by a high blood pressure of creeds and an anemia of deeds! We talk eloquently about our commitment to the principles of Christianity, and yet our lives are saturated with the practices of paganism. We proclaim our devotion to democracy, but we sadly practice the very opposite of the democratic creed. We talk passionately about peace, and at the same time we assiduously prepare for war. We make our fervent pleas for the high road of justice, and then we tread unflinchingly the low road of injustice. This strange dichotomy, this agonizing gulf between the ought and the is, represents the tragic theme of man's earthly pilgrimage.

But in the life of Jesus we find that the gulf is bridged. Never in history was there a more sublime example of the consistency of word and deed. During his ministry in the sunny villages of Galilee, Jesus talked passionately about forgiveness. This strange doctrine awakened the questioning mind of Peter. "How oft," he asked, "shall my brother sin against me, and I forgive him? till seven times?" Peter wanted to be legal and statistical. But Jesus responded by affirming that there is no limit to forgiveness. "I say not unto thee, Until seven times: but, Until seventy times seven." In other words, forgiveness is not a matter of quantity, but of quality. A man cannot forgive up to four hundred and ninety times without forgiveness becoming a part of the habit structure of his being. Forgiveness is not an occasional act; it is a permanent attitude.

Jesus also admonished his followers to love their enemies and to pray for them that despitefully used them. This teaching fell upon the ears of many of his hearers like a strange music from a foreign land. Their ears were not attuned to the tonal qualities of such amazing love. They had been taught to love their friends and hate their enemies. Their lives had been conditioned to seek redress in the time-honored tradition of retaliation. Yet Jesus continued to teach them that only through a creative love for their enemies could they be children of their Father in heaven and also that love and forgiveness were absolute necessities for spiritual maturity.

The moment of testing emerges. Christ, the innocent Son of God, is stretched in painful agony on an uplifted cross. What place is there for love and forgiveness now? How will Jesus react? What will he say? The answer to these questions bursts forth in majestic splendor. Jesus lifts his thorn-crowned head and cries in words of cosmic proportions: "Father, forgive them; for they know not what they do." This was Jesus' finest hour; this was his heavenly response to his earthly rendezvous with destiny.

We sense the greatness of this prayer by contrasting it with nature, which caught in the finality of her own impersonal structure, does not forgive. In spite of the agonizing pleas of men trapped in the path of an onrushing hurricane or the anguishing cry of the builder falling from the scaffold, nature expresses only a cold, serene, and passionless indifference. She must honor everlastingly her fixed, immutable laws. When these laws are violated, she has no alternative except to follow inexorably her path of uniformity. Nature does not and cannot forgive.

Or contrast Jesus' prayer with the slowness of man to forgive. We live according to the philosophy that life is a matter of getting even and of saving face. We bow before the altar of revenge. Samson, eyeless at Gaza, prays fervently for his enemies—but only for their utter destruction. The potential beauty of human life is constantly made ugly by man's ever-recurring song of retaliation.

Or contrast the prayer with a society that is even less prone to forgive. Society must have its standards, norms, and mores. It must have its legal checks and judicial restraints. Those who fall below the standards and those who disobey the laws are often left in a dark abyss of condemnation and have no hope for a second chance. Ask an innocent young lady, who, after a moment of overriding passion, becomes the mother of an illegitimate child. She will tell you that society is slow to forgive. Ask a public official, who, in a moment's carelessness, betrays the public trust. He will tell you that society is slow to forgive. Go to any prison and ask the inhabitants, who have written shameful lines across the pages of their lives. From behind the bars they will tell you that society is slow to forgive. Make your way to death row and speak with the tragic victims of criminality. As they prepare to make their pathetic walk to the electric chair, their hopeless cry is that society will not forgive. Capital punishment is society's final assertion that it will not forgive.

Such is the persistent story of mortal life. The oceans of history are made turbulent by the ever-rising tides of revenge. Man has never risen above the injunction of the *lex talionis*: "Life for life, eye for eye, tooth for tooth, hand for hand, foot for foot." In spite of the fact that the law of revenge solves no social problems, men continue to follow its disastrous leading. History is cluttered with the wreckage of nations and individuals that pursued this self-defeating path.

Jesus eloquently affirmed from the cross a higher law. He knew that the old eye-for-an-eye philosophy would leave everyone blind. He did not seek to overcome evil with evil. He overcame evil with good. Although crucified by hate, he responded with aggressive love.

What a magnificent lesson! Generations will rise and fall; men will continue to worship the god of revenge and bow before the altar of retaliation; but ever and again this noble lesson of Calvary will be a nagging reminder that only goodness can drive out evil and only love can conquer hate.

II

A second lesson comes to us from Jesus' prayer on the cross. It is an expression of Jesus' awareness of man's intellectual and spiritual blindness. "They know not what they do," said Jesus. Blindness was their trouble; enlightenment was their need. We must recognize that Jesus was nailed to the cross not simply by sin but also by blindness. The men who cried, "Crucify him," were not bad men but rather blind men. The jeering mob that lined the roadside which led to Calvary was composed not of evil people but of blind people. They knew not what they did. What a tragedy!

History reverberates with testimonies of this shameful tragedy. Centuries ago a sage named Socrates was forced to drink hemlock. The men who called for his death were not bad men with demonic blood running through their veins. On the contrary, they were sincere and respectable citizens of Greece. They genuinely thought that Socrates was an atheist because his idea of God had a philosophical depth that probed beyond traditional concepts. Not badness but blindness killed Socrates. Saul was not an evil-intentioned man when he persecuted Christians. He was a sincere, conscientious devotee of Israel's faith. He thought he was right. He persecuted Christians, not because he was devoid of integrity, but because he was devoid of enlightenment. The Christians who engaged in infamous persecutions and shameful inquisitions were not evil men but misguided men. The churchmen who felt that they had an edict from God to withstand the progress of science, whether in the form of a Copernican revolution or a Darwinian theory of natural selection, were not mischievous men but misinformed men. And so Christ's words from the cross are written in sharp-etched terms across some of the most inexpressible tragedies of history: "They know not what they do."

This tragic blindness expresses itself in many ominous ways in our own day. Some men still feel that war is the answer to the problems of the world. They are not evil people. On the contrary, they are good, respectable citizens whose ideas are robed in the garments of patriotism. They talk of brinkmanship and a balance of terror. They sincerely feel that a continuation of the arms race will be conducive to more beneficent than maleficent consequences. So they passionately call for bigger bombs, larger nuclear stockpiles, and faster ballistic missiles.

Wisdom born of experience should tell us that war is obsolete. There may have been a time when war served as a negative good by preventing the spread and growth of an evil force, but the destructive power of modern weapons eliminates even the possibility that war may serve as a negative good. If we assume that life is worth living and that man has a right to survival, then we must find an alternative to war. In a day when vehicles hurtle through outer space and guided ballistic missiles carve highways of death through the stratosphere, no nation can claim victory in war. A so-called limited war will leave little more than a calamitous legacy of human suffering, political turmoil, and spiritual disillusionment. A world war—God forbid!— will leave only smouldering ashes as a mute testimony of a human race whose folly led inexorably to untimely death. Yet there are those who sincerely feel that disarmament is an evil and international negotiation is an abominable waste of time. Our world is threatened by the grim prospect of atomic annihilation because there are still too many men who know not what they do.

Notice, too, how the truth of this text is revealed in race relations. Slavery in America was perpetuated not merely by human badness but also by human blindness. True, the causal basis for the system of slavery must to a large extent be traced back to the economic factor. Men convinced themselves that a system which was so economically profitable must be morally justifiable. They formulated elaborate theories of racial superiority. Their rationalizations clothed obvious wrongs in the beautiful garments of righteousness. This tragic attempt to give moral sanction to an economically profitable system gave birth to the doctrine of white supremacy. Religion and the Bible were cited to crystallize the status quo. Science was commandeered to prove the biological inferiority of the Negro. Even philosophical logic

212

was manipulated to give intellectual credence to the system of slavery. Someone formulated the argument of the inferiority of the Negro according to the framework of an Aristotelian syllogism:

> All men are made in the image of God;
> God, as everyone knows, is not a Negro;
> Therefore, the Negro is not a man.

So men conveniently twisted the insights of religion, science, and philosophy to give sanction to the doctrine of white supremacy. Soon this idea was imbedded in every textbook and preached in practically every pulpit. It became a structured part of the culture. And men then embraced this philosophy, not as the rationalization of a lie, but as the expression of a final truth. They sincerely came to believe that the Negro was inferior by nature and that slavery was ordained by God. In 1857, the system of slavery was given its greatest legal support by the deliberations of the Supreme Court of the United States in the *Dred Scott* decision. The Court affirmed that the Negro had no rights which the white man was bound to respect. The justices who rendered this decision were not wicked men. On the contrary, they were decent and dedicated men. But they were victims of spiritual and intellectual blindness. They knew not what they did. The whole system of slavery was largely perpetuated by sincere though spiritually ignorant persons.

This tragic blindness is also found in racial segregation, the not-too-distant cousin of slavery. Some of the most vigorous defenders of segregation are sincere in their beliefs and earnest in their motives. Although some men are segregationists merely for reasons of political expediency and economic gain, not all of the resistance to integration is the rear-guard action of professional big-ots. Some people feel that their attempt to preserve segregation is best for themselves, their children, and their nation. Many are good church people, anchored in the religious faith of their mothers and fathers. Pressed for a religious vindication for their conviction, they will even argue that God was the first segregationist. "Red birds and blue birds don't fly together," they contend. Their views about segregation, they insist, can be rationally explained and morally jus-tified. Pressed for a justification of their belief in the inferiority of the Negro, they turn to some pseudo-scientific writing and argue that the Negro's brain is smaller than the white man's brain. They do not know, or they refuse to know, that the idea of an inferior or superior race has been refuted by the best evidence of the science of anthropology. Great anthropologists, like Ruth Benedict, Margaret Mead, and Melville J. Herskovits, agree that, although there may be inferior and superior individuals within all races, there is no supe-rior or inferior race. And segregationists refuse to acknowledge that science has demonstrated that there are four types of blood and that these four types are found within every racial group. They blindly believe in the eternal validity of an evil called segregation and the timeless truth of a myth called white supremacy. What a tragedy! Millions of Negroes have been crucified by conscientious blindness. With Jesus on the cross, we must look lovingly at our oppressors and say, "Father, forgive them; for they know not what they do."

III

From all that I have attempted to say it should now be apparent that sincerity and conscientiousness in themselves are not enough. His-tory has proven that these noble virtues may degenerate into tragic vices. Nothing in all the world is more dangerous than sincere ignorance and conscientious stupidity. Shakespeare wrote:

> For sweetest things turn sourest by their deeds;
> Lilies that fester smell far worse than weeds.

As the chief moral guardian of the community, the church must implore men to be good and well-intentioned and must extol the virtues of kindheartedness and conscientiousness. But somewhere along the way the church must remind men that, devoid of intelligence, goodness and conscientiousness will become brutal forces leading to shameful crucifixions. Never must the church tire of reminding men that they have a moral responsibility to be intelligent.

Must we not admit that the church has often overlooked this moral demand for enlightenment? At times it has talked as though ignorance were a virtue and intelligence a crime. Through its obscurantism, closed-mindedness, and obstinacy to new truth, the church has often unconsciously encouraged its worshipers to look askance upon intelligence.

But if we are to call ourselves Christians, we had better avoid intellectual and moral blindness. Throughout the New Testament we are reminded of the need for enlightenment. We are commanded to love God, not only with our hearts and souls, but also with our minds. When the Apostle Paul noticed the blindness of many of his opponents, he said, "I bear them record that they have a zeal for God, but not according to knowledge." Over and again the Bible reminds us of the danger of zeal without knowledge and sincerity without intelligence.

So we have a mandate both to conquer sin and also to conquer ignorance. Modern man is presently having a rendezvous with chaos, not merely because of human badness, but also because of human stupidity. If Western civilization continues to degenerate until it, like twenty-four of its predecessors, falls hopelessly into a bottomless void, the cause will be not only its undeniable sinfulness, but also its appalling blindness. And if American democracy gradually disintegrates, it will be due as much to a lack of insight as to a lack of commitment to right. If modern man continues to flirt unhesitatingly with war and eventually transforms his earthly habitat into an inferno such as even the mind of Dante could not imagine, it will have resulted from downright badness and also from downright stupidity.

"They know not what they do," said Jesus. Blindness was their besetting trouble. And the crux of the matter lies here: we do need to be blind. Unlike physical blindness that is usually inflicted upon individuals as a result of natural forces beyond their control, intellectual and moral blindness is a dilemma which man inflicts upon himself by his tragic misuse of freedom and his failure to use his mind to its fullest capacity. One day we will learn that the heart can never be totally right if the head is totally wrong. Only through the bringing together of head and heart—intelligence and goodness—shall man rise to a fulfillment of his true nature. Neither is this to say that one must be a philosopher or a possessor of extensive academic training before he can achieve a good life. I know many people of limited formal training who have amazing intelligence and foresight. The call for intelligence is a call for open-mindedness, sound judgment, and love for truth. It is a call for men to rise above the stagnation of closed-mindedness and the paralysis of gullibility. One does not need to be a profound scholar to be open-minded, nor a keen academician to engage in an assiduous pursuit for truth.

Light has come into the world. A voice crying through the vista of time calls men to walk in the light. Man's earthly life will become a tragic cosmic elegy if he fails to heed this call. "This is the condemnation," says John, "that light is come into the world, and men loved the darkness rather than light."

Every time I look at the cross I am reminded of the greatness of God and the redemptive power of Jesus Christ. I am reminded of the beauty of sacrificial love and the majesty of unswerving devotion to truth. It causes me to say with John Bowring:

> In the cross of Christ I glory,
> Towering o'er the wrecks of time;
> All the light of sacred story
> Gathers round its head sublime.

It would be wonderful were I to look at the cross and sense only such a sublime reaction. But somehow I can never turn my eyes from that cross without also realizing that it symbolizes a strange mixture of greatness and smallness, of good and evil. As I behold that uplifted cross I am reminded not only of the unlimited power of God, but also of the sordid weakness of man. I think not only of the radiance of the divine, but also of the tang of the human. I am reminded not only of Christ at his best, but of man at his worst.

We must see the cross as the magnificent symbol of love conquering hate and of light overcoming darkness. But in the midst of this glowing affirmation, let us never forget that our Lord and Master was nailed to that cross because of human blindness. Those who crucified him knew not what they did.

Loving Your Enemies

CHAPTER V OF *STRENGTH TO LOVE*

"Modern psychology recognizes what Jesus taught centuries ago: hate divides the personality and love in an amazing and inexorable way unites it."

Ye have heard that it hath been said. Thou shalt love thy neighbour, and hate thine enemy. But I say unto you, Love your enemies, bless them that curse you, do good to them that hate you, and pray for them which despitefully use you, and persecute you; that ye may be children of your Father which is in heaven.

MATT. 5:43–45, KJV

Probably no admonition of Jesus has been more difficult to follow than the command to "love your enemies." Some men have sincerely felt that its actual practice is not possible. It is easy, they say, to love those who love you, but how can one love those who openly and insidiously seek to defeat you? Others, like the philosopher Nietzsche, contend that Jesus' exhortation to love one's enemies is testimony to the fact that the Christian ethic is designed for the weak and cowardly, and not for the strong and courageous. Jesus, they say, was an impractical idealist.

In spite of these insistent questions and persistent objections, this command of Jesus challenges us with new urgency. Upheaval after upheaval has reminded us that modern man is traveling along a road called hate, in a journey that will bring us to destruction and damnation. Far from being the pious injunction of a Utopian dreamer, the command to love one's enemy is an absolute necessity for our survival. Love even for enemies is the key to the solution of the problem of our world. Jesus is not an impractical idealist; he is the practical realist.

I am certain that Jesus understood the difficulty inherent in the act of loving one's enemy. He never joined the ranks of those who talk glibly about the easiness of the moral life. He realized that every genuine expression of love grows out of a consistent and total surrender to God. So when Jesus said "Love your enemy," he was not unmindful of its stringent qualities. Yet he meant every word of it. Our responsibility as Christians is to discover the meaning of this command and seek passionately to live it out in our daily lives.

I

Let us be practical and ask the question, *How do we love our enemies?*

First, we must develop and maintain the capacity to forgive. He who is devoid of the power to forgive is devoid of the power to love. It is impossible even to begin the act of loving one's enemies without the prior acceptance of the necessity, over and over again, of forgiving those who afflict evil and injury upon us. It is also necessary to realize that the forgiving act must always be initiated by the person who has been wronged, the victim of some great hurt, the recipient of some tortuous injustice, the absorber of some terrible act of oppression. The wrongdoer may request forgiveness. He may come to himself, and, like the prodigal son, move up some dusty road, his heart palpitating with the desire for forgiveness. But only the injured neighbor, the loving father back home, can really pour out the warm waters of forgiveness.

Forgiveness does not mean ignoring what has been done or putting a false label on an evil act. It means, rather, that the evil act no longer remains as a barrier to the relationship. Forgiveness is a catalyst creating the atmosphere necessary for a fresh start and a new beginning. It is the lifting of a burden or the canceling of a debt. The words "I will forgive you, but I'll never forget what you've done" never explain the real nature of forgiveness. Certainly one can never forget, if that means erasing it totally from his mind. But when we forgive, we forget in the sense that the evil deed is no longer a mental block impeding a new relationship. Likewise, we can never say, "I will forgive you, but I won't have anything further to do with you." Forgiveness means reconciliation, a coming together again. Without this, no man can love his enemies. The degree to which we are able to forgive determines the degree to which we are able to love our enemies.

Second, we must recognize that the evil deed of the enemy-neighbor, the thing that hurts, never quite expresses all that he is. An element of goodness may be found even in our worst enemy. Each of us is something of a schizophrenic personality, tragically divided against ourselves. A persistent civil war rages within all of our lives. Something within us causes us to lament with Ovid, the Latin poet, "I see and approve the better things, but follow worse," or to agree with Plato that human personality is like a charioteer having two headstrong horses, each wanting to go in a different direction, or to repeat with the Apostle Paul, "The good that I would I do not: but the evil which I would not, that I do."

This simply means that there is some good in the worst of us and some evil in the best of us. When we discover this, we are less prone to hate our enemies. When we look beneath the surface, beneath the impulsive evil deed, we see within our enemy-neighbor a measure of goodness and know that the viciousness and evilness of his acts are not quite representative of all that he is. We see him in a new light. We recognize that his hate grows out of fear, pride, ignorance, prejudice, and misunderstanding, but in spite of this, we know God's image is ineffably etched in his being. Then we love our enemies by realizing that they are not totally bad and that they are not beyond the reach of God's redemptive love.

Third, we must not seek to defeat or humiliate the enemy but to win his friendship and understanding. At times we are able to humiliate our worst enemy. Inevitably, his weak moments come and we are able to thrust in his side the spear of defeat. But this we must not do. Every word and deed must contribute to an understanding with the enemy and release those vast reservoirs of goodwill which have been blocked by impenetrable walls of hate.

The meaning of love is not to be confused with some sentimental outpouring. Love is something much deeper than emotional bosh. Perhaps the Greek language can clear our confusion at this point. In the Greek New Testament are three words for love.* The word eros is a sort of aesthetic or romantic love. In the Platonic dialogues eros is a yearning of the soul for the realm of the divine. The second word is philia, a reciprocal love and the intimate affection and friendship between friends. We love those whom we like, and we love because we are loved. The third word is agape, understanding and creative, redemptive goodwill for all men. An overflowing love which seeks nothing in return, agape is the love of God operating in the human heart. At this level, we love men

---

* While the Greek language has three words for love, "eros" does not appear in the Greek New Testament.

not because we like them, nor because their ways appeal to us, nor even because they possess some type of divine spark; we love every man because God loves him. At this level, we love the person who does an evil deed, although we hate the deed that he does.

Now we can see what Jesus meant when he said, "Love your enemies." We should be happy that he did not say, "Like your enemies." It is almost impossible to like some people. "Like" is a sentimental and affectionate word. How can we be affectionate toward a person whose avowed aim is to crush our very being and place innumerable stumbling blocks in our path? How can we like a person who is threatening our children and bombing our homes? This is impossible. But Jesus recognized that love is greater than like. When Jesus bids us to love our enemies, he is speaking neither of eros nor philia; he is speaking of agape, understanding and creative, redemptive goodwill for all men. Only by following this way and responding with this type of love are we able to be children of our Father who is in heaven.

II

Let us move now from the practical how to the theoretical *why: Why should we love our enemies?* The first reason is fairly obvious. Returning hate for hate multiplies hate, adding deeper darkness to a night already devoid of stars. Darkness cannot drive out darkness; only light can do that. Hate cannot drive out hate; only love can do that. Hate multiples hate, violence multiplies violence, and toughness multiplies toughness in a descending spiral of destruction. So when Jesus says "Love your enemies," he is setting forth a profound and ultimately inescapable admonition. Have we not come to such an impasse in the modern world that we must love our enemies—or else? The chain reaction of evil—hate begetting hate, wars producing more wars—must be broken, or we shall be plunged into the dark abyss of annihilation.

Another reason why we must love our enemies is that hate scars the soul and distorts the personality. Mindful that hate is an evil and dangerous force, we too often think of what it does to the person hated. This is understandable, for hate brings irreparable damage to its victims. We have seen its ugly consequences in the ignominious deaths brought to six million Jews by a hate-obsessed madman named Hitler, in the unspeakable violence inflicted upon Negroes by bloodthirsty mobs, in the dark horrors of war, and in the terrible indignities and injustices perpetrated against millions of God's children by unconscionable oppressors.

But there is another side which we must never overlook. Hate is just as injurious to the person who hates. Like an unchecked cancer, hate corrodes the personality and eats away its vital unity. Hate destroys a man's sense of values and his objectivity. It causes him to describe the beautiful as ugly and the ugly as beautiful, and to confuse the true with the false and the false with the true.

Dr. E. Franklin Frazier, in an interesting essay entitled "The Pathology of Race Prejudice," included several examples of white persons who were normal, amiable, and congenial in their day-to-day relationships with other white persons, but when they were challenged to think of Negroes as equals or even to discuss the question of racial injustice, they reacted with unbelievable irrationality and an abnormal unbalance. This happens when hate lingers in our minds. Psychiatrists report that many of the strange things that happen in the subconscious, many of our inner conflicts, are rooted in hate. They say, "Love or perish." Modern psychology recognizes what Jesus taught centuries ago: hate divides the personality and love in an amazing and inexorable way unites it.

A third reason why we should love our enemies is that love is the only force capable of transforming an enemy into a friend. We never get rid of an enemy by meeting hate with hate; we get rid of an enemy by getting rid of enmity. By its very nature, hate destroys and tears down; by its very nature, love creates and builds up. Love transforms with redemptive power.

Lincoln tried love and left for all history a magnificent drama of reconciliation. When he was campaigning for the presidency one of his archenemies was a man named [Edwin M.] Stanton. For some reason Stanton hated Lincoln. He used every ounce of his energy to degrade him in the eyes of the public. So deep rooted was Stanton's hate for Lincoln that he uttered unkind words about his physical appearance, and sought to embarrass him at every point with the bitterest diatribes. But in spite of this Lincoln was elected President of the United States. Then came the period when he had to select his cabinet which would consist of the persons who would be his most intimate associates in implementing his program. He started choosing men here and there for the various secretaryships. The day finally came for Lincoln to select a man to fill the all-important post of Secretary of War. Can you imagine whom Lincoln chose to fill this post? None other than the man named Stanton. There was an immediate uproar in the inner circle when the news began to spread. Adviser after adviser was heard saying, "Mr. President, you are making a mistake. Do you know this man Stanton? Are you familiar with all of the ugly things he said about you? He is your enemy. He will seek to sabotage your program. Have you thought this through, Mr. President?" Mr. Lincoln's answer was terse and to the point: "Yes, I know Mr. Stanton. I am aware of all the terrible things he has said about me. But after looking over the nation, I find that he is the best man for the job." So Stanton became Abraham Lincoln's Secretary of War and rendered an invaluable service to his nation and his President. Not many years later Lincoln was assassinated. Many laudable things were said about him. Even today millions of people still adore him as the greatest of all Americans. H. G. Wells selected him as one of the six great men of history. But of all the great statements made about Abraham Lincoln, the words of Stanton remain among the greatest. Standing near the dead body of the man he once hated, Stanton referred to him as one of the greatest men that ever lived and said "He now belongs to the ages." If Lincoln had hated Stanton both men would have gone to their graves as bitter enemies. But through the power of love Lincoln transformed an enemy into a friend. It was this same attitude that made it possible for Lincoln to speak a kind word about the South during the Civil War when feeling was most bitter. Asked by a shocked bystander how he could do this, Lincoln said, "Madam, do I not destroy my enemies when I make them my friends?" This is the power of redemptive love.

We must hasten to say that these are not the ultimate reasons why we should love our enemies. An even more basic reason why we are commanded to love is expressed explicitly in Jesus' words, "Love your enemies . . . *that ye may be [the] children of your Father which is in heaven.*" We are called to this difficult task in order to realize a unique relationship with God. We are potential sons of God. Through love that potentiality becomes actuality. We must love our enemies, because only by loving them can we know God and experience the beauty of his holiness.

The relevance of what I have said to the crisis in race relations should be readily apparent. There will be no permanent solution to the race problem until oppressed men develop the capacity to love their enemies. The darkness of racial injustice will be dispelled only by the light of forgiving love. For more than three centuries American Negroes have been battered by the iron rod of oppression, frustrated by day and bewildered by night by unbearable injustice, and burdened with the ugly weight of discrimination. Forced to live with these shameful conditions, we are tempted to become bitter and to retaliate with a corresponding hate. But if this happens, the new order we seek will be little more than a duplicate of the old order. We must in strength and humility meet hate with love.

Of course, this is not practical. Life is a matter of getting even, of hitting back, of dog eat dog. Am I saying that Jesus commands us to love those who hurt and oppress us? Do I sound like most preachers—idealistic and impractical? Maybe in some distant Utopia, you say, that idea will work, but not in the hard, cold world in which we live.

My friends, we have followed the so-called practical way for too long a time now, and it has led inexorably to deeper confusion and chaos. Time is cluttered with the wreckage of communities which surrendered to hatred and violence. For the salvation of our nation and the salvation of mankind, we must follow another way. This does not mean that we abandon our righteous efforts. With every ounce of our energy we must continue to rid this nation of the incubus of segregation. But we shall not in the process relinquish our privilege and our obligation to love. While abhorring segregation, we shall love the segregationist. This is the only way to create the beloved community.

To our most bitter opponents we say: "We shall match your capacity to inflict suffering by our capacity to endure suffering. We shall meet your physical force with soul force. Do to us what you will, and we shall continue to love you. We cannot in all good conscience obey your unjust laws, because noncooperation with evil is as much a moral obligation as is cooperation with good. Throw us in jail, and we shall still love you. Bomb our homes and threaten our children, and we shall still love you. Send your hooded perpetrators of violence into our community at the midnight hour and beat us and leave us half dead, and we shall still love you. But be ye assured that we will wear you down by our capacity to suffer. One day we shall win freedom, but not only for ourselves. We shall so appeal to your heart and conscience that we shall win you in the process, and our victory will be a double victory."

Love is the most durable power in the world. This creative force, so beautifully exemplified in the life of our Christ, is the most potent instrument available in mankind's quest for peace and security. Napoleon Bonaparte, the great military genius, looking back over his years of conquest, is reported to have said: "Alexander, Caesar, Charlemagne and I have built great empires. But upon what did they depend? They depended on force. But centuries ago Jesus started an empire that was built on love, and even to this day millions will die for him." Who can doubt the veracity of these words? The great military leaders of the past have gone, and their empires have crumbled and burned to ashes. But the empire of Jesus, built solidly and majestically on the foundation of love, is still growing. It started with a small group of dedicated men, who, through the inspiration of their Lord, were able to shake the hinges from the gates of the Roman Empire, and carry the gospel into all the world. Today the vast earthly kingdom of Christ numbers more than 900,000,000 and covers every land and tribe. Today we hear again the promise of victory:

> Jesus shall reign where'er the sun
> Does his successive journeys run;
> His kingdom stretch from shore to shore,
> Till moon shall wax and wane no more.

Another choir joyously responds:

> In Christ there is no East or West,
> In Him no South or North,
> But one great Fellowship of Love
> Throughout the whole wide earth.

Jesus is eternally right. History is replete with the bleached bones of nations that refused to listen to him. May we in the twentieth century hear and follow his words—before it is too late. May we solemnly realize that we shall never be true sons of our heavenly Father until we love our enemies and pray for those who persecute us.

A Knock at Midnight

EXCERPT FROM CHAPTER VI OF *STRENGTH TO LOVE*

"Bewildered by this tendency to reduce man to a card in a vast index, man desperately searches for the bread of love."

[Excerpt]

... There is the deep longing for the bread of love. Everybody wishes to love and to be loved. He who feels that he is not loved feels that he does not count. Much has happened in the modern world to make men feel that they do not belong. Living in a world which has become oppressively impersonal, many of us have come to feel that we are little more than numbers. Ralph Borsodi in an arresting picture of a world wherein numbers have replaced persons writes that the modern mother is often maternity case No. 8434 and her child, after being fingerprinted and footprinted, becomes No. 8003, and that a funeral in a large city is an event in Parlor B with Class B flowers and decorations at which Preacher No. 14 officiates and Musician No. 84 sings Selection No. 174. Bewildered by this tendency to reduce man to a card in a vast index, man desperately searches for the bread of love. . . .

Shattered Dreams

CHAPTER X OF *STRENGTH TO LOVE*

"Too unconcerned to love and too passionless to hate, too detached to be selfish and too lifeless to be unselfish, too indifferent to experience joy and too cold to experience sorrow, they are neither dead nor alive; they merely exist."

Whensoever I take my journey into Spain, I will come to you.

ROMANS 15:24, KJV

One of the most agonizing problems within our human experience is that few, if any, of us live to see our fondest hopes fulfilled. The hopes of our childhood and the promises of our mature years are unfinished symphonies. In a famous painting, George Frederic Watts portrays Hope as a tranquil figure who, seated atop our planet, her head sadly bowed, plucks a single unbroken harpstring. Is there any one of us who has not faced the agony of blasted hopes and shattered dreams?

In Paul's letter to the Roman Christians we find a potent illustration of this vexing problem of disappointed hopes: "Whensoever I take my journey into Spain, I will come to you." One of his ardent hopes was to travel to Spain where, at the edge of the then

229

known world, he might further proclaim the Christian gospel. On his return he wished to have personal fellowship with that valiant group of Roman Christians. The more he anticipated this privilege, the more his heart quickened with joy. His preparations now centered in carrying the gospel to the capital city of Rome and to Spain at the distant fringe of the empire.

What a glowing hope stirred within Paul's heart. But he never got to Rome according to the pattern of his hopes. Because of his daring faith in Jesus Christ, he was indeed taken there but as a prisoner and was held captive in a little prison cell. Nor did he ever walk the dusty roads of Spain, nor look upon its curvaceous slopes, nor watch its busy coastal life. He was put to death, we presume, as a martyr for Christ in Rome. Paul's life is a tragic story of a shattered dream.

Life mirrors many similar experiences. Who has not set out toward some distant Spain, some momentous goal, or some glorious realization, only to learn at last that he must settle for much less? We never walk as free men through the streets of our Rome; instead, circumstances decree that we live within little confining cells. Written across our lives is a fatal flaw and within history runs an irrational and unpredictable vein. Like Abraham, we too sojourn in the land of promise, but so often we do not become "heirs with him of the same promise." Always our reach exceeds our grasp.

After struggling for years to achieve independence, Mahatma Gandhi witnessed a bloody religious war between the Hindus and the Muslims, and the subsequent division of India and Pakistan shattered his heart's desire for a united nation. Woodrow Wilson died before realizing the fulfillment of his consuming vision of a League of Nations. Many Negro slaves in America, having longed passionately for freedom, died before emancipation. After praying in the garden of Gethsemane that the cup might pass, Jesus, nonetheless, drank to the last bitter dregs. And the Apostle Paul repeatedly and fervently prayed that the "thorn" might be removed from his flesh, but the pain and annoyance continued to the end of his days. Shattered dreams are a hallmark of our mortal life.

I

Before we determine how to live in a world where our highest hopes are not satisfied, we must ask, What does one do under such circumstances? One possible reaction is to distill all of our frustrations into a core of bitterness and resentment. The person who pursues this path is likely to develop a callous attitude, a cold heart, and a bitter hatred toward God, toward those with whom he lives, and toward himself. Because he cannot corner God or life, he releases his pent-up vindictiveness in hostility toward other people. He may be extremely cruel to his mate and inhuman to his children. In short, meanness becomes his dominating characteristic. He loves no one and requires love from no one. He trusts no one and does not expect others to trust him. He finds fault in everything and everybody, and he continually complains.

Such a reaction poisons the soul and scars the personality, always harming the person who harbors this feeling more than anyone else. Medical science reveals that such physical ailments as arthritis, gastric ulcer, and asthma have on occasion been encouraged by bitter resentments. Psychosomatic medicine, dealing with bodily sicknesses which come from mental illnesses, shows how deep resentment may result in physical deterioration.

Another common reaction by persons experiencing the blighting of hope is to withdraw completely into themselves and to become absolute introverts. No one is permitted to enter into their lives and they refuse to enter into the lives of others. Such persons give up the struggle of life, lose their zest for living, and attempt to escape by lifting their minds to a transcendent realm of cold indifference. Detachment is the word which best describes them. Too unconcerned to love and too passionless to hate, too detached to be selfish and too lifeless to be unselfish, too indifferent to experience joy and too cold to experience sorrow, they are neither dead nor alive; they merely exist. Their eyes do not see the beauties of nature, their ears are insensitive to the majestic sounds of great music, and their hands are even unresponsive to the touch of a charming little baby. Nothing of the aliveness of life is left in them; only the dull motion of bare existence. Disappointed hopes lead them to a crippling cynicism such as Omar Khayyam described:

> The Worldly Hope men set their Hearts upon
> Turns Ashes—or it prospers; and anon,
> Like Snow upon the Desert's dusty Face,
> Lighting a little hour or two—is gone.

This reaction is based on an attempt to escape from life. Psychiatrists say that when individuals attempt to escape from reality their personalities become thinner and thinner until finally they split. This is one of the causal sources of the schizophrenic personality.

A third way by which persons respond to disappointments in life is to adopt a fatalistic philosophy stipulating that whatever happens must happen and that all events are determined by necessity. Fatalism implies that everything is foreordained and inescapable. People who subscribe to this philosophy succumb to an absolute resignation to that which they consider to be their fate and think of themselves as being little more than helpless orphans cast into the terrifying immensities of space. Because they believe that man has no freedom, they seek neither to deliberate nor to make decisions, but rather they wait passively for external forces to decide for them. They never actively seek to change their circumstances, for they believe that all circumstances, as in the Greek tragedies, are controlled by irresistible and foreordained forces. Some fatalists are very religious people who think of God as the determiner and controller of destiny. This view is expressed in a verse of one of our Christian hymns:

> Though dark my path and sad my lot,
> Let me be still and murmur not,
> But breathe the prayer divinely taught,
> Thy will be done.

Fatalists, believing that freedom is a myth, surrender to a paralyzing determinism which concludes that we are

> But helpless Pieces of the Game He plays
> Upon this Chequer-board of Nights and Days;

and that we need not trouble about the future, for

> The Moving Finger writes; and, having writ.
> Moves on: nor all your Piety nor Wit
> Shall lure it back to cancel half a Line,
> Nor all your Tears wash out a Word of it.

To sink in the quicksands of fatalism is both intellectually and psychologically stifling. Because freedom is a part of the essence of man, the fatalist, by denying freedom, becomes a puppet, not a person. He is, of course, right in his conviction that there is no absolute freedom and that freedom always operates within the context of predestined structure. Common experience teaches that a man is free to go north from Atlanta to Washington or south from Atlanta to Miami, but not north to Miami nor south to Washington. Freedom is always within the framework of destiny. But there is freedom. We are both free and destined. Freedom is the act of deliberating, deciding, and responding within our destined nature. Even though destiny may prevent our going to some attractive Spain, we do have the capacity to accept such a disappointment, to respond to it, and to do something about the disappointment itself. But fatalism stymies the individual, leaving him helplessly inadequate for life.

Fatalism, furthermore, is based on an appalling conception of God, for everything, whether good or evil, is considered to represent the will of God. A healthy religion rises above the idea that God wills evil. Although God permits evil in order to preserve the freedom of man, he does not cause evil. That which is willed is intended, and the thought that God intends for a child to be born blind or for a man to suffer the ravages of insanity is sheer heresy that pictures God as a devil rather than as a loving Father. The embracing of fatalism is as tragic and dangerous a way to meet the problem of unfulfilled dreams as are bitterness and withdrawal.

II

What, then, is the answer? The answer lies in our willing acceptance of unwanted and unfortunate circumstances even as we still cling to a radiant hope, our acceptance of finite disappointment even as we adhere to infinite hope. This is not the grim, bitter acceptance of the fatalist, but the achievement found in Jeremiah's words, "This is a grief, and I must bear it."

You must honestly confront your shattered dream. To follow the escapist method of attempting to put the disappointment out of your mind will lead to a psychologically injurious repression. Place your failure at the forefront of your mind and stare daringly at it. Ask yourself, "How may I transform this liability into an asset? How may I, confined in some narrow Roman cell and unable to reach life's Spain, transmute this dungeon of shame into a haven of redemptive suffering?" Almost anything that happens to us may be woven into the purposes of God. It may lengthen our cords of sympathy. It may break our self-centered pride. The cross, which was willed by wicked men, was woven by God into the tapestry of world redemption.

Many of the world's most influential personalities have exchanged their thorns for crowns. Charles Darwin, suffering from a recurrent physical illness; Robert Louis Stevenson, plagued with tuberculosis; and Helen Keller, inflicted with blindness and deafness, responded not with bitterness or fatalism, but rather by the exercise of a dynamic will transformed negative circumstances into positive assets. Writes the biographer of George Frederick Handel:

> His health and his fortunes had reached the lowest ebb. His right side had become paralyzed, and his money was all gone. His creditors seized him and threatened him with imprisonment. For a brief time he was tempted to give up the fight—but then he rebounded again to compose the greatest of his inspirations, the epic *Messiah*.

The "Hallelujah Chorus" was born, not in a sequestered villa in Spain, but in a narrow, undesirable cell.

How familiar is the experience of longing for Spain and settling for a Roman prison, and how less familiar the transforming of the broken remains of a disappointed expectation into opportunities to serve God's purpose! Yet powerful living always involves such victories over one's own soul and one's situation.

We Negroes have long dreamed of freedom, but still we are confined in an oppressive prison of segregation and discrimination. Must we respond with bitterness and cynicism? Certainly not, for this will destroy and poison our personalities. Must we, by concluding that segregation is within the will of God, resign ourselves to oppression? Of course not, for this blasphemously attributes to God that which is of the devil. To co-operate passively with an unjust system makes the oppressed as evil as the oppressor. Our most fruitful course is to stand firm with courageous determination, move forward nonviolently amid obstacles and setbacks, accept disappointments, and cling to hope. Our determined refusal not to be stopped will eventually open the door of fulfillment. While still in the prison of segregation, we must ask, "How may we turn this liability into an asset?" By recognizing the necessity of suffering in a righteous cause, we may possibly achieve our humanity's full stature. To guard ourselves from bitterness, we need the vision to see in this generation's ordeals the opportunity to transfigure both ourselves and American society. Our present suffering and our nonviolent struggle to be free may well offer to Western civilization the kind of spiritual dynamic so desperately needed for survival.

Some of us, of course, will die without having received the realization of freedom, but we must continue to sail on our charted course. We must accept finite disappointment, but we must never lose infinite hope. Only in this way shall we live without the fatigue of bitterness and the drain of resentment.

This was the secret of the survival of our slave foreparents. Slavery was a low, dirty, and inhuman business. When the slaves were taken from Africa, they were cut off from their family ties and chained to ships like beasts. Nothing is more tragic than to be divorced from family, language, and roots. In many instances, husbands were separated from wives and children from parents. When women were forced to satisfy the biological urges of white masters, slave husbands were powerless to intervene. Yet, in spite of inexpressible cruelties, our foreparents survived. When a new morning offered only the same long rows of cotton, sweltering heat, and the rawhide whip of the overseer, these brave and courageous men and women dreamed of the brighter day. They had no alternative except to accept the fact of slavery, but they clung tenaciously to the hope of freedom. In a seemingly hopeless situation, they fashioned within their souls a creative optimism that strengthened them. Their bottomless vitality transformed the darkness of frustration into the light of hope.

III

I first flew from New York to London in the propeller-type aircraft that required nine and a half hours for a flight now made in six hours by jet. When returning from London to the States, I was told that the flying time would be twelve and a half hours. The distance was the same. Why an additional three hours? When the pilot entered the cabin to greet the passengers, I asked him to explain the difference in flight time. "You must understand something about the winds," he said. "When we leave New York, a strong tail wind is in our favor, but when we return, a strong head wind is against us." Then he added, "Don't worry. These four engines are capable of battling the winds." At times in our lives the tail winds of joy, triumph, and fulfillment favor us, and at times the head winds of disappointment, sorrow, and tragedy beat unrelentingly against us. Shall we permit adverse winds to overwhelm us as we journey across life's mighty Atlantic, or will our inner spiritual engines sustain us in spite of the winds? Our refusal to be stopped, our "courage to be," our determination to go on "in spite of," reveal the divine image within us. The man who has made this discovery knows that no burden can overwhelm him and no wind of adversity can blow his hope away. He can stand anything that can happen to him.

Certainly the Apostle Paul possessed this type of "courage to be." His life was a continual round of disappointments. On every side were broken plans and shattered dreams. Planning to visit Spain, he was consigned to a Roman prison. Hoping to go to Bithynia, he was sidetracked to Troas. His gallant mission for Christ was measured "in journeyings often, in perils of waters, in perils of robbers, in perils by mine own countrymen, in perils by the heathen, in perils in the city, in perils in the wilderness, in perils in the sea, in perils among false brethren." Did he permit these conditions to master him? "I have learned," he testified, "in whatsoever state I am, therewith to be content." Not that Paul had learned to be complacent, for nothing in his life characterizes him as a complacent individual. In his *Decline and Fall of the Roman Empire*, Edward Gibbon records, "Paul has done more to promote the idea of freedom and liberty than any man who set foot on western soil." Does this sound like complacency? Nor did he learn resignation to inscrutable fate. By discovering the distinction between spiritual tranquility and the outward accidents of circumstance, Paul learned to stand tall and without despairing amid the disappointments of life.

Each of us who makes this magnificent discovery will, like Paul, be a recipient of that true peace "which passeth all understanding." Peace as the world commonly understands it comes when the summer sky is clear and the sun shines in scintillating beauty, when the pocketbook is full, when the mind and body are free of ache and pain, and when the shores of Spain have been reached. But this is not true peace. The peace of which Paul spoke is a calmness of soul amid terrors of trouble, inner tranquility amid the howl and rage of outer storm, the serene quiet at the center of a hurricane amid the howling and jostling winds. We readily understand the meaning of peace when everything is going right and when one is "up and in," but we are baffled when Paul speaks of that true peace which comes when a man is "down and out," when burdens lie heavy upon his shoulders, when pain throbs annoyingly in his body, when he is confined by the stone walls of a prison cell, and when disappointment is inescapably real. True peace, a calm that exceeds all description and all explanation, is peace amid storm and tranquility amid disaster.

Through faith we may inherit Jesus' legacy, "Peace I leave with you, my peace I give unto you." Paul at Philippi, incarcerated in a dark and desolate dungeon, his body beaten and bloody, his feet chained, and his spirit tired, joyously sang the songs of Zion at midnight. The early Christians, facing hungry lions in the arena and the excruciating pain of the chopping block, rejoiced that they had been deemed worthy to suffer for the sake of Christ. Negro slaves, bone-weary in the sizzling heat and the marks of whip lashes freshly etched on their backs, sang triumphantly, "By and by I'm goin' to lay down this heavy load." These are living examples of peace that passeth all understanding.

Our capacity to deal creatively with shattered dreams is ultimately determined by our faith in God. Genuine faith imbues us with the conviction that beyond time is a divine Spirit and beyond life is Life. However dismal and catastrophic may be the present circumstance, we know we are not alone, for God dwells with us in life's most confining and oppressive cells. And even if we die there without having received the earthly promise, he shall lead us down that mysterious road called death and at last to that indescribable city he has prepared for us. His creative power is not exhausted by this earthly life, nor is his majestic love locked within the limited walls of time and space. Would not this be a strangely irrational universe if God did not ultimately join virtue and fulfillment, and an absurdly meaningless universe if death were a blind alley leading the human race into a state of nothingness? God through Christ has taken the sting from death by freeing us from its dominion. Our earthly life is a prelude to a glorious new awakening, and death is an open door that leads us into life eternal.

The Christian faith makes it possible for us nobly to accept that which cannot be changed, to meet disappointments and sorrow with an inner poise, and to absorb the most intense pain without abandoning our sense of hope, for we know, as Paul testified, in life or in death, in Spain or in Rome, "that all things work together for good to them that love God, to them who are the called according to his purpose."

Antidotes for Fear

CHAPTER XIV OF *STRENGTH TO LOVE*

"Does love have a relationship to our modern fear of war, economic displacement, and racial injustice? . . . We say that war is a consequence of hate, but close scrutiny reveals this sequence: first fear, then hate, then war, and finally deeper

hatred. Were a nightmarish nuclear war to engulf our world, the cause would be not so much that one nation hated another, but that both nations feared each other."

There is no fear in love; but perfect love casteth out fear: because fear hath torment. He that feareth is not made perfect in love.

I JOHN 4:18, KJV

In these days of catastrophic change and calamitous uncertainty, is there any man who does not experience the depression and bewilderment of crippling fear, which, like a nagging hound of hell, pursues our every footstep?

Everywhere men and women are confronted by fears that often appear in strange disguises and a variety of wardrobes. Haunted by the possibility of bad health, we detect in every meaningless symptom an evidence of disease. Troubled by the fact that days and years pass so quickly, we dose ourselves with drugs which promise eternal youth. If we are physically vigorous, we become so concerned by the prospect that our personalities may collapse that we develop an inferiority complex and stumble through life with a feeling of insecurity, a lack of self-confidence, and a sense of impending failure. A fear of what life may bring encourages some persons to wander aimlessly along the frittering road of excessive drink and sexual promiscuity. Almost without being aware of the change, many people have permitted fear to transform the sunrise of love and peace into a sunset of inner depression.

When unchecked, fear spawns a whole brood of phobias—fear of water, high places, closed rooms, darkness, loneliness, among others—and such an accumulation culminates in phobia or the fear of fear itself.

Especially common in our highly competitive society are economic fears, from which, Karen Homey says, come most of the psychological problems of our age. Captains of industry are tormented by the possible failure of their business and the capriciousness of the stock market. Employees are plagued by the prospect of unemployment and the consequences of an ever-increasing automation.

And consider, too, the multiplication in our day of religious and ontological fears, which include the fear of death and racial annihilation. The advent of the atomic age, which should have ushered in an era of plenty and of prosperity, has lifted the fear of death to morbid proportions. The terrifying spectacle of nuclear warfare has put Hamlet's words, "To be or not to be," on millions of trembling lips. Witness our frenzied efforts to construct fallout shelters. As though even these offer sanctuary from an H-bomb attack! Witness the agonizing desperation of our petitions that our government increase the nuclear stockpile. But our fanatical quest to maintain "a balance of terror" only increases our fear and leaves nations on tiptoes lest some diplomatic faux pas ignite a frightful holocaust.

Realizing that fear drains a man's energy and depletes his resources, Emerson wrote, "He has not learned the lesson of life who does not every day surmount a fear."

But I do not mean to suggest that we should seek to eliminate fear altogether from human life. Were this humanly possible, it would be practically undesirable. Fear is the elemental alarm system of the human organism which warns of approaching dangers and without which man could not have survived in either the primitive or modern worlds. Fear, moreover, is a powerfully creative force. Every great invention and intellectual advance represents a desire to escape from some dreaded circumstance or condition. The fear of darkness led to the discovery of the secret of electricity. The fear of pain led to the marvelous advances of medical science. The fear of ignorance was one reason that man built great institutions of learning. The fear of war was one of the forces behind the birth of the United Nations. Angelo Patri has rightly said, "Education consists in being afraid at the right time." If man were to lose his capacity to fear, he would be deprived of his capacity to grow, invent, and create. So in a sense fear is normal, necessary, and creative.

But we must remember that abnormal fears are emotionally ruinous and psychologically destructive. To illustrate the difference between normal and abnormal fear, Sigmund Freud spoke of a person who was quite properly afraid of snakes in the heart of an African jungle and of another person who neurotically feared that snakes were under the carpet in his city apartment. Psychologists say that normal children are born with only two fears—the fear of falling and the fear of loud noises—and that all others are environmentally acquired. Most of these acquired fears are snakes under the carpet.

It is to such fears that we usually refer when we speak of getting rid of fear. But this is only a part of the story. Normal fear protects us; abnormal fear paralyzes us. Normal fear motivates us to improve our individual and collective welfare; abnormal fear constantly poisons and distorts our inner lives. Our problem is not to be rid of fear but rather to harness and master it. How may it be mastered?

I

First, we must unflinchingly face our fears and honestly ask ourselves why we are afraid. This confrontation will, to some measure, grant us power. We shall never be cured of fear by escapism or repression, for the more we attempt to ignore and repress our fears, the more we multiply our inner conflicts.

By looking squarely and honestly at our fears we learn that many of them are residues of some childhood need or apprehension. Here, for instance, is a person haunted by a fear of death or the thought of punishment in the afterlife, who discovers that he has unconsciously projected into the whole of reality the childhood experience of being punished by parents, locked in a room, and seemingly deserted. Or here is a man plagued by the fear of inferiority and social rejection, who discovers that rejection in childhood by a self-centered mother and a preoccupied father left him with a self-defeating sense of inadequacy and a repressed bitterness toward life.

By bringing our fears to the forefront of consciousness, we may find them to be more imaginary than real. Some of them will turn out to be snakes under the carpet.

And let us also remember that, more often than not, fear involves the misuse of the imagination. When we get our fears into the open, we may laugh at some of them, and this is good. One psychiatrist said, "Ridicule is the master cure for fear and anxiety."

II

Second, we can master fear through one of the supreme virtues known to man: courage. Plato considered courage to be an element of the soul which bridges the cleavage between reason and desire. Aristotle thought of courage as the affirmation of man's essential nature. Thomas Aquinas said that courage is the strength of mind capable of conquering whatever threatens the attainment of the highest good.

Courage, therefore, is the power of the mind to overcome fear. Unlike anxiety, fear has a definite object which may be faced, analyzed, attacked, and, if need be, endured. How often the object of our fear is fear itself! In his *Journal* Henry David Thoreau wrote, "Nothing is so much to be feared as fear." Centuries earlier, Epictetus wrote, "For it is not death or hardship that is a fearful thing, but the fear of hardship and death." Courage takes the fear produced by a definite object into itself and thereby conquers the fear involved. Paul Tillich has written, "Courage is self-affirmation 'in spite of'. . . that which tends to hinder the self from affirming itself." It is self-affirmation in spite of death and nonbeing, and he who is courageous takes the fear of death into his self-affirmation and acts upon it. This courageous self-affirmation, which is surely a remedy for fear, is not selfishness, for self-affirmation includes both a proper self-love and a properly propositioned love of others. Erich Fromm has shown in convincing terms that the right kind of self-love and the right kind of love of others are interdependent.

Courage, the determination not to be overwhelmed by any object, however frightful, enables us to stand up to any fear. Many of our fears are not mere snakes under the carpet. Trouble is a reality in this strange medley of life, dangers lurk within the circumference of every action, accidents do occur, bad health is an ever-threatening possibility, and death is a stark, grim, and inevitable fact of human experience. Evil and pain in this conundrum of life are close to each of us, and we do both ourselves and our neighbors a great disservice when we attempt to prove that there is nothing in this world of which we should be frightened. These forces that threaten to negate life must be challenged by courage, which is the power of life to affirm itself in spite of life's ambiguities. This requires the exercise of a creative will that enables us to hew out a stone of hope from a mountain of despair.

Courage and cowardice are antithetical. Courage is an inner resolution to go forward in spite of obstacles and frightening situations; cowardice is a submissive surrender to circumstance. Courage breeds creative self-affirmation; cowardice produces destructive self-abnegation. Courage faces fear and thereby masters it; cowardice represses fear and is thereby mastered by it. Courageous men never lose the zest for living even though their life situation is zestless; cowardly men, overwhelmed by the uncertainties of life, lose the will to live. We must constantly build dikes of courage to hold back the flood of fear.

III

Third, fear is mastered through love. The New Testament affirms, "There is no fear in love; but perfect love casteth out fear." The kind of love which led Christ to a cross and kept Paul unembittered amid the angry torrents of persecution is not soft, anemic, and sentimental. Such love confronts evil without flinching and shows in our popular parlance an infinite capacity "to take it." Such love overcomes the world even from a rough-hewn cross against the skyline.

But does love have a relationship to our modern fear of war, economic displacement, and racial injustice? Hate is rooted in fear, and the only cure for fear-hate is love. Our deteriorating international situation is shot through with the lethal darts of fear. Russia fears America, and America fears Russia. Likewise China and India, and the Israelis and the Arabs. These fears include another nation's aggression, scientific and technological supremacy, and economic power, and our own loss of status and power. Is not fear one of the major causes of war? We say that war is a consequence of hate, but close scrutiny reveals this sequence: first fear, then hate, then war, and finally deeper hatred. Were a nightmarish nuclear war to engulf our world, the cause would be not so much that one nation hated another, but that both nations feared each other.

What method has the sophisticated ingenuity of modern man employed to deal with the fear of war? We have armed ourselves to the nth degree. The West and the East have engaged in a fever-pitched arms race. Expenditures for defense have risen to mountainous proportions, and weapons of destruction have been assigned priority over all other human endeavors. The nations have believed that greater armaments will cast out fear. But alas! they have produced greater fear. In these turbulent, panic-stricken days we are once more reminded of the judicious words of old, "Perfect love casteth out fear." Not arms, but love, understanding, and organized goodwill can cast out fear. Only disarmament, based on good faith, will make mutual trust a living reality.

Our own problem of racial injustice must be solved by the same formula. Racial segregation is buttressed by such irrational fears as loss of preferred economic privilege, altered social status, intermarriage, and adjustment to new situations. Through sleepless nights and haggard days numerous white people attempt to combat these corroding fears by diverse methods. By following the path of escape, some seek to ignore the question of race relations and to close their mind to the issues involved. Others placing their faith in such legal maneuvers as interposition and nullification, counsel massive resistance. Still others hope to drown their fear by engaging in acts of violence and meanness toward their Negro brethren. But how futile are all these remedies! Instead of eliminating fear, they instill deeper and more pathological fears that leave the victims inflicted with strange psychoses and peculiar cases of paranoia.

Neither repression, massive resistance, nor aggressive violence will cast out the fear of integration; only love and goodwill can do that.

If our white brothers are to master fear, they must depend not only on their commitment to Christian love but also on the Christlike love which the Negro generates toward them. Only through our adherence to love and nonviolence can the fear in the white community be mitigated. A guilt-ridden white minority fears that if the Negro attains power, he will without restraint or pity act to revenge the accumulated injustices and brutality of the years. A parent, who has continually mistreated his son, suddenly realizes that he is now taller than the parent. Will the son use his new physical power to repay for all of the blows of the past?

Once a helpless child, the Negro has now grown politically, culturally, and economically. Many white men fear retaliation. The Negro must show them that they have nothing to fear, for the Negro forgives and is willing to forget the past. *The Negro must convince the white man that he seeks justice for both himself and the white man.* A mass movement exercising love and nonviolence and demonstrating power under discipline should convince the white community that were such a movement to attain strength its power would be used creatively and not vengefully.

What then is the cure of this morbid fear of integration? We know the cure. God help us to achieve it! Love casts out fear.

This truth is not without a bearing on our personal anxieties. We are afraid of the superiority of other people, of failure, and of the scorn or disapproval of those whose opinions we most value. Envy, jealousy, a lack of self-confidence, a feeling of insecurity, and a haunting sense of inferiority are all rooted in fear. We do not envy people and then fear them; first we fear them and subsequently we become jealous of them. Is there a cure for these annoying fears that pervert our personal lives? Yes, a deep and abiding commitment to the way of love. "Perfect love casteth out fear."

Hatred and bitterness can never cure the disease of fear; only love can do that. Hatred paralyzes life; love releases it. Hatred confuses life; love harmonizes it. Hatred darkens life; love illumines it.

IV

Fourth, fear is mastered through faith. A common source of fear is an awareness of deficient resources and of a consequent inadequacy for life. All too many people attempt to face the tensions of life with inadequate spiritual resources. When vacationing in Mexico, Mrs. King and I wished to go deep-sea fishing. For reasons of economy, we rented an old and poorly equipped boat. We gave this little thought until, ten miles from shore, the clouds lowered and howling winds blew. Then we became paralyzed with fear, for we knew our boat was deficient. Multitudes of people are in a similar situation. Heavy winds and weak boats explain their fear.

Many of our abnormal fears can be dealt with by the skills of psychiatry, a relatively new discipline pioneered by Sigmund Freud, which investigates the subconscious drives of men and seeks to discover how and why fundamental energies are diverted into neurotic channels. Psychiatry helps us to look candidly at our inner selves and to search out the causes of our failures and fears. But much of our fearful living encompasses a realm where the service of psychiatry is ineffectual unless the psychiatrist is a man of religious faith. For our trouble is simply that we attempt to confront fear without faith; we sail through the stormy seas of life without adequate spiritual boats. One of the leading physicians and psychiatrists in America has said, "The only known cure for fear is faith."

Abnormal fears and phobias that are expressed in neurotic anxiety may be cured by psychiatry; but the fear of death, nonbeing, and nothingness, expressed in existential anxiety, may be cured only by a positive religious faith.

A positive religious faith does not offer an illusion that we shall be exempt from pain and suffering, nor does it imbue us with the idea that life is a drama of unalloyed comfort and untroubled ease. Rather, it instills us with the inner equilibrium needed to face strains, burdens, and fears that inevitably come, and assures us that the universe is trustworthy and that God is concerned.

Irreligion, on the other hand, would have us believe that we are orphans cast into the terrifying immensities of space in a universe that is without purpose or intelligence. Such a view drains courage and exhausts the energies of men. In his *Confession* Tolstoi wrote concerning the aloneness and emptiness he felt before his conversion:

> "There was a period in my life when everything seemed to be crumbling, the very foundations of my convictions were beginning to give way, and I felt myself going to pieces. There was no sustaining influence in my life and there was no God there, and so every night before I went to sleep, I made sure that there was no rope in my room lest I be tempted during the night to hang myself from the rafters of my room; and I stopped from going out shooting lest I be tempted to put a quick end to my life and to my misery."

Like so many people, Tolstoi at that stage of his life lacked the sustaining influence which comes from the conviction that this universe is guided by a benign Intelligence whose infinite love embraces all mankind.

Religion endows us with the conviction that we are not alone in this vast, uncertain universe. Beneath and above the shifting sands of time, the uncertainties that darken our days, and the vicissitudes that cloud our nights is a wise and loving God. This universe is not a tragic expression of meaningless chaos but a marvelous display of orderly cosmos—"The Lord by wisdom hath founded the earth; by understanding hath he established the heavens." Man is not a wisp of smoke from a limitless smoldering, but a child of God created "a little lower than the angels." Above the manyness of time stands the one eternal God, with wisdom to guide us, strength to protect us, and love to keep us. His boundless love supports and contains us as a mighty ocean contains and supports the tiny drops of every wave. With a surging fullness he is forever moving toward us, seeking to fill the little creeks and bays of our lives with unlimited resources. This is religion's everlasting diapason, its eternal answer to the enigma of existence. Any man who finds this cosmic sustenance can walk the highways of life without the fatigue of pessimism and the weight of morbid fears.

Herein lies the answer to the neurotic fear of death that plagues so many of our lives. Let us face the fear that the atomic bomb has aroused with the faith that we can never travel beyond the arms of the Divine. Death is inevitable. It is a democracy for all of the people, not an aristocracy for some of the people—kings die and beggars die; young men die and old men die; learned men die and ignorant men die. We need not fear it. The God who brought our whirling planet from primal vapor and has led the human pilgrimage for lo these many centuries can most assuredly lead us through death's dark night into the bright daybreak of eternal life. His will is too perfect and his purposes are too extensive to be contained in the limited receptacle of time and the narrow walls of earth. Death is not the ultimate evil; the ultimate evil is to be outside God's love. We need not join the mad rush to purchase an earthly fallout shelter. God is our eternal fallout shelter.

Jesus knew that nothing could separate man from the love of God. Listen to his majestic words:

> Fear them not therefore: for there is nothing covered, that shall not be revealed; and hid, that shall not be known. . . . And fear not them which kill the body, but are not able to kill the soul: but rather fear him which is able to destroy both soul and body in hell. Are not two sparrows sold for a farthing? and one of them shall not fall on the ground without your Father. But the very hairs of your head are all numbered. Fear ye not therefore, ye are of more value than many sparrows.

Man, for Jesus, is not mere flotsam and jetsam in the river of life, but he is a child of God. Is it not unreasonable to assume that God, whose creative activity is expressed in an awareness of a sparrow's fall and the number of hairs on a man's head, excludes from his encompassing love the life of man itself? The confidence that God is mindful of the individual is of tremendous value in dealing with the disease of fear, for it gives us a sense of worth, of belonging, and of at-homeness in the universe.

One of the most dedicated participants in the bus protest in Montgomery, Alabama, was an elderly Negro whom we affectionately called Mother Pollard. Although poverty stricken and uneducated, she was amazingly intelligent and possessed a deep understanding of the meaning of the movement. After having walked for several weeks, she was asked if she were tired. With ungrammatical profundity, she answered, "My feets is tired, but my soul is rested."

On a particular Monday evening, following a tension-packed week which included being arrested and receiving numerous threatening telephone calls, I spoke at a mass meeting. I attempted to convey an overt impression of strength and courage, although I was inwardly depressed and fear-stricken. At the end of the meeting. Mother Pollard came to the front of the church and said, "Come here, son." I immediately went to her and hugged her affectionately. "Something is wrong with you," she said. "You didn't talk strong tonight." Seeking further to disguise my fears, I retorted, "Oh, no, Mother Pollard, nothing is wrong. I am feeling as fine as ever." But her insight was discerning. "Now you can't fool me," she said. "I knows something is wrong. Is it that we ain't doing things to please you? Or is it that the white folks is bothering you?" Before I could respond, she looked directly into my eyes and said, "I don told you we is with you all the way." Then her face became radiant and she said in words of quiet certainty, "But even if we ain't with you, God's gonna take care of you." As she spoke these consoling words, everything in me quivered and quickened with the pulsing tremor of raw energy.

Since that dreary night in 1956, Mother Pollard has passed on to glory and I have known very few quiet days. I have been tortured without and tormented within by the raging fires of tribulation. I have been forced to muster what strength and courage I have to withstand howling winds of pain and jostling storms of adversity. But as the years have unfolded the eloquently simple words of Mother Pollard have come back again and again to give light and peace and guidance to my troubled soul. "God's gonna take care of you."

This faith transforms the whirlwind of despair into a warm and reviving breeze of hope. The words of a motto which a generation ago were commonly found on the wall in the homes of devout persons need to be etched on our hearts:

> Fear knocked at the door.
> Faith answered.
> There was no one there.

Pilgrimage to Nonviolence

EXCERPT FROM CHAPTER XVII OF *STRENGTH TO LOVE*

"I had almost despaired of the power of love to solve social problems. The turn-the-other-cheek and the love-your-enemies philosophies are valid, I felt, only when individuals are in conflict with other individuals; when racial groups and nations are in conflict, a more realistic approach is necessary."

II

[Excerpt]

... Not until I entered theological seminary ... did I begin a serious intellectual quest for a method that would eliminate social evil. I was immediately influenced by the social gospel. In the early 1950s I read Walter Rauschenbusch's *Christianity and the Social Crisis*, a book which left an indelible imprint on my thinking. Of course, there were points at which I differed with Rauschenbusch. I felt that he was a victim of the nineteenth-century "cult of inevitable progress," which led him to an unwarranted optimism concerning human nature. Moreover, he came perilously close to identifying the Kingdom of God with a particular social and economic system, a temptation to which the church must never surrender. But in spite of these shortcomings, Rauschenbusch gave to American Protestantism a sense of social responsibility that it should never lose. The gospel at its best deals with the whole man, not only his soul but also his body, not only his spiritual well-being but also his material well-being. A religion that professes a concern for the souls of men and is not equally concerned about the slums that damn them, the economic conditions that strangle them, and the social conditions that cripple them, is a spiritually moribund religion.

After reading Rauschenbusch, I turned to a serious study of the social and ethical theories of the great philosophers. During this period I had almost despaired of the power of love to solve social problems. The turn-the-other-cheek and the love-your-enemies philosophies are valid, I felt, only when individuals are in conflict with other individuals; when racial groups and nations are in conflict, a more realistic approach is necessary.

Then I was introduced to the life and teachings of Mahatma Gandhi. As I read his works I became deeply fascinated by his campaigns of nonviolent resistance. The whole Gandhian concept of *satyagraha* (*satya* is truth which equals love and *graha* is force; *satyagraha* thus means truth-force or love-force) was profoundly significant to me. As I delved deeper into the philosophy of Gandhi, my skepticism concerning the power of love gradually diminished, and I came to see for the first time that the Christian doctrine of love, operating through the Gandhian method of nonviolence, is one of the most potent weapons available to an oppressed people in their struggle for freedom. At that time, however, I acquired only an intellectual understanding and appreciation of the position, and I had no firm determination to organize it in a socially effective situation.

When I went to Montgomery, Alabama, as a pastor in 1954, I had not the slightest idea that I would later become involved in a crisis in which nonviolent resistance would be applicable. After I had lived in the community about a year, the bus boycott began. The Negro people of Montgomery, exhausted by the humiliating experiences that they had constantly faced on the buses, expressed in a massive act of noncooperation their determination to be free. They came to see that it was ultimately more honorable to walk the streets in dignity than to ride the buses in humiliation. At the beginning of the protest, the people called on me to serve as their spokesman. In accepting this responsibility, my mind, consciously or unconsciously, was driven back to the Sermon on the Mount and the Gandhian method of nonviolent resistance. This principle became the guiding light of our movement. Christ furnished the spirit and motivation and Gandhi furnished the method.

The experience in Montgomery did more to clarify my thinking in regard to the question of nonviolence than all of the books that I had read. As the days unfolded, I became more and more convinced of the power of nonviolence. Nonviolence became more than a method to which I gave intellectual assent; it became a commitment to a way of life. Many issues I had not cleared up intellectually concerning nonviolence were now resolved within the sphere of practical action.

My privilege of traveling to India had a great impact on me personally, for it was invigorating to see firsthand the amazing results of a nonviolent struggle to achieve independence. The aftermath of hatred and bitterness that usually follows a violent campaign was found nowhere in India, and a mutual friendship, based on complete equality, existed between the Indian and British people within the Commonwealth.

I would not wish to give the impression that nonviolence will accomplish miracles overnight. Men are not easily moved from their mental ruts or purged of their prejudiced and irrational feelings. When the underprivileged demand freedom, the privileged at first react with bitterness and resistance. Even when the demands are couched in nonviolent terms, the initial response is substantially the same. I am sure that many of our white brothers in Montgomery and throughout the South are still bitter toward the Negro leaders, even though these leaders have sought to follow a way of love and nonviolence. But the nonviolent approach does something to the hearts and souls of those committed to it. It gives them new self-respect. It calls up resources of strength and courage that they did not know they had. Finally, it so stirs the conscience of the opponent that reconciliation becomes a reality.

III

More recently I have come to see the need for the method of nonviolence in international relations. Although I was not yet convinced of its efficacy in conflicts between nations, I felt that while war could never be a positive good, it could serve as a negative good by preventing the spread and growth of an evil force. War, horrible as it is, might be preferable to surrender to a totalitarian system. But I now believe that the potential destructiveness of modern weapons totally rules out the possibility of war ever again achieving a negative good. If we assume that mankind has a right to survive, then we must find an alternative to war and destruction. In our day of space vehicles and guided ballistic missiles, the choice is either non-violence or nonexistence.

I am no doctrinaire pacifist, but I have tried to embrace a realistic pacifism which finds the pacifist position as the lesser evil in the circumstances. I do not claim to be free from the moral dilemmas that the Christian nonpacifist confronts, but I am convinced that the church cannot be silent while mankind faces the threat of nuclear annihilation. If the church is true to her mission, she must call for an end to the arms race.

Some of my personal sufferings over the last few years have also served to shape my thinking. I always hesitate to mention these experiences for fear of conveying the wrong impression. A person who constantly calls attention to his trials and sufferings is in danger of developing a martyr complex and impressing others that he is consciously seeking sympathy. It is possible for one to be self-centered in his self-sacrifice. So I am always reluctant to refer to my personal sacrifices. But I feel somewhat justified in mentioning them in this essay because of the influence they have had upon my thought.

Due to my involvement in the struggle for the freedom of my people, I have known very few quiet days in the last few years. I have been imprisoned in Alabama and Georgia jails twelve times. My home has been bombed twice. A day seldom passes that my family and I are not the recipients of threats of death. I have been the victim of a near-fatal stabbing. So in a real sense I have been battered by the storms of persecution. I must admit that at times I have felt that I could no longer bear such a heavy burden, and have been tempted to retreat to a more quiet and serene life. But every time such a temptation appeared, something came to strengthen my determination. I have learned now that the Master's burden is light precisely when we take his yoke upon us.

My personal trials have also taught me the value of unmerited suffering. As my sufferings mounted I soon realized that there were two ways in which I could respond to my situation—either to react with bitterness or seek to transform the suffering into a creative force. I decided to follow the latter course. Recognizing the necessity for suffering, I have tried to make of it a virtue. If only to save myself from bitterness, I have attempted to see my personal ordeals as an opportunity to transfigure myself and heal the people involved in the tragic situation which now obtains. I have lived these last few years with the conviction that unearned suffering is redemptive. There are some who still find the Cross a stumbling block, others consider it foolishness, but I am more convinced than ever before that it is the power of God unto social and individual salvation. So like the Apostle Paul I can now humbly, yet proudly, say, "I bear in my body the marks of the Lord Jesus."

The agonizing moments through which I have passed during the last few years have also drawn me closer to God. More than ever before I am convinced of the reality of a personal God. True, I have always believed in the personality of God. But in the past the idea of a personal God was little more than a metaphysical category that I found theologically and philosophically satisfying. Now it is a living reality that has been validated in the experiences of everyday life. God has been profoundly real to me in recent years. In the midst of lonely days and dreary nights I have heard an inner voice saying, "Lo, I will be with you." When the chains of fear and the manacles of frustration have all but stymied my efforts, I have felt the power of God transforming the fatigue of despair into the buoyancy of hope. I am convinced that the universe is under the control of a loving purpose, and that in the struggle for righteousness man has cosmic companionship. Behind the harsh appearances of the world there is a benign power. To say that this God is personal is not to make him a finite object besides other objects or attribute to him the limitations of human personality; it is to take what is finest and noblest in our consciousness and affirm its perfect existence in him. It is certainly true that human personality is limited, but personality as such involves no necessary limitations. It means simply self-consciousness and self-direction. So in the truest sense of the word, God is a living God. In him there is feeling and will, responsive to the deepest yearnings of the human heart: *this* God both evokes and answers prayer.

The past decade has been a most exciting one. In spite of the tensions and uncertainties of this period something profoundly meaningful is taking place. Old systems of exploitation and oppression are passing away; new systems of justice and equality are being born. In a real sense this is a great time to be alive. Therefore, I am not yet discouraged about the future. Granted that the easygoing optimism of yesterday is impossible. Granted that we face a world crisis which leaves us standing so often amid the surging murmur of life's restless sea. But every crisis has both its dangers and its opportunities. It can spell either salvation or doom. In a dark, confused world the Kingdom of God may yet reign in the hearts of men.

Eulogy for the Martyred Children

EXCERPT FROM ADDRESS GIVEN AT THE
SIXTH AVENUE BAPTIST CHURCH

Birmingham, Alabama

"They died not in a den or dive, nor were they hearing and telling filthy jokes at the time of their death. They died within the sacred walls of the church after discussing a principle as eternal as love."

On September 15, 1963, a racist terrorist planted a bomb under the stairs of the 16th Street Baptist Church in Birmingham, Alabama, as people gathered for 11 a.m. church services. The explosion killed four young girls who had been preparing in the basement for the church's Youth Day: Addie Mae Collins, Carole Robertson, and Cynthia Wesley, all fourteen-year-olds, and Denise McNair, who was eleven. The blast injured many more.

Birmingham had been a focal point of racial equality protests due to the extremity of its segregation enforcement—King called it "perhaps the most segregated city in America." It was known as "Bombingham" because of the twenty-one bombings at the homes of Black Americans from 1955 to 1963, including at the houses of King's brother, A. D., and Arthur Shores, a lawyer for the NAACP. When King visited Birmingham, he stayed at the Gaston Motel, and in May that motel was bombed as well.

On September 9, 1963, President John F. Kennedy had taken control of the Alabama National Guard from Governor George Wallace, who was using his state forces to block the desegregation of schools.

When King heard of the terrorist attack, he sent a telegram to Governor Wallace, saying: "The blood of our little children is on your hands." Three days later, King spoke at the memorial services, where some eight thousand people gathered to mourn. His eulogy is excerpted here.

[Excerpt]

... At times, life is hard, as hard as crucible steel. It has its bleak and painful moments. Like the ever-flowing waters of a river, life has its moments of drought and its moments of flood. Like the ever-changing cycle of the seasons, life has the soothing warmth of the summers and the piercing chill of its winters. But through it all, God walks with us. Never forget that God is able to lift you from fatigue of despair to the buoyancy of hope, and transform dark and desolate valleys into sunlit paths of inner peace.

Your children did not live long, but they lived well. The quantity of their lives was disturbingly small, but the quality of their lives was magnificently big. Where they died and what they were doing when death came will remain a marvelous tribute to each of you and an eternal epitaph to each of them. They died not in a den or dive, nor were they hearing and telling filthy jokes at the time of their death. They died within the sacred walls of the church after discussing a principle as eternal as love.

Shakespeare had Horatio utter some beautiful words over the dead body of Hamlet. I paraphrase these words today as I stand over the last remains of these lovely girls: "Good night, sweet princesses; may the flight of angels take thee to thy eternal rest."

Marching for Equality
Saint Augustine, Florida

"We love everybody."

This was the chant of young Black protesters in early July 1964 in Saint Augustine, Florida, the oldest city in the country. King described Saint Augustine that year "as the most lawless city in America" due to the rampant intimidation of Black citizens by white racists.

Protests had begun in the deeply segregated city as early as 1963, with the Klan interrupting those demonstrations with violence. After the Klan beat protesters, the local courts supported the Klan leaders against the protesters.

King first addressed the community in May 1964, urging them to keep hope, and the Southern Christian Leadership Council called for northern white college students to visit the city to support the protesters during their Easter break. Some one hundred students were jailed, and high bails were set. King himself was arrested that summer when he asked to be served at a segregated restaurant.

On June 18, 1964, a grand jury ordered him to leave the city for disrupting racial harmony. He and the Southern Christian Leadership Conference left on July 1, the day before Lyndon B. Johnson signed the 1964 Civil Rights Bill, with King looking on.

Nobel Peace Prize Acceptance Speech

AUDITORIUM AT UNIVERSITY OF OSLO

Oslo, Norway

"**I refuse to accept the cynical notion that nation after nation must spiral down a militaristic stairway into the hell of thermonuclear destruction. I believe that unarmed truth and unconditional love will have the final word in reality.**"

King was named the winner of the Nobel Prize for Peace on October 14, 1964, for "his non-violent struggle for civil rights for the Afro-American population." He told the *New York Times*, "I do not consider this merely an honor to me personally, but a tribute to the disciplined, wise restraint and majestic courage of gallant Negro and white persons of goodwill who have followed a nonviolent course in seeking to establish a reign of justice and a rule of love across this nation of ours."* He said he would donate the prize money to the civil rights struggle.

---

* "Martin Luther King Awarded Nobel Peace Prize," *The Learning Network* (blog), *New York Times*, October 14, 2011, https://archive.nytimes.com/learning.blogs .nytimes.com/2011/10/14/oct-14-1964-martin-luther-king-awarded-nobel-peace -prize/.

In his acceptance speech in December 1964, reproduced here in full, King refers to the threat of nuclear war, which had escalated over the Cold War years and with China's first successful nuclear bomb test on October 16. Just over a year earlier, President John F. Kennedy had been assassinated, marking a new step in the turmoil of the United States.

Your Majesty, Your Royal Highness, Mr. President, Excellencies, Ladies and Gentlemen:

I accept the Nobel Prize for Peace at a moment when 22 million Negroes of the United States of America are engaged in a creative battle to end the long night of racial injustice. I accept this award on behalf of a civil rights movement which is moving with determination and a majestic scorn for risk and danger to establish a reign of freedom and a rule of justice. I am mindful that only yesterday in Birmingham, Alabama, our children, crying out for brotherhood, were answered with fire hoses, snarling dogs and even death. I am mindful that only yesterday in Philadelphia, Mississippi, young people seeking to secure the right to vote were brutalized and murdered. And only yesterday more than 40 houses of worship in the State of Mississippi alone were bombed or burned because they offered a sanctuary to those who would not accept segregation. I am mindful that debilitating and grinding poverty afflicts my people and chains them to the lowest rung of the economic ladder.

Therefore, I must ask why this prize is awarded to a movement which is beleaguered and committed to unrelenting struggle; to a movement which has not won the very peace and brotherhood which is the essence of the Nobel Prize.

After contemplation, I conclude that this award which I receive on behalf of that movement is a profound recognition that non-violence is the answer to the crucial political and moral question of our time—the need for man to overcome oppression and violence without resorting to violence and oppression. Civilization and violence are antithetical concepts. Negroes of the United States, following the people of India, have demonstrated that nonviolence is not sterile passivity, but a powerful moral force which makes for social transformation. Sooner or later all the people of the world will have to discover a way to live together in peace, and thereby transform this pending cosmic elegy into a creative psalm of brotherhood. If this is to be achieved, man must evolve for all human conflict a method which rejects revenge, aggression and retaliation. The foundation of such a method is love.

The tortuous road which has led from Montgomery, Alabama to Oslo bears witness to this truth. This is a road over which millions of Negroes are travelling to find a new sense of dignity. This same road has opened for all Americans a new era of progress and hope. It has led to a new Civil Rights Bill, and it will, I am convinced, be widened and lengthened into a super highway of justice as Negro and white men in increasing numbers create alliances to overcome their common problems.

I accept this award today with an abiding faith in America and an audacious faith in the future of mankind. I refuse to accept despair as the final response to the ambiguities of history. I refuse to accept the idea that the "isness" of man's present nature makes him morally incapable of reaching up for the eternal "oughtness" that forever confronts him. I refuse to accept the idea that man is mere flotsam and jetsam in the river of life, unable to influence the unfolding events which surround him. I refuse to accept the view that mankind is so tragically bound to the starless midnight of racism and war that the bright daybreak of peace and brotherhood can never become a reality.

I refuse to accept the cynical notion that nation after nation must spiral down a militaristic stairway into the hell of thermonuclear destruction. I believe that unarmed truth and unconditional love will have the final word in reality. This is why right temporarily defeated is stronger than evil triumphant. I believe that even amid today's mortar bursts and whining bullets, there is still hope for a brighter tomorrow. I believe that wounded justice, lying prostrate on the blood-flowing streets of our nations, can be lifted from this dust of shame to reign supreme among the children of men. I have the audacity to believe that peoples everywhere can have three meals a day for their bodies, education and culture for their minds, and dignity, equality and freedom for their spirits. I believe that what self-centered men have torn down men other-centered can build up. I still believe that one day mankind will bow before the altars of God and be crowned triumphant over war and bloodshed, and nonviolent redemptive good will proclaim the rule of the land. "And the lion and the lamb shall lie down together and every man shall sit under his own vine and fig tree and none shall be afraid." I still believe that we *Shall overcome!*

This faith can give us courage to face the uncertainties of the future. It will give our tired feet new strength as we continue our forward stride toward the city of freedom. When our days become dreary with low-hovering clouds and our nights become darker than a thousand midnights, we will know that we are living in the creative turmoil of a genuine civilization struggling to be born.

Today I come to Oslo as a trustee, inspired and with renewed dedication to humanity. I accept this prize on behalf of all men who love peace and brotherhood. I say I come as a trustee, for in the depths of my heart I am aware that this prize is much more than an honor to me personally.

Every time I take a flight, I am always mindful of the many people who make a successful journey possible—the known pilots and the unknown ground crew.

So you honor the dedicated pilots of our struggle who have sat at the controls as the freedom movement soared into orbit. You honor, once again, Chief [Albert] Lutuli of South Africa, whose struggles with and for his people, are still met with the most brutal expression of man's inhumanity to man. You honor the ground crew without whose labor and sacrifices the jet flights to freedom could never have left the earth. Most of these people will never make the headline and their names will not appear in *Who's Who*. Yet when years have rolled past and when the blazing light of truth is focused on this marvellous age in which we live—men and women will know and children will be taught that we have a finer land, a better people, a more noble civilization—because these humble children of God were willing to suffer for righteousness' sake.

I think Alfred Nobel would know what I mean when I say that I accept this award in the spirit of a curator of some precious heirloom which he holds in trust for its true owners—all those to whom beauty is truth and truth beauty—and in whose eyes the beauty of genuine brotherhood and peace is more precious than diamonds or silver or gold.

The Quest for Peace and Justice

EXCERPT FROM NOBEL LECTURE AT UNIVERSITY OF OSLO

Oslo, Norway

"Love is somehow the key that unlocks the door which leads to ultimate reality."

The day after King's Nobel Prize acceptance speech, he delivered a lecture in the same venue to an audience that included students. His presentation, which was international in scope, combined elements of his previous sermons.

He began by talking about his joy in accepting this award on behalf of his fellow protesters in the United States. He then talked about the spiritual challenges for modern people in a world of great technological invention. He gave an overview of the oppressed peoples of the world, proclaiming that they would not stay oppressed forever, that the world was seeing changes on various continents.

In this excerpt from his lecture, King spoke of love as a form of dedication.

[Excerpt]

. . . Some years ago a famous novelist died. Among his papers was found a list of suggested story plots for future stories, the most prominently underscored being this one: "A widely separated family inherits a house in which they have to live together." This is the great new problem of mankind. We have inherited a big house, a great "world house" in which we have to live together—Black and white, easterners and westerners, Gentiles and Jews, Catholics and Protestants, Muslim and Hindu, a family unduly separated in ideas, culture, and interests who, because we can never again live without each other, must learn, somehow, in this one big world, to live with each other.

This means that more and more our loyalties must become ecumenical rather than sectional. We must now give an overriding loyalty to mankind as a whole in order to preserve the best in our individual societies.

This call for a worldwide fellowship that lifts neighborly concern beyond one's tribe, race, class, and nation is in reality a call for an all-embracing and unconditional love for all men. This oft misunderstood and misinterpreted concept, so readily dismissed by the Nietzsches of the world as a weak and cowardly force, has now become an absolute necessity for the survival of man. When I speak of love, I am not speaking of some sentimental and weak response which is little more than emotional bosh. I am speaking of that force which all of the great religions have seen as the supreme unifying principle of life. Love is somehow the key that unlocks the door which leads to ultimate reality. This Hindu-Muslim-Christian-Jewish-Buddhist belief about ultimate reality is beautifully summed up in the First Epistle of Saint John:

> Let us love one another: for love is of God; and every one that
> loveth is born of God, and knoweth God.
> He that loveth not knoweth not God; for God is love.

If we love one another, God dwelleth in us, and His
love is perfected in us.*

Let us hope that this spirit will become the order of the day. As Arnold Toynbee says, "Love is the ultimate force that makes for the saving choice of life and good against the damning choice of death and evil. Therefore the first hope in our inventory must be the hope that love is going to have the last word."† We can no longer afford to worship the God of hate or bow before the altar of retaliation. The oceans of history are made turbulent by the ever-rising tides of hate. History is cluttered with the wreckage of nations and individuals that pursued this self-defeating path of hate. Love is the key to the solution of the problems of the world.

Let me close by saying that I have the personal faith that mankind will somehow rise up to the occasion and give new directions to an age drifting rapidly to its doom. In spite of the tensions and uncertainties of this period, something profoundly meaningful is taking place. Old systems of exploitation and oppression are passing away, and out of the womb of a frail world new systems of justice and equality are being born. Doors of opportunity are gradually being opened to those at the bottom of society. The shirtless and barefoot people of the land are developing a new sense of "somebodiness" and carving a tunnel of hope through the dark mountain of despair. "The people who sat in darkness have seen

---

* 1 John 4:7–8, 12, KJV

† Arnold Joseph Toynbee (1889–1975) was a British historian whose monumental work is the twelve-volume *A Study of History* (London: Oxford University Press, 1934–1961).

a great light."* Here and there an individual or group dares to love and rises to the majestic heights of moral maturity. So in a real sense this is a great time to be alive. Therefore, I am not yet discouraged about the future. Granted that the easygoing optimism of yesterday is impossible. Granted that those who pioneer in the struggle for peace and freedom will still face uncomfortable jail terms, painful threats of death; they will still be battered by the storms of persecution, leading them to the nagging feeling that they can no longer bear such a heavy burden, and the temptation of wanting to retreat to a more quiet and serene life. Granted that we face a world crisis which leaves us standing so often amid the surging murmur of life's restless sea. But every crisis has both its dangers and its opportunities. It can spell either salvation or doom. In a dark, confused world the Kingdom of God may yet reign in the hearts of men.

---

* This quotation may be based on a phrase from Luke 1:79 ("To give light to them that sit in darkness and in the shadow of death") or from Psalms 107:10 ("Such as sit in darkness and in the shadow of death"). Or it might be based on a line from Mark Twain's essay "To the Person Sitting in Darkness" (1901): "The people who sit in darkness have noticed it."

The Casualties of the War in Vietnam

EXCERPT FROM SPEECH AT THE NATION INSTITUTE

Los Angeles, California

**"Those of us who love peace must organize as effectively as
the war hawks."**

In this speech, King laid out the myriad ways the war in Vietnam was
causing US losses—not only the loss of American lives but also the
loss of the nation's international and moral stature. In his conclusion,
reprinted here, he reflected on love of country and the need for a
beloved community.

[Excerpt]

... Let me say finally that I oppose the war in Vietnam because I love
America. I speak out against it not in anger but with anxiety and
sorrow in my heart, and above all with a passionate desire to see our
beloved country stand as the moral example of the world. I speak out
against this war because I am disappointed with America. There can
be no great disappointment where there is no great love. I am disappointed with our failure to deal positively and forthrightly with the
triple evils of racism, extreme materialism, and militarism. We are presently moving down a dead-end road that can lead to national disaster.

It is time for all people of conscience to call upon America to return to her true home of brotherhood and peaceful pursuits. We cannot remain silent as our nation engages in one of history's most cruel and senseless wars. During these days of human travail, we must encourage creative dissenters. We need them because the thunder of their fearless voices will be the only sound stronger than the blasts of bombs and the clamor of war hysteria.

Those of us who love peace must organize as effectively as the war hawks. As they spread the propaganda of war, we must spread the propaganda of peace. We must combine the fervor of the civil rights movement with the peace movement. We must demonstrate, teach, and preach until the very foundations of our nation are shaken. We must work unceasingly to lift this nation that we love to a higher destiny, to a new plateau of compassion, to a more noble expression of humaneness.

I have tried to be honest. To be honest is to confront the truth. To be honest is to realize that the ultimate measure of a man is not where he stands in moments of convenience and moments of comfort, but where he stands in moments of challenge and moments of controversy. However unpleasant and inconvenient the truth may be, I believe we must expose and face it if we are to achieve a better quality of American life.

Just the other day, the distinguished American historian Henry Steele Commager told a Senate committee: "Justice Holmes used to say that the first lesson a judge had to learn was that he was not God.... We do tend, perhaps more than other nations, to transform our wars into crusades.... Our current involvement in Vietnam is cast, increasingly, into a moral mold.... It is my feeling that we do not have the resources—material, intellectual, or moral—to be at once an American power, a European power, and an Asian power."

I agree with Mr. Commager. And I would suggest that there is, however, another kind of power that America can and should be. It is a moral power, a power harnessed to the service of peace and human beings, not an inhumane power unleashed against defenseless people. All the world knows that America is a great military power. We need not be diligent in seeking to prove it. We must now show the world our moral power.

We still have a choice today: nonviolent coexistence or violent co-annihilation. History will record the choice we made. It is still not too late to make the proper choice. If we decide to become a moral power, we will be able to transform the jangling discords of this world into a beautiful symphony of brotherhood. If we make the wise decision, we will be able to transform our pending cosmic elegy into a creative psalm of peace. This will be a glorious day. In reaching it we can fulfill the noblest of American dreams.

Where Do We Go from Here?

EXCERPT FROM SPEECH AT THE CONVENTION OF THE
SOUTHERN CHRISTIAN LEADERSHIP CONFERENCE

Atlanta, Georgia

**"And I say to you, I have . . . decided to stick with love, for I
know that love is ultimately the only answer to mankind's
problems. And I'm going to talk about it everywhere I go."**

The speech excerpted here echoes King's earlier speeches but shows
the development of his idea of love and power.

[Excerpt]

. . . Now a lot of us are preachers, and all of us have our moral
convictions and concerns, and so often we have problems with
power. But there is nothing wrong with power if power is used
correctly.

You see, what happened is that some of our philosophers got off
base. And one of the great problems of history is that the concepts
of love and power have usually been contrasted as opposites, po-
lar opposites, so that love is identified with a resignation of power,
and power with a denial of love. It was this misinterpretation that
caused the philosopher Nietzsche, who was a philosopher of the

will to power, to reject the Christian concept of love. It was this same misinterpretation which induced Christian theologians to reject Nietzsche's philosophy of the will to power in the name of the Christian idea of love.

Now, we got to get this thing right. What is needed is a realization that power without love is reckless and abusive, and that love without power is sentimental and anemic. [*Audience: Yes*] Power at its best, [*applause*] power at its best is love (*Yes*) implementing the demands of justice, and justice at its best is love correcting everything that stands against love. (*Speak*) And this is what we must see as we move on.

Now what has happened is that we've had it wrong and mixed up in our country, and this has led Negro Americans in the past to seek their goals through love and moral suasion devoid of power, and white Americans to seek their goals through power devoid of love and conscience. It is leading a few extremists today to advocate for Negroes the same destructive and conscienceless power that they have justly abhorred in whites. It is precisely this collision of immoral power with powerless morality which constitutes the major crisis of our times. (*Yes*) . . .

[Excerpt]
This is no time for romantic illusions and empty philosophical debates about freedom. This is a time for action. (*All right*) What is needed is a strategy for change, a tactical program that will bring the Negro into the mainstream of American life as quickly as possible. So far, this has only been offered by the nonviolent movement. Without recognizing this we will end up with solu-

tions that don't solve, answers that don't answer, and explanations that don't explain. [*applause*]

And so I say to you today that I still stand by nonviolence. (*Yes*) And I am still convinced, [*applause*] and I'm still convinced that it is the most potent weapon available to the Negro in his struggle for justice in this country.

And the other thing is, I'm concerned about a better world. I'm concerned about justice; I'm concerned about brotherhood; I'm concerned about truth. (*That's right*) And when one is concerned about that, he can never advocate violence. For through violence you may murder a murderer, but you can't murder murder. (*Yes*) Through violence you may murder a liar, but you can't establish truth. (*That's right*) Through violence you may murder a hater, but you can't murder hate through violence. (*All right, That's right*) Darkness cannot put out darkness; only light can do that. [*applause*]

And I say to you, I have also decided to stick with love, for I know that love is ultimately the only answer to mankind's problems. (*Yes*) And I'm going to talk about it everywhere I go. I know it isn't popular to talk about it in some circles today. (*No*) And I'm not talking about emotional bosh when I talk about love; I'm talking about a strong, demanding love. (*Yes*) For I have seen too much hate. (*Yes*) I've seen too much hate on the faces of sheriffs in the South. (*Yeah*) I've seen hate on the faces of too many Klansmen and too many White Citizens Councilors in the South to want to hate, myself, because every time I see it, I know that it does something to their faces and their personalities, and I say to myself that hate is too great a burden to bear. (*Yes, That's right*) I have decided to love. [*applause*] If you are seeking the highest good, I think you can find it through love. And the beautiful thing is that we aren't moving wrong when we do it, because John was right, God is love. (*Yes*) He who hates does not know God, but he who loves has the key that unlocks the door to the meaning of ultimate reality.

And so I say to you today, my friends, that you may be able to speak with the tongues of men and angels; (*All right*) you may have the eloquence of articulate speech; but if you have not love, it means nothing. (*That's right*) Yes, you may have the gift of prophecy; you may have the gift of scientific prediction (*Yes sir*) and understand the behavior of molecules (*All right*); you may break into the storehouse of nature (*Yes sir*) and bring forth many new insights; yes, you may ascend to the heights of academic achievement (*Yes sir*) so that you have all knowledge; (*Yes sir, Yes*) and you may boast of your great institutions of learning and the boundless extent of your degrees; but if you have not love, all of these mean absolutely nothing. (*Yes*) You may even give your goods to feed the poor; (*Yes sir*) you may bestow great gifts to charity; (*Speak*) and you may tower high in philanthropy; but if you have not love, your charity means nothing. (*Yes sir*) You may even give your body to be burned and die the death of a martyr, and your spilt blood may be a symbol of honor for generations yet unborn, and thousands may praise you as one of history's greatest heroes; but if you have not love, (*Yes, All right*) your blood was spilt in vain. What I'm trying to get you to see this morning is that a man may be self-centered in his self-denial and self-righteous in his self-sacrifice. His generosity may feed his ego, and his piety may feed his pride. (*Speak*) So without love, benevolence becomes egotism, and martyrdom becomes spiritual pride. . . .

Drum Major Instinct

EXCERPT FROM SERMON AT EBENEZER BAPTIST CHURCH

Atlanta, Georgia

"I'd like for somebody to say . . . that Martin Luther King Jr. tried to love somebody. . . . I want you to say that I tried to love and serve humanity."

North Vietnamese forces had attacked South Vietnam's Saigon—the Tet Offensive—less than a week before this sermon, marking an escalation in the war.

This speech was delivered in the last two months of King's life—he would be assassinated in April—and seems to resound with the idea that he knew that the enormous number of threats he had received over his lifetime might one day be made real. It reflects the endurance of his belief in the power of love and his desire to be known for that effort to hold on to love, no matter the trial.

This sermon marked his last sermon at the church where he and his father were co-pastors.

[Excerpt]

This morning I would like to use as a subject from which to preach: "The Drum Major Instinct." "The Drum Major Instinct." And our text for the morning is taken from a very familiar passage in the tenth chapter as recorded by Saint Mark. Beginning with the thirty-fifth verse of that chapter, we read these words: "And James and John, the sons of Zebedee, came unto him saying, 'Master, we would that thou shouldest do for us whatsoever we shall desire.' And he said unto them, 'What would ye that I should do for you?' And they said unto him, 'Grant unto us that we may sit, one on thy right hand, and the other on thy left hand, in thy glory.' But Jesus said unto them, 'Ye know not what ye ask: Can ye drink of the cup that I drink of? and be baptized with the baptism that I am baptized with?' And they said unto him, 'We can.' And Jesus said unto them, 'Ye shall indeed drink of the cup that I drink of, and with the baptism that I am baptized withal shall ye be baptized: but to sit on my right hand and on my left hand is not mine to give; but it shall be given to them for whom it is prepared.'" And then Jesus goes on toward the end of that passage to say, "But so shall it not be among you: but whosoever will be great among you, shall be your servant: and whosoever of you will be the chiefest, shall be servant of all."

The setting is clear. James and John are making a specific request of the master. They had dreamed, as most of the Hebrews dreamed, of a coming king of Israel who would set Jerusalem free and establish his kingdom on Mount Zion, and in righteousness rule the world. And they thought of Jesus as this kind of king. And they were thinking of that day when Jesus would reign supreme as this new king of Israel. And they were saying, "Now when you establish your kingdom, let one of us sit on the right hand and the other on the left hand of your throne."

Now very quickly, we would automatically condemn James and John, and we would say they were selfish. Why would they make such a selfish request? But before we condemn them too quickly, let us look calmly and honestly at ourselves, and we will discover that we too have those same basic desires for recognition, for importance. That same desire for attention, that same desire to be first. Of course, the other disciples got mad with James and John, and you could understand why, but we must understand that we have some of the same James and John qualities. And there is deep down within all of us an instinct. It's a kind of drum major instinct—a desire to be out front, a desire to lead the parade, a desire to be first. And it is something that runs the whole gamut of life.

And so before we condemn them, let us see that we all have the drum major instinct. We all want to be important, to surpass others, to achieve distinction, to lead the parade. Alfred Adler, the great psychoanalyst, contends that this is the dominant impulse. Sigmund Freud used to contend that sex was the dominant impulse, and Adler came with a new argument, saying that this quest for recognition, this desire for attention, this desire for distinction is the basic impulse, the basic drive of human life, this drum major instinct. . . .

[Excerpt]

I want you to see what Jesus was really saying. What was the answer that Jesus gave these men? It's very interesting. One would have thought that Jesus would have condemned them. One would have thought that Jesus would have said, "You are out of your place. You are selfish. Why would you raise such a question?"

But that isn't what Jesus did; he did something altogether different. He said, in substance, "Oh, I see, you want to be first. You want to be great. You want to be important. You want to be significant. Well, you ought to be. If you're going to be my disciple, you must be." But he reordered priorities. And he said, "Yes, don't give up this instinct. It's a good instinct if you use it right. [*Congregation:*] (*Yes*) It's a good instinct if you don't distort it and pervert it. Don't give it up. Keep feeling the need for being important. Keep feeling the need for being first. But I want you to be first in love. (*Amen*) I want you to be first in moral excellence. I want you to be first in generosity. That is what I want you to do."

And he transformed the situation by giving a new definition of greatness. And you know how he said it? He said, "Now brethren, I can't give you greatness. And really, I can't make you first." This is what Jesus said to James and John. "You must earn it. True greatness comes not by favoritism, but by fitness. And the right hand and the left are not mine to give; they belong to those who are prepared." (*Amen*)

And so Jesus gave us a new norm of greatness. If you want to be important—wonderful. If you want to be recognized—wonderful. If you want to be great—wonderful. But recognize that he who is greatest among you shall be your servant. (*Amen*) That's a new definition of greatness.

And this morning, the thing that I like about it: by giving that definition of greatness, it means that everybody can be great, (*Everybody*) because everybody can serve. (*Amen*) You don't have to have a college degree to serve. (*All right*) You don't have to make your subject and your verb agree to serve. You don't have to know about Plato and Aristotle to serve. You don't have to know Einstein's theory of relativity to serve. You don't have to know the second theory of thermodynamics in physics to serve. (*Amen*) You only need a heart full of grace, (*Yes, sir, Amen*) a soul generated by love. (*Yes*) And you can be that servant.

I know a man—and I just want to talk about him a minute, and maybe you will discover who I'm talking about as I go down the way (*Yeah*) because he was a great one. And he just went about serving. He was born in an obscure village, (*Yes, sir*) the child of a poor peasant woman. And then he grew up in still another obscure village, where he worked as a carpenter until he was thirty years old. (*Amen*) Then for three years, he just got on his feet, and he was an itinerant preacher. And he went about doing some things. He didn't have much. He never wrote a book. He never held an office. He never had a family. (*Yes*) He never owned a house. He never went to college. He never visited a big city. He never went two hundred miles from where he was born. He did none of the usual things that the world would associate with greatness. He had no credentials but himself.

He was only thirty-three when the tide of public opinion turned against him. They called him a rabble-rouser. They called him a troublemaker. They said he was an agitator. (*Glory to God*) He practiced civil disobedience; he broke injunctions. And so he was turned over to his enemies and went through the mockery of a trial. And the irony of it all is that his friends turned him over to them. (*Amen*) One of his closest friends denied him. Another of his friends turned him over to his enemies. And while he was dying, the people who killed him gambled for his clothing, the only possession that he had in the world. (*Lord help him*) When he was dead, he was buried in a borrowed tomb, through the pity of a friend.

Nineteen centuries have come and gone and today he stands as the most influential figure that ever entered human history. All of the armies that ever marched, all the navies that ever sailed, all the parliaments that ever sat, and all the kings that ever reigned put together (*Yes*) have not affected the life of man on this earth (*Amen*) as much as that one solitary life. His name may be a familiar one.

(*Jesus*) But today I can hear them talking about him. Every now and then somebody says, "He's King of Kings." (*Yes*) And again I can hear somebody saying, "He's Lord of Lords." Somewhere else I can hear somebody saying, "In Christ there is no East nor West." (*Yes*) And then they go on and talk about, "In Him there's no North and South, but one great Fellowship of Love throughout the whole wide world." He didn't have anything. (*Amen*) He just went around serving and doing good.

This morning, you can be on his right hand and his left hand if you serve. (*Amen*) It's the only way in.

Every now and then I guess we all think realistically (*Yes, sir*) about that day when we will be victimized with what is life's final common denominator—that something that we call death. We all think about it. And every now and then I think about my own death, and I think about my own funeral. And I don't think of it in a morbid sense. And every now and then I ask myself, "What is it that I would want said?" And I leave the word to you this morning.

If any of you are around when I have to meet my day, I don't want a long funeral. And if you get somebody to deliver the eulogy, tell them not to talk too long. (*Yes*) And every now and then I wonder what I want them to say. Tell them not to mention that I have a Nobel Peace Prize—that isn't important. Tell them not to mention that I have three or four hundred other awards—that's not important. Tell them not to mention where I went to school. (*Yes*) I'd like somebody to mention that day that Martin Luther King Jr. tried to give his life serving others.

I'd like for somebody to say that day that Martin Luther King Jr. tried to love somebody. I want you to say that day that I tried to be right on the war question. (*Amen*) I want you to be able to say that day that I did try to feed the hungry. (*Yes*) And I want you to be able to say that day that I did try in my life to clothe those who were naked. (*Yes*) I want you to say on that day that I did try in my life to visit those who were in prison. (*Lord*) I want you to say that I tried to love and serve humanity. (*Yes*)

Yes, if you want to say that I was a drum major, say that I was a drum major for justice. (*Amen*) Say that I was a drum major for peace. (*Yes*) I was a drum major for righteousness. And all of the other shallow things will not matter. (*Yes*) I won't have any money to leave behind. I won't have the fine and luxurious things of life to leave behind. But I just want to leave a committed life behind. (*Amen*) And that's all I want to say.

[King quotes multiple lines of the hymn ending with these]

If I can bring salvation to a world once wrought,
If I can spread the message as the master taught,
Then my living will not be in vain.

Yes, Jesus, I want to be on your right or your left side, (*Yes*) not for any selfish reason. I want to be on your right or your left side, not in terms of some political kingdom or ambition. But I just want to be there in love and in justice and in truth and in commitment to others, so that we can make of this old world a new world.

APRIL 9, 1968

Eulogy for King by Benjamin Mays

MOREHOUSE COLLEGE

Atlanta, Georgia

"[King] went up and down the length and breadth of this
world preaching nonviolence and the redemptive power of
love. He believed with all of his heart, mind, and soul that
the way to peace and brotherhood is through nonviolence,
love, and suffering..."

King and his mentor, Benjamin Mays, had made a pact to deliver each
other's eulogies, depending on who died first. Mays, whom King described as his "spiritual mentor" and "my intellectual father," had been
the president of Morehouse College in Atlanta during King's studies
there. King was assassinated on April 4, 1968. An audio recording of
his "Drum Major Instinct" sermon played during the private memorial service at Ebenezer Baptist Church on April 9. A public service,
televised to a national audience, was held later that day at Morehouse
College, with the eulogy delivered by Mays.

[Excerpt]
... Coupled with moral courage was Martin Luther King Jr.'s
capacity to love people. Though deeply committed to a program

of freedom for Negroes, he had love and concern for all kinds of peoples. He drew no distinction between the high and low; none between the rich and the poor. He believed especially that he was sent to champion the cause of the man farthest down. He would probably say that if death had to come, I am sure there was no greater cause to die for than fighting to get a just wage for garbage collectors. He was supra-race, supra-nation, supra-denomination, supra-class, and supra-culture. He belonged to the world and to mankind. Now he belongs to posterity.

But there is a dichotomy in all this. This man was loved by some and hated by others. If any man knew the meaning of suffering, King knew. House bombed; living day by day for thirteen years under constant threats of death; maliciously accused of being a Communist; falsely accused of being insincere and seeking lime-light for his own glory; stabbed by a member of his own race; slugged in a hotel lobby; jailed thirty times; occasionally deeply hurt because his friends betrayed him—and yet this man had no bitterness in his heart, no rancor in his soul, no revenge in his mind; and he went up and down the length and breadth of this world preaching nonviolence and the redemptive power of love. He believed with all of his heart, mind, and soul that the way to peace and brotherhood is through nonviolence, love, and suffering. . . .

More from the Martin Luther King Jr. Library at HarperOne

HARDCOVER

I Have a Dream *(foreword by Amanda Gorman)*

Yo Tengo Un Sueño *(Spanish Edition)*

The Dream Journal

Beyond Vietnam *(foreword by Viet Thanh Nguyen)*

Our God Is Marching On *(foreword by Clyde W. Ford)*

I've Been to the Mountaintop *(foreword by Eric D. Tidwell, Esq.)*

PAPERBACK

I Have a Dream: 60th Anniversary Edition
*(forewords and afterword by Martin Luther King III,
Dr. Bernice A. King, and Dexter Scott King)*